PATRISTIC MONOGRAPH SERIES, NO. 5

THE USE OF SACRIFICIAL IDEAS IN GREEK CHRISTIAN WRITERS FROM THE NEW TESTAMENT TO JOHN CHRYSOSTOM

by

Frances M. Young

Wipf & Stock
PUBLISHERS
Eugene, Oregon

Wipf and Stock Publishers
199 W 8th Ave, Suite 3
Eugene, OR 97401

The Use of Sacrificial Ideas in Greek Christian Writers
from the New Testament to John Chrysostom
By Young, Frances M.

ISBN: 1-59244-928-X
Publication date 10/6/2004
Previously published by The Philadelphia Patristic Foundation, Ltd, 1979

TABLE OF CONTENTS

∞ ∞ ∞ ∞ ∞ ∞ ∞ ∞

ABBREVIATIONS

CQR	Church Quarterly Review
GCS	Die Griechischen Christlichen Schriftstelle der ersten drei Jahrhunderte
HTR	Harvard Theological Review
JEH	Journal of Ecclesiastical History
JTS	Journal of Theological Studies
MPG	Migne, Patrologia Graeca
SJT	Scottish Journal of Theology
ZAW	Zeitschrift für die alttestamentliche Wissenschaft

PREFACE

The work involved in preparing this dissertation for the degree of Doctor of Philosophy, University of Cambridge, was carried out between October 1963 and March 1967. It is with some hesitation that I now offer it for publication, since the passage of time has led to a certain dissatisfaction with its presentation. A more discursive and suggestive style would suit the material better than this somewhat rigid and argumentative analysis. However, the documentary evidence remains unchanged and, generally speaking, I stand by most of the conclusions. I have therefore complied with the editor's request that it should be published with a minimum of modifications. Most of the minor alterations made occur in the chapter on the Eucharist.

My thanks are due to my two research supervisors, the Rev. Professor Maurice F. Wiles and Dr. Robert M. Grant; to the staff of the University Libraries at Cambridge and Chicago; to Girton College, where I held research studentships during the preparation of this thesis; and to the Ministry of Education for Northern Ireland for financial support throughout the period of research. Finally, I should like to thank the Philadelphia Patristic Foundation, and particularly Donald F. Winslow, for encouraging me to offer this dissertation for publication.

Some of the material presented here has already been published in other contexts:

"The Idea of Sacrifice in Neoplatonic and Patristic Texts" (presented to the Fifth International Conference on Patristic Studies, September, 1967), *Studia Patristica*, XI.

"Insight or Incoherence? The Greek Fathers on God and Evil," *Journal of Ecclesiastical History*, Vol. 24 (1973), pp. 113-26.

"Temple, Cult and Law in Early Christianity: A Study in the Relations between Jews and Christians in the Early Centuries," *New Testament Studies*, Vol. 19 (1973), pp. 325-38.

The copyright of the latter two papers is held by Cambridge University Press. In each case, the main argument is largely independent of this thesis, although related to it and utilising overlapping evidence.

Frances M. Young

INTRODUCTION

The subject of Christ's sacrifice on the Cross has mainly been treated in the context of general discussions of Atonement theory. This is inevitable, but when it occurs, his sacrifice tends to be confused with theories of substitution, satisfaction and propitiation, in which case its nature is understood according to *a priori* assumptions concerning the proper rationale of sacrifice. The result of this situation is that, according to their own convictions, historians of the Doctrine of the Atonement have either tended to accept sacrificial language in the Greek Fathers as evidence of the presence of the later Western theory of the Atonement, at any rate, in germ;[1] or they have dismissed it as no more than the use of traditional Christian expressions which do not represent the real Doctrine held by the authors with whom we are concerned.[2]

In addition to this, the treatment of sacrificial language as one of the modes of expressing Atonement has meant that, in modern studies, the subject of Christ's sacrifice has been divorced from consideration of the sacrificial worship and service of the Church. The fact that it formed part of the apologetic of the first movement that claimed to be a religion despite having no outward and visible sacrificial cult has been overlooked. Nor has the importance of contemporary religious and philosophical ideas been recognised in most attempts to examine the nature of sacrifice, except in so far as Old Testament ideas have been appealed to in exegesis of the sacrificial language used in the New Testament.

The aim of this study is to try to correct the balance, to emphasize the importance and diversity of sacrificial concepts in the theology and life of the

---

[1]E.g., J. Rivière, *The Doctrine of the Atonement* (London, 1909).

[2]E.g., H. Rashdall, *The Idea of Atonement in Christian Theology* (London, 1919).

early Eastern Church, and so to throw light on the usually confused treatment, not only of Christ's atoning death, but also of the sacrifice of the Eucharist. We set out to examine the use of sacrificial terminology by Greek-speaking Christians in every kind of context in which it occurs, and with contemporary religious views in mind. It is plain that the East was not dominated by one concept of sacrifice. The Christian position was worked out both in opposition to current views and at the same time under the influence of both the Jewish and Greek backgrounds. On the one hand, sacrifice was repudiated and polemic against the practice conducted; on the other hand, sacrificial terminology was embraced as a suitable mode of expression for Christian worship, moral life, and self-offering in martyrdom. This kind of "spiritual sacrifice" is deeply imbedded in the moral theology of the Eastern Church, the fullest expression of it being in imitation of and participation in the perfect and supreme sacrifice of Christ. The nature of the atoning efficacy of Christ's sacrifice is discussed within the whole context of the sacrificial thought of the Greek Church.

The plan of the study is to outline, in Section One, the Jewish and Greek background under the influence of which Christian ideas were developed. In Section Two, we trace the Christian rejection of material sacrifice and examine the character of the spiritual cult which replaced it. In Section Three, the nature of Christ's sacrifice is discussed, with particular reference to ideas of Atonement, and, in Section Four, we consider the relation of Christ's sacrifice to the sacrificial life of the Church.

The method adopted is to analyse the various types of sacrifice. This pattern runs throughout the study, Christian sacrifices and the sacrifice of Christ being distinguished according to the types of sacrifice found in the background cultures. Propitiatory sacrifice is thus shown to be but one type, and a much richer and more varied range of ideas beyond that one type is emphasized. Apart from the emphasis placed on sacrifices of worship and thanksgiving, and sacrifices of communion, other types of sin-offering (that is, other than propitiatory sin-offerings) are found to have played a considerable part in Christian thought.

The intended result is to demonstrate that the use of sacrificial language in the Greek Fathers does not necessarily imply the presence of a propitiatory theory of Atonement; yet neither can such a theory be dismissed as alien to the real thought of those authors who discuss the Atonement. Indeed, it played a vital part in the belief and worship of Greek Christians of the early Church, and, even though it received a number of different interpretations, it was of great importance in their attempts to understand the full meaning of Christ's death.

SECTION ONE

BACKGROUND

INTRODUCTION TO SECTION ONE

In the Ancient World, the offering of sacrifice was a universal practice of religion. The various tribes and nations that eventually made up the Roman Empire each had their traditional cults, in all of which sacrifice played a central part. It was not merely the practice of the less civilised people of, for example, North Africa and Gaul; it was even the normal mode of worship in the more sophisticated cultures of the Jews, Greeks, Egyptians and Romans up to the reign of Constantine and beyond. This is not to claim that there was no change or development in the religious thought of these people, but it does help to explain why there is a complete lack of any attempt to define sacrifice in literature spanning approximately two thousand years. It never occurred to anyone that explanation or definition was necessary.[1] Sacrifice was assumed, and played an essential part in everything which claimed to be a religion.

---

[1]It was suggested to me by the Rev. Massey Shepherd that the first definition of sacrifice is to be found in Augustine, <u>City of God</u>, X.6: verum sacrificium est omne opus quo agitur ut sancta societate inhaereamus Deo, relatum scilicet ad illum finem boni quo veraciter beati esse possimus. That the earliest definition should be so late emphasises the fact that sacrifice was taken for granted in the ancient world. Simply because its meaning was not consciously defined, we must expect unconscious presuppositions to dominate the use of sacrificial terminology throughout the period covered by this study, and this limits the extent to which clarity can be achieved. Augustine's definition provides no guidance for a general understanding of the implications of sacrifice in the ancient world, as it is obviously under the influence of the spiritualisation of sacrifice developed by philosophy and by Christianity.

The term sacrifice tends to suggest the slaughtering of animals; in the Ancient World, however, it covered all forms of material offering to the gods.[2] Sacrifice included the offering as much of first-fruits of the crops, of wine, honey or flour, as of ritually slain animals. Generally speaking, however, the latter was regarded as the richer and better offering - reasonably enough, for in that time, meat was a luxury item.

Sacrifice was performed with a number of differing rites and with many different intentions; during the course of recorded time, it received a variety of interpretations. To provide background for the study of the use of sacrificial concepts and language in the Greek Christian Church, some attempt is made in the chapters of this section to classify the various types of sacrifice that can be broadly distinguished, firstly in the traditional religion of Greece, and secondly, in the highly complex sacrificial system that was maintained in Jerusalem on the basis of the sacred books of the Law. Besides this, the attempts of Greek and Jewish thinkers to interpret sacrifice and criticise popular practices are briefly surveyed, with the pur-

---

[2]Anthropological disputes about the origins of sacrifice do not form a part of the present discussion. As background to the use of sacrificial ideas in the Greek Church, only the accepted forms of sacrifice in classical Greece, Hellenistic and Rabbinic Judaism, and the Roman Empire are strictly relevant. I do not, therefore, by this definition intend to support the "Gift Theory" as an explanation of the origin of sacrifice. Whatever the origin, I am convinced that G. B. Gray is right in his book, <u>Sacrifice in the Old Testament</u> (Oxford, 1925), when he argues that the idea of <u>gift</u> was actually associated with all the various sacrifices of Judaism at some period in history, and predominated in the Hellenistic and Roman periods. Likewise all Greek sacrifices can be regarded as gifts, particularly in the light of the over-riding importance of votive-offerings in Greek religion. For further details, see my discussion below.

pose of unearthing not only conscious attitudes, but also beliefs that were traditional and subconscious. In the light of this background material, the Christian use of sacrificial ideas will become clearer.

CHAPTER ONE
SACRIFICE IN GREEK RELIGION

A. Classification of Types

(a) Votive-offerings: The votive-offering plays a large role in the religion of Greece, so much so that many regard this type of offering as the basis for the interpretation of all Greek sacrifices. A city or individual in distress or need, or motivated by some selfish desire, would vow to give a particular deity some gift in the future, provided he satisfied his present greed or came to his immediate aid.[1] Prayer in the Homeric poems has been described by one scholar as a "negotium," a business transaction:[2] a man argues his case with the gods on the basis of how many sacrifices he has offered, or promises future sacrifices in return for their answer to his requests; the gods are obligated to help men by their acceptance of these sacrificial gifts. This concept of prayer and

---

[1]E.g., before the Battle of Marathon the Athenians vowed to Artemis, pledging that, if they won, they would sacrifice to her she-goats equal in number to the number of enemy dead. So many were slain that the vow was paid off at the rate of five hundred per year; and, when Xenophon wrote, they were still sacrificing (_Anabasis_ 3.2.12). See R. K. Yerkes, _Sacrifice in Greek and Roman Religion and Early Judaism_ (London, 1953), to which I am indebted for the above example.

[2]H. Schmidt, _Veteres philosophi quomodo iudicaverint de precibus_ (Giessen, 1908), p. 1. A clear example of this appeal to former offerings is found in the prayer of Chryses to Apollo in Iliad, 1.37. Of interest also is the following remark: "La prière antique, ou le sacrifice qui en est une forme, n'est qu'un marche entre l'homme et la divinité, le premier cherchant à s'assurer une faveur ou en remerciant après l'avoir obtenue." Guy Soury, _Aperçus de philosophe religieuse chez Maxime de Tyre_ (Paris, 1942), Ch. 2.

the general prevalence of votive-offerings in literature and in excavated temples[3] has led to the suggestion that Greek sacrifice was solely a kind of bargain with the gods: "do ut des" is the Latin phrase commonly used to describe this.

(b) The great festivals: It cannot, however, be argued that the great religious festivals of the city-states were such mercenary transactions with their patron-deity. For example, Athena would naturally protect Athens, regardless of the correct celebration of the Panathenaia. The majority of sacrifices (thusiai), and particularly the great religious festivals, were occasions of rejoicing and feasting, worship and thanksgiving. The slaughtered animals were eaten by the worshippers and the requisite portions burnt on the altar for the consumption of the god, who was present as the head of the family or as an honoured guest at a banquet. All feasted together, and the worshippers praised the greatness of the god and thanked him for his protection and support.

The "bargain" idea cannot therefore be extended to cover the meaning of all sacrifices in Classical Greece, because in the great festivals, we find sacrifices of genuine worship and thanksgiving, untainted by mercenary motives. Nor was the custom of offering first-fruits the result of a bargain with the gods;

---

[3]See W. D. Rouse, Greek Votive Offerings (Cambridge, 1902) for large numbers of examples of the type of gift offered: they included just about everything from terracotta statuettes to money, workman's tools, clothing, and jewelry. The occasions for votive offerings included sickness, plague, war, election to office, success at games, the birth of a child, etc. Rouse includes first-fruits among such offerings, but I am unwilling to agree that they had anything to do with the fulfillment of a vow. Not all freewill offerings should be described as votive, as Rouse seems to think.

it arose rather out of gratitude for the power that made the crops grow and provided a successful harvest.[4]

(c) Holocausts: The sacrifices we have discussed so far were all offered, whether disinterestedly or not, to powers regarded as basically friendly, and their object was to please them and keep their protecting influence near. But Greek religion had another side as well. It "contained two diverse, even opposite factors: on the one hand, the element of service (θεραπεία), on the other, the element of aversion (ἀποτροπή)." The rites of service were connected by tradition with the Olympians, or, as they are sometimes called, the Ouranians; the rites of aversion with ghosts, heroes and underground divinities. The rites of service were of a cheerful and rational character, the rites of aversion gloomy and tending to superstition.[5] The object of sacrifice to the Chthonians, the gods of the earth and the underworld, was to placate the evil spirits who caused disease, old age and death, to remove pollution and appease the powers below. It was of quite a different character from sacrifice to the Olympians. The malevolent powers were not welcome guests at a common feast, but received the gift whole, either buried or entirely consumed by fire (i.e., as holocausts - wholly burnt). The rites were performed at night rather than during the day, and with "shuddering" rather than joy. The worship of the Chthonians is usually regarded as the most primitive aspect of Greek religion, and with it are associated ancient

---

[4]Originally, the offering of first-fruits seems to have been based on primitive taboos. It is clear, however, that this was not the motive for offering them in our period; e.g., Porphyry assumes the practice is based on gratitude (*De abs.*, II, 12, 13).

[5]J. E. Harrison, *Prologomena to the Study of Greek Religion* (3rd Edition; Cambridge, 1922), p. 10. This distinction is commonly accepted in books on Greek religion since Harrison's work. See Yerkes, op. cit.; G. Murray, *Five Stages of Greek Religion* (Oxford, 1925); H. J. Rose, *Religion in Greece and Rome* (New York, 1959).

taboos and scapegoat rituals for the removal of sins and impurities.

(d) Placatory sacrifices: Does our discussion of holocausts imply that placatory intent is entirely absent from sacrifice to the Ouranians? This is what Yerkes[6] tries to maintain, arguing that when a god had been offended, only proper obedience and restoration of the fault could regain the favour of the god. This contention is based on the story in <u>Iliad</u> I of Apollo and the pestilence he sent upon the Greeks: the Greeks appeased Apollo's anger, not by offering propitiatory sacrifices, but by returning the girl they had stolen, after which they were able to hold a joyful sacrificial feast of worship in honour of Apollo. His contention cannot, however, apply to the majority of cases, the most extreme example being the case of Iphigeneia who was offered as a human sacrifice in response to the demand of the goddess Artemis to placate her anger.

Strictly speaking this type of sacrifice must be closely associated with the votive-offerings (Type a) discussed above. It was regarded as a kind of payment to buy off the anger of an offended deity.

(e) Communion-sacrifices: The great festivals were sacrifices of communion in the sense that the worshipper shared a communion-meal with the god. But in Greece there was another form of communion-sacrifice in which the worshipper actually partook of the nature of the god himself. The most well-known example is provided by the cult of Dionysus, in which ecstatic and frenzied worshippers wandered over the mountains, tearing at the raw flesh of a bull that was thought to be the actual embodiment of the god. By eating this flesh, the worshipper believed he received a little of the god's power and character.[7]

---

[6]Op. cit., Ch. 6.

[7]See particularly E. R. Dodds' edition of Euripides' <u>Bacchae</u>. Dodds says (p. xvi), "We may regard the [eating of raw flesh], then, as a rite in which the god was in some sense present in his beast-vehicle and was, in that shape, torn and eaten by his people." See also Dodds' Appendix on Maenadism in his <u>The</u>

B. Explanations and Criticisms of Sacrifice

In the earliest period revealed to us by archaeology, it is clear that the Greeks, like so many other primitive peoples, thought that the gods and the dead needed everything that men need for life. Throughout Greek history, the offering of meat, honey and wine, and the sacrificing of animals continued to be regarded as a means of feeding the gods. The persistence of this picture of sacrifice is confirmed by the fact that all the later philosophical discussions of sacrifice find it necessary to insist that the gods do not need to be fed by sacrifice. For the ordinary worshipper, it was natural to think that, if the gods were dependent on sacrifices for their food, they would be very displeased if the requisite sacrifices were not forthcoming. The omission would have to be made up, and probably an additional gift provided as compensation, before the anger of the deity could be appeased.

At variance with the view that the gods were dependent on men for their food, was the picture of the happy Olympians in need of nothing but nectar and ambrosia. However, it was felt that, even if the gods did not actually need sacrifices to obtain food, they certainly enjoyed an occasional feast when it was offered. This was the basis of the primary interpretation of sacrifice that was both consciously and unconsciously accepted in the Greek world, the view that it was a bribe, or man's part of a bargain with the gods. All the types of sacrifice enumerated above could be explained in this way, including even the religious festivals which we preferred to explain as occasions of worship and thanksgiving. That this was the usual interpretation of sacrifice is confirmed by the fact that later criticisms of sacrifice were directed against the idea that sacrifice was an attempt to get the gods to accomplish something on behalf of

---

Greeks and the Irrational (Berkeley, 1951). Note that, since their rites did not involve any new idea of sacrifice, the mystery-religions are not relevant to our study.

the person offering the sacrifice. It was assumed that the whole object of religious practices was to see that the gods were for us, not against us. Fear of the consequences of not keeping the gods happy, an attitude far from absent in the Classical period, became even more prominent in the Hellenistic age of superstition and pessimism.

It will be noticeable that so far no mention has been made of sin. A passing acquaintance with Greek religion suggests that the carefree Olympians were not overconcerned with the morality of their worshippers. But Greek religion certainly had moral content, and this became increasingly important. There were many traditional ritual purifications,[8] and in the context of Orphism, these acquired importance as an expiation of the sin of the individual soul.[9] In literature, the gods were seen as the guardians of justice, whose anger was aroused by the injustice of men.[10] Desire to appease their anger became associated, therefore, not merely with failure to offer the right sacrifices, but with the moral sins of the worshipper.

The rise of philosophy brought moral criticism to bear on the traditional religion. Some like the Sophists rejected the gods outright on the grounds that they were unworthy of worship because they did not respect the normal moral standards of human beings; Zeus' many love affairs provided obvious material for their ridicule.[11] For others, however, acceptance of

---

[8]See above, sacrifices of Type 'c.' There were also many rites of purification not involving actual sacrifice, e.g., lustrations.

[9]For increased concern with guilt and sin, see E. R. Dodds, op. cit., especially Ch. 2; also H. J. Rose, op. cit., Ch. 5.

[10]Hesiod was followed by Aeschylus in his zealous insistence on the close connection between Zeus and Diké (Justice). See especially his *Agamemnon*.

[11]This criticism of Homeric gods began with the Presocratics and was popularised by the Sophists. The problem of the gods' lack of morality was resolved by regarding them as personifications of natural forces.

a more worthy concept of the gods and morality led to criticism of the current attitudes to sacrifice. Socrates[12] insisted that sacrifice made no difference; it was the sincere and prayerful desire for virtue that alone was of value in the endeavour to keep the favour of the gods. His influence was felt by Plato and Aristotle, Diogenes and the Cynics, as well as, of course, the long line of Stoic moralists, for whom the moral character of the worshipper was far more important than any sacrifice.

The close connection between sacrifice and prayer was quickly recognised in the Ancient World. Sacrifice was regarded as a reinforcement of prayer, and prayer gave content and meaning to the sacrifice, whether a man was requesting riches, purification from his sins, or return to the favour of a deity he had offended. It was natural then that vain petitions for riches, good health, a son and heir, or other such material comforts, which were the main content of popular prayers, should be criticised in the light of the idea that a multitude of sacrifices could not make up for moral shortcomings. The only worthwhile prayer in the eyes of the moral philosophers was for spiritual qualities, particularly that of virtue. Sacrifice with selfish mercenary motives received its due criticism, from a moral stand-point.

Meanwhile, sacrifice of this kind had also received theological criticism. Euripides suggested that it was unworthy of the dignity and sanctity of the gods,[13] and philosophers like Plato refused to allow that the gods could be bribed.[14] Although

---

[12]What Socrates actually taught is notoriously subject to dispute, but both Plato and Xenophon bear witness to his religious outlook and to his insistence on the close connection between morality and piety. See, for example, Xenophon, *Memorabilia*, I.3 and Plato, *Phaedrus*, 279 B-C.

[13]For references, see H. Schmidt, op. cit., p. 5.

[14]*Laws*, 716 E - 717 A. See *Euthyphro*, 14 E, where sacrifice is called an ἐμπορική τις τέχνη. I am indebted to Dodds, op. cit., p. 222, for these references.

this cut at the root of the traditional interpretation of sacrifice, it did not prevent it from remaining the popular assumption throughout the Hellenistic period. The majority continued to agree that the gods should be worshipped for what you could get out of them,[15] even though philosophers and satirists ridiculed sacrifice as an attempt to corrupt the gods.[16]

Nor was it merely the integrity of the gods that was called in question by the practice of sacrifice. Intelligent men began to realise how ridiculous it was to suppose that the gods were dependent on men for their sustenance or gratification. The idea that the gods would starve if one did not sacrifice was recognised as a "reductio ad absurdum".[17] The superiority of gods to men was assumed in every concept of god, however crude, and the realisation that sacrifice, as commonly interpreted, treated the gods as if they were inferior to men, should have undermined this interpretation.[18]

---

[15]This attitude lies behind Cicero's criticism of Epicurean theology: Quid est enim cur deos ab hominibus colendos dicas, cum dei non modo homines non colant sed omnino nihil curent, nihil agant? (*De natura deorum*, 1.115).

[16]E.g., Persius, Satire, 2 and Maximus of Tyre, *Dissertations*, 11.

[17]Lucian, the 2nd century A.D. satirist, has a delightful burlesque on current attitudes to sacrifice. He questions the piety of those who think so meanly of God as to suppose that he needs anything from the hands of men, takes pleasure in their flattery, or is wounded by their neglect. He pictures the gods in heaven looking down and waiting for sacrifices to be offered. If a sacrifice is being performed, all mouths are open to feast upon the smoke; like flies they settle on the altar to drink up the trickling streams of blood (Περὶ θυσίων, 1 and 9). This satire is a remarkable testimony to the persistence of the primitive interpretation of sacrifice which we have outlined.

[18]This argument seems to date from Aristotle. By the 4th century A.D., it was sufficiently common to warrant consideration by the Neoplatonists in their defence of sacrifice. A. S. Pease, in his commentary on

With the spread of belief in fate, necessity, or chance during the Hellenistic period, philosophers pointed out that sacrifice was quite useless. A rigidly determined world, whether ruled by gods or not, was incapable of change, while the object of sacrifice was to effect a change in one's favour. The popularity of astrology strengthened this deterministic outlook, which logically excluded sacrifice.[19] The widespread cult of Τύχη (Chance) was even more irrational; how could random happenings be affected by sacrifice? The Stoics' impersonal Providence left no room for sacrifice; in any case, for them, virtue was the only thing that mattered, ultimately, and this could only be attained by a man's own efforts.[20] The Epicurean gods

---

Cicero: De natura deorum (Cambridge, Mass., 1955-8), gives references to Aristotle, Apollonius of Tyana, Philodemus, Lucretius, Lucian, Apuleius, Julian, Porphyry, and Sallustius. It is not surprising that the same view was to be found in Jewish and Christian writers. Pease refers also to the Maccabees, Josephus, Aristides, and Láctantius, a list which must be far from exhaustive.

[19]A. D. Nock, in his _Conversion_ (Oxford, 1933), p. 101, gives the example of a professional astrologer, Valens Vettius, who said: "It is impossible for any man by prayers and sacrifices to overcome what is fixed from the beginning and to alter it to his taste; what has been assigned to us will happen without praying for it, what is not fated will not happen for our prayers." He also points out that Tiberius is described by Suetonius as neglecting worship as useless in view of the certainty of astrological predestination.

[20]Seneca regards prayer and sacrifice as useles because of (i) the tenets of Stoic morality (_Ep_. 31.5; 41.1) and (ii) fate or providence (e.g., _Ep_. 77.12), although in fact he prayed himself (_De beneficiis_, VII.4.6). (I am indebted to H. Schmidt, op. cit., for these references.) See R. D. Hicks, _Stoic and Epicurean_ (London, 1910), p. 136 on Seneca and Marcus Aurelius. The same attitude towards morality is found in the "Neopythagorean" Apollonius of Tyana, who says in his

had no concern with men, so there was no point in sacrificing to them.[21] The Platonism of the early Christian centuries insisted more and more on the unchangeability of the Supreme God of the Universe. This again suggested that sacrifice was pointless: God would give each man his due whether he prayed and sacrificed or not.[22]

Epistle to the priests at Olympia (Loeb Edition, XXVI): "The gods are in no need of sacrifices. What then can one do in order to win their favour? One can in my opinion acquire wisdom, and so far as one can, do good to such men as deserve it. This pleases the gods; atheists, however, can sacrifice. (Compare the Epicurean attitude, *infra*, n. 21.) N.B. also the story of Apollonius' visit to the temple of Asclepius in Philostratus' *Life*, I.11. The point of the story is the teaching that God will give blessings and punishments in accordance with justice and desert; one's situation is not dependent on sacrifice.

[21]But see A. J. Festugière, *Epicurus and His Gods* (Oxford, 1955), and Pease, op. cit. In spite of the charge of atheism, and the assumption that if the gods felt no concern for men there was no point in sacrificing, there are many testimonies to the piety of Epicurus, who worshipped the gods for what they were, because they were immortal and happy, and this was the ideal to which men aspired. Because he believed that the gods had nothing to do with human affairs, his advocacy of the cult was from purely disinterested motives, unlike most of his avowedly religious contemporaries.

[22]See Maximus of Tyre, *Dissertations*, XI. He deals with the implications of the various beliefs in fate, providence, chance, etc. in relation to prayer, which also implies sacrifice. He also mentions the philosophical commonplace that it is undignified for a man to change his mind, and all the more so for a god. This makes all attempts to influence the gods in one's favour pointless. Soury's judgement (op. cit., Ch. 2) of Maximus' treatise is that it is not marked by original thought or rigorous logic, but is an amalgam of the

The ideal of the "philosopher's prayer" owed much to criticism of popular religious practices. This ideal is admirably disclosed in the meditations of Marcus Aurelius, and was conceived as intercourse between god and man, based on their kinship and likeness, and dependent on the virtue of man and his endeavour to imitate the gods. But although the spirituality of Marcus Aurelius is profound for paganism, it is the Hermetic Corpus which has been called "The higher religion of Hellenism."[23] It is probable that this group of writings dates, in its present form, from the early third century (though perhaps some parts are older), and that it developed in Egypt. It purports to be accounts of special revelations given particularly by "Hermes."[24] Here is found a common ideal of piety, based on a philosophical monotheism which combined the transcendence of Platonism with the immanence of Stoicism. There was never such a thing as a "Hermetic sect," though the prime interest of the writings is religious. Religion being inseparable from sacrifice in the Ancient World, it is not surprising to find discussion of it here, and what we find is a "radical spiritualisation"[25] of it. God needs nothing; he is everything and all things are in him. We should adore him by giving thanks. Even

---

essential views of ancient philosophy on the subject of prayer. Maximus recognises the weakness of the current conceptions of prayer and opposes to them the idea of the prayer of the philosopher. He traces this concept of the philosopher's prayer to Socrates. It appears frequently, e.g., in the religious meditations of Marcus Aurelius. I take Maximus' treatise as typical of the thought of the enlightened pagan in the early Christian centuries.

[23]C. H. Dodd, The Interpretation of the Fourth Gospel (Cambridge, 1953), p. 10.

[24]For discussion, see Dodd, op. cit., and his The Bible and the Greeks (London, 1935); G. van Moorsel, The Mysteries of Hermes Trismegistus (Utrecht, 1955); A. -J. Festugière, Personal Religion among the Greeks (Berkeley, 1954).

[25]G. van Moorsel, op. cit., p. 38.

burning incense, the purest form of material sacrifice, is regarded as an abomination to God who is above all matter. Material sacrifice is abolished and replaced by λογικαὶ θυσίαι which are variously interpreted in terms of the height of religious ecstasy, or of moral qualities.[26] Such rational sacrifices figure more frequently in Jewish and Christian writings than in pagan, so we have here one example of the Jewish influence that is certainly present throughout these writings.[27] But such a reinterpretation of sacrifice is not inconsistent with the tradition of criticism we have found in the philosophies which contributed to Hermeticism. The prayer of the philosopher has been overlayed with an "oriental Mysticism," but the theological ideas are not out of tune with the philosophical developments that led eventually to Neoplatonism.

Complete repudiation of material sacrifice was, however, extremely rare.[28] Compromise was the keynote of most philosophy under the Romans, and in spite of all the criticisms that were produced and all the illogicalities that were revealed, sacrifice continued undiminished, even being actively supported by philosophy. The Stoics, for example, found a way of reconciling their philosophy with popular religion, and together with the Sceptics,[29] of all companions, they

---

[26] Asclepius, 41; Corpus Hermeticum, I.31; XII, 23; XIII.18, 21.

[27] Jewish influence is the subject of C. H. Dodd's discussion in his The Bible and the Greeks (London, 1935).

[28] Even those who rejected the sacrifice of animals on vegetarian grounds would offer first-fruits and other material offerings.

[29] The Sceptics refused to have an opinion on anything. On the basis of the common agreement of all mankind that gods exist, however, and the common experience that religion is a good thing and irreligion a bad thing, they were able to support the religious customs of their forefathers. See P. Hallie, Scepticism, Man and God (Middletown, Conn., 1964) and E. Bevan, Stoic and Sceptic (Oxford, 1913).

worked to uphold the state religion of Rome,[30] without which they feared for the sanctity of the oath and the moral qualities which had made Rome great.[31] Even Marcus Aurelius frequently sacrificed to the gods. Under the Empire sacrifice to the genius of the Emperor became a test of loyalty to the state. Polytheism is essentially tolerant of all faiths, and every nation accepted the Emperor cult except the Jews who had a special exemption. Every philosophy was able to subscribe to it, and intelligent, educated men who believed in a Supreme God of the Middle Platonic type, allowed the existence of subsidiary deities to whom it was right to sacrifice, and among whom were included the genius of the Emperor as well as the gods of traditional popular religion. Christianity alone held out against such "liberal" views, and here it came into conflict with Rome; a Christian would not compromise his position by sacrificing to the gods. The situation was such that the great Monistic rival to Christianity, Neoplatonism, which grew up in the Third and Fourth Centuries A.D., found itself in the position of defender of sacrifice, and therefore under an obligation to discuss all objections to the practice and account for its supposed effectiveness.

---

[30] I have not felt it necessary to discuss Roman religion in detail, as the special traits of Roman religion did not affect the thinking of the East very much. By the period of the Empire, Rome had assimilated Greek literature and philosophy. While the state religion continued to be officially performed on the basis of a kind of legal undertaking with the gods that they would continue to make Rome prosper as long as they received due worship and respect, the satirists made use of Greek criticism of popular religion, and educated men were theologically sceptical or adopted Stoic philosophy.

[31] See Cicero, De natura deorum, I.4, 14, 77. N.B. III.5 where Cotta, the Sceptic in philosophy, is Pontifex Maximus in religion (or, should we say, politics). See also Epictetus, Enchiridion, 31, and the discussion in R. D. Hicks, op. cit., pp. 133-4.

C. The Neoplatonist Discussion of Sacrifice

The views of the Neoplatonists concerning sacrifice were formulated under the same influences as, and to some extent in opposition to, Christianity. Besides this, their writings provide the most comprehensive discussion of sacrifice in Ancient literature. For these reasons, it is now proposed to survey their arguments in greater detail than those of their predecessors.

For the Neoplatonists, the subject was opened by Porphyry's argument, based on the vegetarian principle, that slaying of animals, even for sacrificial purposes, could not be morally right. This apparently radical idea for conformist pagan philosophers can be traced to the Pythagoreans,[32] under whose influence Theophrastus wrote a treatise which seems to have been

---

[32]It is not entirely true that all the philosophers compromised over sacrifice, and the Pythagorean stand against animal sacrifice was an exception to the general rule. Apollonius of Tyana, a Neopythagorean, is represented in Philostratus' _Life_ (VIII.7) as holding similar views on the subject of vegetarianism and sacrifice. See also Apollonius, _Epistle_ XXVII (Loeb Edition): "The altar should not be defiled with blood; it is courting the displeasure of the gods." (There is a difficulty here, however, since Philostratus also says _Life_, III.41 that Apollonius wrote a treatise on sacrifice in four books which was to be found in a number of temples in various cities. How this could be when he opposed sacrifice on vegetarian grounds is not clear, but perhaps, like Porphyry, it was only animal sacrifices he opposed, and the book mentioned might have contained teaching on other kinds of sacrifice.) The need for philosophers to compromise with traditional cults is reflected, however, in Porphyry's remark that his intention was not to overthrow all customs and religious laws (_De. abs._, II.33); tradition was too ingrained and respected by this time. Compare the Christians' need to prove that they were not innovators by claiming that their faith was based on foundations older than the Greek religion.

an important source for Porphyry's discussion.[33] Porphyry accepts Theophrastus' suggestion that animal sacrifice originated in time of famine when lack of crops drove men to seek other forms of food.[34] Now, however, sacrifice had become merely an excuse for the satisfaction of human greed, made respectable by the supposed religious value of the practice.[35] To take the life of any other living creature was wrong, and since the gods were not worse than men, it was impossible to think that they demanded an immoral act as worship.[36]

Porphyry's opposition to sacrifice is, however, only based on his refusal to take the life of another creature; he does believe that men should repay the gods for their gifts and he recommends the offering of first-fruits, of crops, honey and wine.[37] His main concern is that the sacrifices offered should be worthy of the gods,[38] and he particularly insists that experience has shown that the gods are not pleased with extravagant offerings, but by the purified character of the worshipper.[39] The simplest gifts can provide a feast for gods and men, and the more costly and supposedly better animal sacrifices are simply not necessary.[40]

---

[33]On Porphyry's debt to Theophrastus, see J. Bernays, Theophrastus Schrift über Frommigkeit (Berlin, 1866). This work isolates large passages of Porphyry's De abstinentia, regarding them as direct quotations from the lost work of Theophrastus.

[34]In support of this, Porphyry points out that the ritual taboos which decide what is clean and unclean are very convenient; it is because of their function in reproduction that female animals are ineligible as sacrificial victims (De abs., II.10, 11). Only animals that are edible are sacrificed, not snakes or apes (ibid., II.25).

[35]De abs., II.27. [36]Ibid., II.12, 22, 23.

[37]Ibid., II.12, 13. [38]Ibid., II.33.

[39]Ibid., II.14, 15, 19.

[40]Ibid., II.14, 15, 19, 33.

This argument reveals that Porphyry is conscious of the interdependence of interpretations of sacrifice and the nature of the gods. This appears again in his Letter to Anebo, which was a deliberate attempt to raise such questions about religious practices as how can it be that the gods enjoy sacrifices if they are απαθεῖς. What is impassive cannot be allured, compelled or necessitated, so offerings must be in vain whether regarded as a method of appeasing the anger of the gods or as providing necessities for them.[41] In the light of this passage, it is not surprising to find that propitiation is omitted from the list of motives for sacrifice which Porphyry gives in the De Abstinentia. The three purposes he allows are διὰ τιμήν, διὰ χάριν, and διὰ χρείαν τῶν ἀγαθῶν.[42] Quite how Porphyry understood the third of these suggestions is not clear; it seems to reflect the popular "bargain" interpretation of sacrifice, but Porphyry's own argument about the changeless nature of the gods should have excluded the possibility of obtaining benefits from the gods by the offering of sacrificial bribes, just as much as it excluded placation. Apart from this difficulty, however, it is clear that he allowed only worship and thanksgiving as motives for offering sacrifice, since these alone were consistent with the advanced theological belief that the gods could not be persuaded to change their minds as a result of sacrifice.

Porphyry's consciousness of the relation between the nature of the gods and suitable worship is further revealed by his division of deities into various grades to which different types of sacrifice are proper. To the Supreme God we should not sacrifice, he says, for even a word is too material. He can only be worshipped by pure silence, holy sacrifice being offered to him simply by close contact with him and being transformed

---

[41] Letter to Anebo, 4, 5.

[42] De abs., II.24. The context of his discussion of the purpose of sacrifice is an argument to show that animal sacrifice simply does not serve any of these purposes.

to his likeness, until the offering is perfected by achieving ἀπάθεια of soul and contemplation (θεωρία) of God.[43] There are however, lower heavenly beings; to the νοητοὶ θεοί may be offered hymns and words the "first-fruits of beautiful thoughts,"[44] and to beings further down the scale, those material offerings which Porphyry has said should be presented according to ancestral custom, provided that animal sacrifice is excluded. This lowest order of gods includes the planets, who should receive thanks for their providential oversight of human lives,[45] and the good daemons who administer the world and act as intermediaries between gods and men.[46]

---

[43]Ibid., II.34-5. [44]Ibid. [45]Ibid., II.37.

[46]Ibid., II.37-9. Iamblichus also divides the deities into grades, regarding this as the only way to come to the right view of sacrifice. His scheme is rather different: there are no evil daemons. Material offerings are suitable for the daemons who rule the world, whereas, when we honour the μονοειδεῖς θεοί , we should worship them with means that are free from matter, with intellectual gifts, that is, which will harmonize with the life of the immaterial. Iamblichus posits a third class of deities, intermediary gods who provide the link between the lower and higher orders, and to these a mixture of material and immaterial gifts may be offered (<u>De mysteriis</u>, V.19). Unlike Porphyry, Iamblichus also distinguishes different grades of worshipper. Some souls, being freer of the influence of matter, have less needs of material forms of worship, although few in this life will get beyond offering a mixture of material and spiritual worship. Those that are entirely occupied with material pursuits quite rightly will offer only worship in a material way to the gods who govern material affairs (ibid., V.18), but since the whole universe is in communion, such material offerings ultimately touch even the most supernatural beings and set the divine causes in operation (see, e.g., V.9). The various forms of sacrifice all contribute to restoring things to their proper order and to making the world perfect (ibid., V.20, 24). Compare also Celsus'

Since, in Porphyry's view, the only possible motive for sacrifice is gratitude, it is quite wrong to think that the good daemons are angry if they do not receive due worship. If they are good they can do no evil, and therefore the common belief that they have to be propitiated is false.[47] It is not the good daemons that have to be propitiated, but the evil daemons who cause famine, crop failure, earthquakes and other natural disasters. They do this in order to get sacrifices out of men, for they thrive on the fat of bloody sacrifices. So, according to Porphyry, apart from the principle of vegetarianism, there is a much more compelling reason for refusing to offer any animal sacrifice, namely, that it only strengthens the evil daemons for their evil works.[48]

Iamblichus continued the Neoplatonist discussion of sacrifice by setting out to answer point by point the problems raised in Porphyry's _Letter to Anebo_.[49] Unlike Porphyry, Iamblichus is concerned to defend animal sacrifice, and for this reason he deliberately disagrees with certain of Porphyry's statements in the _De Abstinentia_ and goes beyond Porphyry in seeking a rationale of sacrifice. Where Porphyry used the popular notion that the gods were fed by bloody sacrifices to warn against offering them to evil daemons, Iamblichus rejects the very idea that sacrifice provides meat for the gods; the fact that the animal is consumed by fire in sacrifice means that it is quite

---

suggestion that the Supreme God is worshipped through offering material sacrifices to the lower gods (_C. Cels._, VIII.2).

[47] _De abs._, II.37-39. This is a slightly different argument from that already seen in the _Letter to Anebo_; there the argument was based on the _apatheia_ of the gods, here on their unalterable goodness. The conclusion reached, however, is essentially the same.

[48] Ibid., II.40-3.

[49] See the introduction to the _De mysteriis_, especially I.12.

unsuitable for food.[50] Although he regards the division of deities into various grades as essential to find the right view of sacrifice,[51] evil daemons have no place in Iamblichus' universe - no doubt, because his position depends on the unity and harmony of the whole universe. This view also affects his attitude to placation. In answer to Porphyry's perplexities about the possibility of affecting the gods if they are απαθεῖς, Iamblichus maintains that this is the wrong kind of question, because it completely misunderstands the point of sacrifice. Prayer and sacrifice do not affect the gods, for the divine nature is indeed incapable of being fed, allured or changed. Sacrifice is a means whereby lower orders of being can ascend to higher; through sacrifices the gods impart their light to men, calling their souls upwards into union with themselves, so effecting the salvation of their souls.[52] The supposed anger of the gods is interpreted as a deliberate rejection of their light by men, not a passion of the gods. Rather than influencing the gods in our favour, "appeasement" actually converts us to participation in the divinity.[53]

It is his view that the whole universe works together which provides Iamblichus with his rationale of sacrifice. The rites are effective because of the common life and sympathetic union of all grades of being.[54] Iamblichus insists that the result of this is not to reduce sacrifice to a link in an automatic chain of causes and effects; since the being of the gods is not confined within nature nor bound by nature's necessities, it cannot be just a latent power in matter which inevitably reacts to sacrifice.[55] The gods are independent supernatural causes, moved simply by the bonds of kinship and love which relate creatures

---

[50]<u>De mysteriis</u>, V.11. Iamblichus also uses the stock argument that it is inconceivable that the creator should leave superior beings dependent on men for their food supply when he has provided for every other creature (ibid., V.10).

[51]Ibid., V.20, 23. See <u>supra</u>, n. 45.

[52]Ibid., I.12. [53]Ibid., I.13. [54]Ibid., V.7.

[55]Ibid., V.8.

to their creator.[56] The life of the sacrificed animal unites daemons and men and becomes a link between them, because it has something in common with both, namely, with men, ψυχή (life), and with daemons, freedom from matter acquired by being sublimated in sacrifice.[57] The sacrificial fire is an imitation of the divine fire, purifying what is offered and freeing it from the chains of matter.[58] Sacrifice is thus turned into an acted parable of the union and sympathy of the universe. As the fire assimilates the sacrifice to itself, so we are assimilated to the gods. Prayer is an essential part of sacrifice; without prayer, sacrifice is incomplete, but together they create an indissoluble bond of fellowship with the gods, the aim of both being to fill the worshipper with divine fire.[59]

The surprising thing is that it is not the sacrifices of worship and thanksgiving allowed by Porphyry that Iamblichus defends by this rationale. He deliberately opposes his predecessor,[60] stating that the best reason for sacrifice is the aversion of evil. Without sacrifices, we are not liberated from pestilence or famine, nor do we obtain seasonable rains, nor even emancipation from the process of "becoming" and salvation of our souls.[61] Sacrifice is thus

---

[56]Iamblichus explains that when a living thing is taken, an animal without blemish which perfectly fulfills the intentions of the Creator, it is a witness to the common creaturely origin of both sacrificer and victim, and the Creator is moved by it (ibid., V.9).

[57]Ibid., VI.3. [58]Ibid., V.12. [59]Ibid., V.26.

[60]It is obviously with the words of Porphyry in mind that Iamblichus states that sacrifices should not be offered for τιμή only, as we honour benefactors, not for the sake of returning thanks for the good things imparted to us by the gods, nor as remuneration for their gifts, as in the case of first-fruits (ibid., V.6).

[61]Ibid., V.6. The need to sacrifice to the gods that have to be averted appears in a number of writings in the Christian era, showing that this primitive as-

associated with purification from the "wheel of birth" in a way that is reminiscent of Orphism. For several centuries, philosophers sought such an escape from the transient in a rational and moral way through imitation of the gods; Iamblichus associates this imitation of the divine with the most superstitious practice of rites of aversion, justifying them as a kind of sacramental symbol of union with the gods.

Iamblichus justified the traditional practices of paganism by a symbolic interpretation, and he was followed by the avowed defenders of paganism against the encroaching power of Christianity. Julian, the Apostate Emperor, felt he had been commanded by the gods to restore their worship in its utmost purity, and this meant the restoration of sacrifices, even though the practice had almost entirely disappeared, the temples were in disrepair, and most educated men had learned to abhor the whole business.[62] Sallustius' treatise, On the Gods and the Universe, was probably an appeal to intelligent men to support Julian's programme.[63] Sallustius adopts the commonly accepted view that the gods are not subject to change

---

pect of Greek religion had by no means died out. Josephus distinguishes between gods who give blessing and gods to have to be averted (Contra Apionem, II.249). Julian followed Iamblichus. See also Eusebius' quotations from Porphyry in Praep. Evan., IV.9.

62Julian, Ep. 8 (Loeb), on the need to restore sacrifices. Since Julian confesses that not many know how to sacrifice, even though they do not refuse to do so, it appears that the practice had almost died out. Ammianus Marcellinus disapproved of Julian's hecatombs (XXII.12.6). (I am indebted to A. D. Nock's introduction to this edition of Sallustius p. lxxxiii and to Gilbert Murray, op. cit., p. 180, for this reference.) Nock (Conversion, p. 224) describes Julian as Ammianus' hero, so his disapproval is all the more significant.

63That the treatise should be ascribed to the friend of Julian is argued by Murray (op. cit., p. 171) and accepted by Nock in his edition.

or passion, and, anger being a passion, he agrees with Iamblichus that the gods cannot be appeased by gifts; when we are good, we have union with them because we are like them, whereas if we are bad we make them our enemies, not because they are angry but because our sins do not allow them to shed their light upon us. By sacrifice we do not affect the gods, but heal our own evil by returning to enjoy their goodness.[64] In Sallustius' rationale of sacrifice, union with the gods is dependent on the mediation of life, namely the life of the animal sacrificed. The form of the argument is not identical with that of Iamblichus, but clearly, like Iamblichus, Sallustius is committed to a defense of animal sacrifice by means of symbolism and to the construction of a sophisticated interpretation of sacrifice out of traditional ideas. Like Iamblichus he regards prayer as an essential element in sacrifice, maintaining their interdependence: prayers without sacrifice are mere words, whereas, together, sacrifice gives life to the word of prayer, and the word gives power to the life offered in sacrifice.[65] Sacrifice is an allegory of our union with the gods, but, for Sallustius, fire does not play the important role that it has in Iamblichus. He says that the animals are symbols of our "unreasonable" (ἄλογος) life and prayers of the intellectual element, in the same way as temples are copies of heaven, altars of earth, and images of life (which is the reason images are made in the likeness of living creatures).[66]

One difference from Iamblichus is that Sallustius does emphasise the offering of first-fruits as an obligation in return for the goodness of the gods, though he differs from Porphyry in including the first-fruits of flocks and herds - which is hardly surprising since the mediation of the life of an animal is so important in his rationale of sacrifice.[67] Again, unlike Iamblichus, Sallustius makes nothing of

---

[64]Sallustius, *On the Gods and the Universe*, XIV and XV.

[65]Ibid., XVI. [66]Ibid., XV.

[67]Ibid., XVI.

aversion sacrifices, but Julian certainly did. Whereas earlier pagan Emperors had persecuted the Christians by trying to force them to sacrifice, Julian would not allow anyone to sacrifice without first undergoing purification and offering sacrifices to the ἀποτρόπαιοι θεοί.[68] He was haunted by ancient taboos to such an extent that he forbade daytime funerals to avoid the ill-omen of a corpse passing-by during a sacrifice.[69] He believed that Moses had sacrificed to these abominable deities who avert evil, the scapegoat ritual and the sin-offerings of the Old Testament being proof of this.[70] However, his rationale of sacrifice, as far as it can be detected, seems to have followed Sallustius' view of the mediation of life.[71]

The basic problem of the Neoplatonists was to explain their sacrificial practices when their philosophical concept of God had rendered traditional ideas about how sacrifice worked completely unacceptable. The Christian Platonists were faced with an identical problem, and we shall find many points of contact with Neoplatonism. Whether the cult defended was the traditional offering of material gifts or the new purely spiritual worship, the problem of how it affected a passionless and changeless God was common to both religious philosophies. The protagonists of

---

[68]Julian, Ep. 41. [69]Ibid., Ep. 56.

[70]Julian (Loeb Edition, Vol. 3), pp. 402-4. The treatise Against the Galilaeans is excerpted by the Loeb editor (W. C. Wright) from Cyril of Alexandria's reply to it and thus is, as it stands, somewhat fragmentary and disconnected.

[71]This is reflected in Julian's exegesis of the sacrifices offered by Abel and Cain. In Against the Galilaeans (Loeb, pp. 418-20), he quotes the exegesis given him by a bishop and then proceeds to give a more adequate explanation: the things on earth that have life are more precious to the living God who is the cause of life, in as much as they have a share of life and a soul more akin to his. Therefore, the sacrifice of a living creature was more perfect in the eyes of God.

both were chiefly concerned to justify their cult practices as suitable sacrifices worthy of God as they conceived him, and to explain exactly how sacrifice "worked." Neoplatonism was the final statement of Greek religion on sacrifice, and it was produced under many of the same influences as Christian ideas. For this reason, it provides most important background to our study.

D. Conclusion

Popular religion in the Hellenistic world remained traditional in its practices, sacrifice being a feature of daily life until late in the Roman Empire. This situation continued in spite of the earlier philosophers, who found the popular conceptions of how sacrifice worked completely irrational in the light of a more advanced theology. Later, the philosophically inclined moved from practical compromise to deliberate attempts to rationalise sacrifice in accordance with their theology. It was at this stage that conflict with Christianity began, since the new faith had rejected sacrifice in favour of a spiritual cult. In spite of this basic difference, however, Christianity found itself faced by many of the same problems in rationalising its worship, and we shall find a number of contacts, particularly in the work of the pagan and Christian Platonists.

CHAPTER TWO
SACRIFICE IN JEWISH RELIGION

A. Classification of types

The Old Testament has a very complex vocabulary for sacrifice,[1] but it is possible to make a broad classification into three types, the "zebachs" or communion-sacrifices, the holocausts, and the expiatory sacrifices.[2]

(a) Communion-sacrifices: This term is intended to cover all the sacrifices of which the offerer, his family and guests, and the priest partook.[3] Originally it was performed at local altars whenever meat was eaten, part of the slaughtered animal being offered to God on the same principle as the first-fruits, namely that God's gift of food should not be enjoyed without offering part to him in gratitude.[4] Those who partook of the sacrifice had to be in a state of

---

[1]The number of terms for sacrifice in Hebrew is enormous, but most of them define not the reason for the sacrifice but the way in which the victim was treated, whether slain, burnt, or "waved," for example. For a full discussion of the various terms for sacrifice, and their etymologies and probable meanings, see G. B. Gray, _Sacrifice in the Old Testament_ (Oxford, 1925).

[2]This classification follows Ezekiel and Philo, _De victimis_, 4; see Gray, op. cit., pp. 64-5. It is followed by Yerkes, _Sacrifice in Greek and Roman Religion and in Early Judaism_ (London, 1953); Roland de Vaux, _Ancient Israel_, Vol. II (London, 1961) and _Les sacrifices de l'Ancien Testament_ (Paris, 1964).

[3]For the rituals, see _Lev._ 3 and 7.

[4]The origin of the offering of first-fruits was undoubtedly some sort of taboo idea, but see _infra_, Ch. II, sec. D, for its reinterpretation in terms of gratitude for God's gifts. They were still regarded as "sacred" and God's by right. See H. H. Rowley, _The Meaning of Sacrifice in the Old Testament_ (republished in _From Moses to Qumran_, London, 1964), p. 78.

ritual purity, that is, fit to feast in the presence of Jahweh.[5] This type of sacrifice was translated θυσία by the LXX, and it closely resembles the Greek festivals in which part was eaten and part given to the deity.[6]

After the centralisation of the cult at Jerusalem, provisions were made for the secular slaughtering of animals for meat,[7] and this type of sacrifice became less important; in the ritual manual of the Second Temple,[8] however, it is still prescribed for many occasions, including the fulfilment of vows. Votive-offerings had their place in Hebrew religion as in Greek, but the type of vow that predominated in later Judaism was not the "do ut des" variety,[9] but the religious vow of, for example, the Nazirite. The faithful fulfilment of the obligations undertaken was consummated by a communion-sacrifice.

The communion involved in the sacrifice is simply the fellowship of sharing in a meal. As the relationship of guest and host established a special bond

---

[5]See Yerkes, op. cit., pp. 154-5 and de Vaux, _Ancient Israel_, II, p. 418.

[6]Yerkes, op. cit., p. 146 and de Vaux, op. cit., p. 440.

[7]See _Deut_, 12.15-16, 20-25.

[8]By this term, reference is made to _Lev_. 1-7, the main source for ritual prescriptions. These chapters belong to the final redaction of the Pentateuch and may be regarded as the source for the developed sacrificial system of Judaism which formed the background of NT and Christian thought.

[9]Such vows are certainly found in some early OT narratives, e.g., _Judges_ 11.30-40, where Jephthah, by a vow, puts himself into the position of having to sacrifice his own daughter. This was presumably a holocaust, not a communion-sacrifice. See also 2 _Sam_. 15.7-9. The variety of votive-offerings can be seen in, e.g., _Gen_. 28.20-1, a vow to set up a holy place to Jahweh; and 1 _Sam_. 1.22,28, the dedication of a child to lifelong temple service. For discussions, see De Vaux, op. cit., pp. 465ff and Yerkes, op. cit., pp. 64ff.

between men,[10] so this common meal represented the special covenant, the "peace" (zebach shelamin = peace offering) between Jahweh and his worshippers. The sacrifice was a joyful one in which ideas of thanksgiving were present as well as the idea of communion.[11]

If Jahweh was invited to a meal, it was a not unnatural assumption that he was fed by sacrifices, and a few Old Testament references do indeed suggest this.[12] This primitive idea has, however, mostly been edited out. The ancient traditional phrase *lereach nichoch laAdonai* probably reflects the first stage of sophistication, replacing the crudest concept of feeding god with the idea that God enjoyed the smell of offerings; but in the late Priestly Document (P), even this has become fossilised,[13] and is merely used as a metaphor for God's pleasure in the dutiful devotion of his worshippers. Since it was inconceivable to the Jews that the author of all things was dependent on men for anything, there was no need for the constant reminder found in the Greek philosophers and Roman satirists that God had no need for food.[14]

---

[10]De Vaux, op. cit., p. 453. [11]Ibid., p. 417.

[12]Ibid., pp. 449ff and *Sacrifices*, pp. 38ff; G. von Rad, *Old Testament Theology* (Edinburgh, 1962), Vol. I, p. 254, n. 160. In discussing communion-sacrifices, von Rad refers especially to the meal at Sinai in *Exod*. 24. It is noticeable that this account omits any reference to God consuming his portions, although saying (v. 11), "They beheld God and ate and drank," i.e., they feasted in the presence of Yahweh.

[13]For its fossilisation, see Gray, op. cit., pp. 74, 76-81, and p. 22: ". . . in later literature such as *Ezechiel* and P the terms were merely petrified expressions preserving the forms of once living but long dead beliefs." See also Yerkes, op. cit., p. 129. *Lereach nichoch laAdonai* is translated in the LXX as ὀσμὴ εὐωδίας.

[14]A very occasional protest is found; see Ps. 50. 12-13. The idea that the heathen fed their idols with sacrifices is found in the OT and in Jewish polemical writings.

Communion-sacrifices were not a very important element in the thinking of later Judaism. While it must be admitted that Paul wrote of Jewish sacrifices "Are not they who eat the victims in communion with the altar?",[15] this does not refute the fact that for the Diaspora Jew participation in sacrifice was more or less unknown, and the practice of commutation (that is the offering of money instead of an animal victim) suggests that by this time the dominant idea of sacrifice was that of gift.[16]

(b) Holocausts: The whole-burnt offering[17] was the best gift that could be offered to God, and it expressed the worshipper's praise and thanksgiving. This should be contrasted with Greek religion, where, as we saw earlier, the holocaust was an offering of aversion to the underworld powers.[18] In the later Temple the priests offered daily burnt-offerings on behalf of the nation, so performing a continual act of praise to God for his mercies.[19]

---

[15] *1 Cor.* 10.18.

[16] See Gray, op. cit., pp. 33ff.

[17] The term "holocaust" is used in the LXX to translate both *'olah* and *kalil*. The meaning of the first term is disputed, but it probably comes from the root meaning "to go up," and most likely refers to the ascent of the smoke of the sacrifice which goes up to God when the victim is burned. The second is a later term used to describe the sacrifice by its characteristic feature, namely, that the whole victim is consumed by fire and offered to God, none of it being consumed by either the priests or the offerer. See de Vaux, *Institutions*, pp. 415ff and *Sacrifices*, p. 28. The rituals for these offerings are given in *Lev.* 1.

[18] See Yerkes, op. cit., p. 128; de Vaux, *Institutions*, pp. 440ff and *Sacrifices*, p. 46.

[19] *Num.* 28.3-4. See de Vaux, *Sacrifices*, p. 36: "L'holocauste est principalement un acte d'hommage qui s'exprime par un don. Il est ainsi devenu le type du sacrifice parfait, de l'hommage fait à Dieu par un don total . . ."

That the gift sacrifice was open to crude interpretations must be admitted. The criticisms of the prophets indicate that costly gifts were thought to gain God's favour,[20] but in later Judaism such an attitude was not general. Because man owes everything to God, it is right that tribute should be paid to him, especially of those things that are vital to his life, which meant in an earlier age, his flocks and herds or his crops, and later his money. The complete destruction of the offering on the altar, whatever crude ideas about God needing food may have originated the practice, came to signify the irrevocable nature of the gift.[21] How God received the gift was overshadowed by the fact that the giver gave up something for God, and so fasting became an adequate substitute for sacrifice after the loss of the Temple.[22]

In early Israel, the holocaust was occasionally offered to propitiate the wrath of Jahweh, especially in times of crisis.[23] This usage is absent from later

---

[20]Gray, op. cit., p. 42. See *infra*, Ch. 2 at n. 76.

[21]De Vaux, *Institutions*, p. 452.

[22]Gray, op. cit., p. 49.

[23]It is possible that the phrase *reach nichoch laAdonai* originally referred to propitiation. Etymologically the phrase means a "rest-giving smell," that is, possibly, a smell which quiets the anger of Jahweh or placates him. This suggestion finds support in the one text where the phrase is used outside the ritual texts: "And Yahweh smelled the soothing odour; and Jahweh said in his heart, I will not again curse the ground any more for man's sake" (*Gen*. 8.21). See also 1 *Sam*. 26.19: If it be Jahweh that hath incited thee against me, let him smell an offering." This propitiatory sense is used in P. It has become simply a symbol of God's pleasure in the obedience of his people; hence the Greek paraphrase ὀσμὴ εὐωδίας has no sense of propitiation. For the above discussion, see Gray, op. cit., pp. 74, 76-81. Many early OT stories tell of propitiatory offerings; see Gray, op. cit., Ch. 6 and V. Taylor, *Jesus and His Sacrifice*

Judaism, though the increasing concern with the cleansing of sin led to the attribution of expiatory significance to all sacrifices including the holocaust.[24]

(c) Expiatory sacrifices: These sacrifices dominate the Levitical ritual. Evidence for their existence prior to the exile is slim, and the terms first appear in the writings of the prophet-priest, Ezechiel. While it is unlikely that these sacrifices were post-exilic innovations,[25] it is certain that they received greater prominence after the exile, presumably because the exile heightened the sense of national sin and emphasized the need for constant expiation to prevent such a disaster occurring again.

The ritual for the expiatory sacrifices[26] differs from that of the two types of sacrifice we have so far considered. As in the communion-offering, only specified parts of the victim were offered to God, but by contrast, the one who needed purification was not permitted to eat the flesh of the sacrifice;[27] it was

---

(London, 1959), p. 50. One good example is 2 Sam. 24.25: "And David built there an altar to the Lord, and offered burnt-offerings and peace-offerings. So the Lord heeded his supplications for the land, and the plague was averted from Israel."

[24]See Lev. 1.4; 16.24; von Rad, op. cit., p. 256 and de Vaux, Sacrifices, p. 36.

[25]Gray argues for the existence of these sacrifices in pre-exilic Israel; op. cit., pp. 64-6; and de Vaux argues also that they were not an innovation but were given greater prominence after the exile; Institutions, pp. 429ff and Sacrifices, pp. 93-5. Similarly, H. H. Rowley, op. cit., p. 80.

[26]There are two sacrifices referred to by this term, the sin-offering (chattat) and the guilt-offering (asham). It is virtually impossible to distinguish between them, or to find any consistence in the various matters for which they are respectively prescribed. See de Vaux, Institutions, pp. 420ff and Sacrifices, pp. 88-91; von Rad, op. cit., p. 259. The rituals for the expiatory sacrifice are given in Lev. 4-7.

[27]One eating the flesh of sacrifice had to be in a state of ritual purity.

therefore eaten by the priests, unless the sacrifice was offered on the priests' behalf, in which case, it was thrown outside and burned. The blood ritual was more elaborate than in other types of sacrifice, because the blood was considered to be the efficacious agent in expiating sin.[28]

The object of these offerings was the removal of ritual impurities, whether of the altar, the sacred vessels, the priests, the nation or the individual. P saw itself as the upholder of exact and strict observances given by God for the express purpose of re-establishing the covenant whenever unwitting sin and defilement had caused its annulment,[29] but this stress on purity was ritually conceived. Unintentional infringement of cultic regulations broke the Law as much as moral offences,[30] and an essential part of the purificatory rites was the expiation of the pollution of the altar caused by sin. There was no sacrificial expiation for sins committed with "a high-hand," that is, deliberate and premeditated refusal to do right whether cultically or morally,[31] though some such sins

---

[28]See discussion of the meaning of blood, infra, Ch. 2, at n. 69.

[29]von Rad, op. cit., p. 260 and de Vaux, Institutions, p. 453. There are repeated warnings that the ritual must be performed exactly or the sacrifice will not be acceptable; e.g., Lev. 7.18; 19.5; 22.19 etc.

[30]This was so right up to the fall of the Temple. See E. O. James, Sacrifice and Sacrament (London, 1962), p. 109.

[31]Num. 15.22-9. See von Rad, op. cit., p. 258; Yerkes, op. cit., p. 169; James, op. cit., p. 110; Taylor, op. cit., p. 51; de Vaux, Sacrifices, p. 85; and the discussion in H. H. Rowley, op. cit., pp. 92ff. Rowley points out that unwitting sins cannot mean simply sins committed in ignorance, because they include robbery and oppression, wrongful retention of lost property, and false dealing with a neighbor. In many cases, unwitting sin means accidental violation of ritual laws, but the above were not unconscious sins in this sense. Rowley suggests that sins committed

could be expiated by the ritual of the Day of Atonement.[32] Otherwise the only possible solution was excommunication from the covenant people and its worship of God, since the prosperity of the nation depended on the removal of all impurities.[33]

These sacrifices were not simply gifts to turn away God's wrath, since only part was given to Jahweh. The purpose of the offerings is described as lekhapper, a term whose origin is disputed, but which has come to mean technically "to make atonement for."[34] In the Old Testament it is construed with the priests or Jahweh as

---

with a high-hand must be defined as deliberate sins, perpetrated of set purpose, as over against sins committed through human weakness; the latter could find atonement through sacrifice but the former, which includes such acts as murder and adultery, could not. But although there was no sacrificial rite to cover them, atonement was possible: see the story of David and Uriah where the prophet Nathan says to David, when he has recognized and repented of his fault, "The Lord has put away thy sin" (2 Sam. 12.13). This cleansing was an act of God (though not performed through sacrifice) in response to penitence.

32See Taylor, op. cit., p. 56.

33James, op. cit., p. 53; Yerkes, op. cit., pp. 168-9; von Rad, op. cit., pp. 262ff, where the author stresses the importance of the corporate sense of sin and guilt in the OT.

34The etymology of the phrase is disputed; some compare it with a Syriac root which means to "wipe away," and others with an Arabic root meaning "cover." Whichever it should be, the term is certainly a fixed cultic formula in ritual texts, and therefore its meaning can be sought only in context. See Yerkes, op. cit., p. 178ff; Gray, op. cit., p. 68ff, especially p. 73 on its fixture as a cultic technical term; von Rad, op. cit., p. 262, refuses to discuss the question of etymology, regarding it as irrelevant to the problem of what the technical term meant to those who used it. James, op. cit., p. 110, suggests comparison with the Babylonian cultic term "kuppuru" which means "purge" or "purify."

the subject, and the Temple, altar or iniquity as the object. The object is never God, though the action is performed in God's presence.[35] The only possible conclusion is that the rites were not propitiatory, but were expiatory, a means given by God to wipe away sin and cope with the problem of failure to fulfil the Law. God acted through these cultic instruments to keep Israel from sin and calamity, making her ritually clean so that she could offer him fitting worship.[36]

B. Jewish Feasts

Only two of the Jewish feasts are of special importance as background to Christian thought, the Day of Atonement ritual and the Passover; so, I propose to confine discussion to these, although there were many other feasts which had an important place in Jewish religion.

(a) The Feast of the Passover: The origins of this feast are extremely interesting, but not relevant here. In all the Old Testament traditions, the combined festival of the Passover and Unleavened Bread has become a memorial of the escape from Egypt, and in fact, this tradition is so dominant that the Exodus has been regarded by some scholars as an aetiological myth constructed to explain the significance of the feast.[37] It is more likely, however, that a very ancient nomadic feast which accompanied removal to summer pastures was reinterpreted in the light of the

---

[35]Yerkes, op. cit., p. 182; Gray, op. cit., p. 68, 74; Taylor, op. cit., pp. 52-3.

[36]Philo says of sin-offerings that they are offered for deliverance from evils and for the cure of those offences which the soul had committed (*De victimis*, 4). Therefore he does not regard them as propitiatory.

[37]de Vaux (*Sacrifices*, p. 23) differs from J. Pedersen in *ZAW*, 3 (1934), pp. 161-75 and in his *Israel, its Life and Culture* (London, 1926). See also de Vaux, *Institutions*, pp. 492-3.

most important migration in the history of Israel, from Egypt to the Promised Land.[38]

According to Biblical traditions, God gave the command to Moses that each household should slaughter a lamb, smear its blood on the doorposts of the house, roast it and eat it with unleavened bread and bitter herbs, all dressed for immediate flight. The Angel of Destruction would slay all the first-born in Egypt, except where the sign of the blood protected the inmates of the house. So the command to celebrate the Passover was the means whereby God delivered his people, and hereafter the same ritual was to be performed year after year to commemorate this supreme act of salvation in Israel's history.[39] This traditional account of the origin of the Passover retains in a modified form the primitive significance of the blood: namely that it was "Apotropaeic," a means of protecting the household from evil powers.[40]

---

[38]de Vaux (Sacrifices, pp. 22-3) refers to M. Noth, Ueberlieferungs geschichte des Pentateuchs (1948), pp. 72-3.

[39]Exod. 12. von Rad (op. cit., p. 253) comments: "The interpretation in Exod. 12 and Deut. 16.1ff, which connects it with the saving-history, sees in its performance an actualisation of Jahweh's redemptive action in history."

[40]That blood was originally "apotropaeic" in significance (i.e., was a means of driving away evil powers from home and flocks, like the aversion sacrifices in Greek religion) is argued against by Gray (op. cit., Ch. 23, passim) and de Vaux (Sacrifices, pp. 11-2) but accepted by Yerkes (op. cit., pp. 48-9), de Vaux (Institutions, p. 489), and von Rad (op. cit., p. 253). de Vaux (Sacrifices, p. 22) draws attention to the way in which the legend of the tenth plague provided a reinterpretation of this atropaeic significance in the light of developing beliefs in the sole authority of Jahweh and his special saving grace in the deliverance of Israel. Gray cites Jubilees to show that the atropaeic idea reappeared surprisingly late, although modified by the theological idea that

Because the Passover lamb was regarded as a sacrifice,[41] _Deuteronomy_'s law of the one sanctuary required that it be slain in the Temple at Jerusalem.[42] This transformed the Passover from a family festival to a national pilgrimage festival, and required an alteration in the blood ritual, since it could no longer be applied to the doorposts of the house where it was celebrated. Consequently the simplest blood ritual was adopted, the blood being poured out at the base of the altar as an offering to God.[43] The lambs were slain in the Temple in the afternoon preceding the Holy Day, and then roasted and eaten in houses in Jerusalem that evening. This was the procedure in New Testament times, when the Passover had become the chief pilgrimage festival of the Jewish calenaar.[44]

Jahweh controlled the evil powers: "And do thou command the children of Israel to observe the Passover throughout their days, every year once a year, on the day of its fixed time, and it shall come for a memorial before the Lord and no plague shall come upon them to slay or to smite in that year in which they celebrate the Passover in its season in every respect according to his command." (_Jubilees_, 49.15; Gray, op. cit., p. 365).

[41]The Passover is described as a "sacrifice to Jahweh" or "Jahweh's pesach," and the expression "to sacrifice the Passover" is also used. _Exod_. 12.11, 27, 48; _Deut_. 16.2, 5, 6; _Lev_. 23.5; 2 _Kings_ 23.21, etc.

[42]_Deut_. 16.1-8.

[43]_See_ von Rad, op. cit., p. 253 and discussion in Gray, op. cit., p. 365. Gray draws attention to the fact that the Passover sacrifice was unique. The victim has to be male as with a burnt-offering, the meat is consumed as in the zebach (though in fact there is a difference here, for the whole victim is consumed by the worshippers and none burnt on the altar), and the blood-offering is similar to the sin-offering, though no ideas of atonement were ever associated with the Passover sacrifice. See pp. 351 and 366.

[44]The fact that the Passover was the chief pilgrimage feast is obvious from the Gospels; _Lk_. 2.41: "Now

The feast continued to be celebrated after the destruction of the Temple, but without the sacrificial lamb. The implication of this is that the sacrifice in the Temple and the blood ritual had become relatively insignificant, and the central act of the feast was the family meal. Ideas of communion are not associated with this meal in later Jewish literature,[45] the feast being simply a memorial in the developed tradition. The Rabbis followed the Old Testament in regarding it as a sacred meal of thanksgiving, commemoratively associated with God's supreme act of redemption, the Exodus from Egypt. Traditionally, the son of the family would ask what the significance of the feast was during the course of the meal, and the father's liturgical response followed the lines of the *Exodus* text: "It is the sacrifice of the Lord's Passover, for he passed over the houses of the people of Israel in Egypt, when he slew the Egyptians but spared our houses."[46] In Rabbinic times, prayers were added which expressed the hope of the people for future

---

his parents went to Jerusalem every year at the feast of the Passover." Jesus had gone to Jerusalem for the Passover when he was finally arrested, and the fact that Jerusalem was crowded with pilgrims for the feast is clear from the narratives. See de Vaux, *Institutions*, p. 484 and *Sacrifices*, p. 7.

[45]Gray, op. cit., p. 381.

[46]*Exod*. 12.26-7. The ritual referred to acquired elaborations, but basically followed the idea of the *Exod*. verse quoted. The longer ritual account of the redemption from Egypt, applied in *Deut*. to the first-fruits ritual (*Deut*. 26.5ff) was used, according to the Mishnah. See Gray, op. cit., pp. 378-9. The victim was regarded as a symbol of the fact that God passed over the houses of the fathers in Egypt, the unleavened bread of their redemption, and the bitter herbs of the bitter life they had led in Egypt. The association with redemption led to the inclusion of praise, thanksgiving, and hymn singing. See also de Vaux, *Sacrifices*, p. 25.

redemption and the restoration of the glory of Israel.[47]

(b) The Day of Atonement: The "Yom hakkippurim," the Day of Atonement, developed very late by comparison with many Jewish festivals. There is no evidence for it even by the comparatively late date of Nehemiah and Ezra, though the ritual is given fully in *Leviticus*.[48] Its origin is obscure, but clearly its importance rested on the accentuated interest in purification which we have already noticed as a characteristic of post-exilic Judaism. By New Testament and Rabbinic times it had become known as "The Day," and was the most solemn feast of the Jewish calendar.[49]

The rituals of the Day of Atonement combine two quite different ceremonies. In the first, a bull was sacrificed as a sin-offering for the priests, and a goat as a sin-offering for the people. These rituals were exactly similar to the Levitical sin-offerings already outlined, except that on this one day of the year, the High-Priest entered the Holy of Holies and sprinkled the blood of each sin-offering on the mercy-seat itself. Expiation for the priests and people had apparently become linked with a ritual for the purification of the very heart of the sanctuary.[50]

The second ceremony was quite different. Another goat was "presented alive before the Lord,"[51] and the High-Priest laid his hands on its head, confessing over it all the sins of the people of Israel. In this way, the sins were transferred to the goat and it was sent out into the desert bearing them all away with it.

---

[47]See Gray, op. cit., p. 379ff, where he gives Rabbinic evidence for the future hopes associated with the Passover. Also de Vaux, *Sacrifices*, pp. 25-6.

[48]*Lev*. 16 and 23.26-32.

[49]For the late development of the feast, see de Vaux, *Institutions*, p. 510 and James, op. cit., p. 110. For the importance of "The Day," see de Vaux, *Institutions*, p. 507 and Gray, op. cit., p. 318ff.

[50]de Vaux, *Institutions*, p. 508 and *Sacrifices*, p. 86; von Rad, op. cit., p. 271.

[51]*Lev*. 16.10.

These two ceremonies were integrated by the fact that the two goats were brought forward together and set before Jahweh, no distinction being made between them at this stage. Lots were cast, and one goat designated for Jahweh and the other for "Azazel." The goat for Jahweh was sacrificed as a sin-offering for the people as described above, but the other goat was not sacrificed either to Jahweh or Azazel, because once it had received all the sins of the people it was impure and therefore could not be used as a sacrificial victim.[52] The man who escorted it away into the desert became unclean by association with it, and before re-joining the people had to wash himself and his clothes.

This "scapegoat" ceremony is obviously very primitive in origin, and many analogies to it from other primitive peoples were collected by Sir James Frazer.[53] There is one analogy in Hebrew ritual namely the offering made by a man cured from leprosy; a bird is allowed to fly away carrying with it the sin and disease of the leper.[54]

Azazel was clearly a supernatural being of some sort parallel to Jahweh; in the book of _Enoch_ he is called the prince of the devils.[55] It is apparently to him that the sins of the people are carried; but the important thing about the transaction as it is given in _Leviticus_ is that this primitive rite has

---

[52]de Vaux, _Institutions_, p. 509 and _Sacrifices_, p. 87.

[53]J. G. Fraser, _The Golden Bough_ (ii.3 and vi). One example may be quoted from "The Scapegoat" (p. 209); in some parts of Breadalbane it was formerly the custom on New Year's Day to take a dog to the door, give him a bit of bread, and drive him out, saying, "Get away, you dog! Whatever death of men or loss of cattle would happen in this house to the end of the year, may it all light upon your head."

[54]_Lev_. 14.1-9.

[55]_Enoch_, IX.6; X.4-8. See de Vaux, _Sacrifices_, op. cit., p. 87 and _Institutions_, p. 509; Gray, op. cit., p. 316; James, op. cit., p. 110.

been "exorcised"[56] by its close association with more sophisticated beliefs about Jahweh. Azazel is by no means Jahweh's equal, and he plays no active part in the ritual. Until the lots were cast there was no distinction between the goats and both are set before Jahweh. The removal of sin depends on confession over the goat in the presence of Jahweh, and it is by the power of Jahweh that the sins are transferred by the rite and so removed. The whole transaction takes place because Jahweh wills it and Azazel is merely the passive recipient of the sins. The prayer of confession in the Rabbinic treatise on the Day of Atonement emphasizes the point that Jahweh alone is active in expiating the sins of the people.[57]

Since the Day could atone for some premeditated sins, (unlike the regular sin-offerings), there was a grave danger inherent in the ritual, namely that it should be regarded as automatically effective. The Rabbis specifically deal with this problem: "If one says, 'I will sin and the Day of Atonement will procure atonement for me,' the Day of Atonement procures for him no atonement." The need for genuine repentance is a constant refrain in their casuistry which determined

---

[56]This is de Vaux' expression in Institutions, p. 509 and Sacrifices, p. 87. See Gray's discussion (op. cit., p. 317) of the way the primitive rite has been incorporated into Jahweh worship and so transformed.

[57]"O Jahweh, thy people the house of Israel have committed iniquity, transgressed and sinned before thee; O Jahweh expiate now the transgressions which thy people, the house of Israel, have committed, transgressed and sinned, before thee; as it is written in the Law of Moses, 'For on that day he shall make expiation for you to cleanse you from all your sins; before Jahweh ye shall be clean" (Yoma, 6.2); quoted by Gray, op. cit., p. 317. See also C. G. Montefiore and H. Loewe, A Rabbinic Anthology (London, 1938), p. 151: "Who makes you clean? Your Father in heaven."

which sins were atoned for by the Day.[58] For them, the Day had become a national Day of repentance and confession. Even prior to the Fall of the Temple, the Day affected all Jews, not merely those attending the rituals in the Temple at Jerusalem, since, being a High Sabbath and a fast-day, no work of any kind was allowed, and services of confession and penitence were observed in the synagogues throughout the Diaspora. Already, emphasis had shifted, for the majority of Jews, away from rituals whereby sins were mechanically removed, to the need for repentance and purification of the heart.[59] Atonement depended ultimately on the power of Jahweh to expiate sin, but his will to exercise this power depended on the individual's genuine repentance.

---

[58]See S. Baron and J. Blau (ed.), _Judaism, Postbiblical and Talmudic Period_ (New York, 1954), pp. 143ff. Some statements reveal a belief in the automatic atoning efficacy of the Day, but for high-handed sins, repentance was required: "For all the transgressions of the commands of the Torah, _whether one repented or not_, does the Day of Atonement procure atonement, except in the case of one who throws off the yoke of the Torah, interprets the Torah unlawfully, or breaks the covenant of Abraham our father. In these cases, if he repented, the Day of Atonement procures atonement; if not, not" (ibid., pp. 144-5). Presumably the point is that it is impossible, strictly speaking, to repent of sins committed in ignorance. Against this, see the following: "Sin-offering and guilt-offering and death and the Day of Atonement all of them together do not expiate sin without repentance" (Montefiore & Loewe, op. cit., p. 323).

[59]See James, op. cit., pp. 112-3.

C. The Rationale of Sacrifice

In modern discussions of the significance of Old Testament sacrifices, it is frequently claimed that the animal victim died as a substitute for the offerer:[60] by the laying on of hands, the man offering the sacrifice transferred his sins to the head of the victim so that they could be wiped out by the destruction of the animal; and, in the blood rituals, the life of the victim was poured out as a symbol of the life of the sacrificer offered to God.

This rationale of sacrifice is clearly dependent on particular interpretations of two ritual acts, the laying on of hands and the manipulation of the blood. The validity of these interpretations must therefore be examined.

(a) The Laying on of Hands: Two suggestions have been made as to the meaning of this action. The first argues that human sacrifice was the original form of sacrifice and when animals were substituted for men, the laying on of hands symbolised the fact that the animal was to die in the offerer's stead.[61] The flaw in this argument is that it is extremely unlikely that a man ever sacrificed himself. Even where human sacrifice was practised, one man was sacrificed by another or by the community. In any case, evidence that human sacrifice was the most primitive form is apparently non-existent; it is merely an inference, which is hardly justified, since human sacrifice in fact seems to have flourished among semi-civilised peoples rather than the most primitive.[62] Besides this, the action occurs with the communion-sacrifices as well as the others, and the sacrificer could hardly

---

[60]E.g., James and Rowley. For detailed references, see discussion *infra*.

[61]James, *op. cit.*, p. 34. Rowley (*op. cit.*, p. 83) takes this even further; the action is said to imply not merely substitution but identification with the victim, so that the death of the victim symbolizes his death to sin, or whatever hampered the continuance of the covenant relation with God.

[62]de Vaux, *Sacrifices*, Ch. 3, *passim*.

have thought that the animal was to die in his stead when he was about to eat the meat as part of the ritual.[63]

The second suggestion has already been mentioned above, and is based more nearly on Old Testament evidence. In general, where the laying on of hands is prescribed, no interpretation of the action is given, but there is one occasion when we are told what it was supposed to signify, namely, when it is used in the scapegoat ritual; there, as we have already seen, it implied that the sins of the people were transferred to the goat. By analogy, it is claimed, the sacrificial victim was made to bear the sins of the offerer by this symbolic act, and so the victim died as his substitute to expiate his sins. This interpretation is also suspect. The victim cannot have been regarded as loaded with sin, firstly because of the law that every sacrificial victim must be pure and faultless if it is to be acceptable, and secondly because in the case of the sin-offering, it was eaten as a "most holy thing" by the priests.[64] It is precisely because the scapegoat was loaded with sin that it was banished into the desert; it was defiled and unworthy to be sacrificed.[65] The sacrificial victim was well-pleasing to God,[66] and in consideration of it, he removed the sin of the offerer.

---

[63]It is possible the action was transferred from the sin-offering to all sacrifices by P in order to give expiatory significance to every kind of sacrifice. See von Rad, op. cit., p. 256. But even so, we are largely concerned with the thoughts of people in NT times when they sacrifice, and in this case our argument holds.

[64]de Vaux, _Institutions_, p. 419 and _Sacrifices_, p. 29.

[65]de Vaux, _Institutions_, p. 416 and _Sacrifices_, p. 29. The fact that the laying on of hands cannot have meant the transference of sin is confirmed by Philo's allegorisation of it. He says (_De victimis_, 5) that it is the symbol of an irreproachable life.

[66]de Vaux, _Institutions_, p. 419 and _Sacrifices_, pp. 84-5.

Ritual actions tend to be traditional and to be performed without any search for rationale. Even in its origin, this action probably had no more significance than the identification by the offerer of the victim which was offered on his behalf by the priest.[67] This is consistent with the fact that the action occurs with all kinds of sacrifice and not just the sin-offering, the victim being offered "à son bénéfice, non pas à sa place."[68]

(b) The Blood Rituals: Debate over the meaning of the blood rituals is heated, simply because the exegesis of many most important New Testament texts is felt to depend on the conclusions reached.[69] The generally accepted view is that the practices should be interpreted in the light of the one clue given in Leviticus, "For the life of the flesh is in the blood,"[70] a view found also in Deuteronomy.[71] This interpretation of the significance of the blood is supported by the suggestions of anthropologists concerning the rites of other primitive peoples, and such practices as the blood-covenant made between individuals.[72] To the primitive mind it would be obvious that life resides in the blood, for when the blood is shed life ends. Because the whole animal world is united with the world of men in a common life represented by the blood, the

---

[67]de Vaux, Institutions, p. 416 and Sacrifices, p. 29; Yerkes, op. cit., p. 134; H. Wheeler Robinson, Redemption and Revelation (London, 1952), p. 251; Taylor, op. cit., pp. 50-1.

[68]de Vaux, Sacrifices, p. 59.

[69]See, for instance, the debate begun by Leon Morris in the Journal of Theological Studies (1952) with an article entitled "The Biblical Use of the Term Blood," answered by L. Dewar in the same journal in 1953 with an article of the same title, with Morris, in 1955, defending himself, again under the same title.

[70]Lev. 7.11. [71]Deut. 12.23.

[72]See James, op. cit., Ch. 3 and Yerkes, op. cit., Ch. 5. Examples from Greek literature include the fact that Odysseus administers blood to revive the spirits in Hades before they can speak to him.

blood of a sacrificed animal must be given directly to Jahweh, the originator of life. Hence the practice of offering the blood to Jahweh in both the 'olah and the zebach, and the prohibition against eating blood.[73]

Against this commonly held opinion, an attempt has been made by Leon Morris[74] to show that in the Old Testament blood means not life but death, and specifically death with violence. He presents statistics: of 360 occasions of the word "blood," 203 are of violent death, only 3 specifically interpret death as life, and 103, being sacrificial, are the subject of the dispute. Against him, Leon Morris has the actual text of Leviticus and Deuteronomy, both of which purport to be explaining the significance of blood rituals and taboos. The idiomatic use of blood to signify death can surely be explained in terms of responsibility for the loss of lifeblood. His statistics seem to be irrelevant to the discussion.

The actual issue in the dispute is whether the essential act of sacrifice was the death of the victim or the offering of lifeblood. The form of the rituals definitely suggests that the blood ritual was more important, and that it signified more than merely the death or destruction of the victim. The owner of the victim killed it, the immolation being merely the preparation for the sacrifice;[75] the priest manipulated the blood in accordance with the precise rituals laid down for each type of sacrifice. There can be no doubt that the blood was held to be particularly sacred, and indeed to have extraordinary powers. It was the blood that effected atonement and expiation. The Leviticus passage already referred to, continues by saying that God has given the blood "for you upon the altar to make atonement for your souls; for it is the blood that makes atonement by reason of the life . . . ." The blood is the efficacious agent in the

---

[73]In the Deut. passage and in Lev. 17.14, the blood is said to be the life in order to explain the prohibition against eating it.

[74]Morris, op. cit.

[75]See de Vaux, Institutions, p. 452.

expiation of sin because, being especially sacred to Jahweh, it can cover or wipe away pollution by means of its holy powers.[76] Why this efficacy for expiation if the blood signified no more than the death of the victim?

In addition to his use of statistics, Leon Morris argued that the assumptions usually made about sacrifice not merely stretch the meaning of the texts in question far beyond the actual evidence,[77] but are also inconsistent with the fact that beliefs about an after-life developed late, and when they did develop, incorporeal existence was so inconceivable that a resurrection of the body was postulated. We should certainly heed this warning against putting too sophisticated an interpretation on the offering of life to the deity, even if, against Leon Morris, we accept the statement of the Law-books that the blood was the life. It is extremely unlikely that the blood should be regarded as a symbol of the worshipper's life surrendered to Jahweh.[78] The idea has much more primitive roots and was never dependent on the fact that the idea of an after-life gave it "spiritualised" significance. The blood, as essential to life, was regarded as the life-principle (nephesh). The life-principle was released

---

[76]Ibid., p. 419; James, op. cit., p. 111.

[77]Morris quoted Vincent Taylor as an example of assumptions made about sacrificial blood which go far beyond the evidence: "The victim is slain in order that its life, in the form of blood, may be released. . . The aim is to make it possible for the life to be presented as an offering to the deity. . . The bestowal of life is the fundamental idea in sacrificial worship."

[78]Dewar's argument (op. cit., p. 26, n. 4) to this effect depends on interpreting the laying on of hands as an act substituting the victim for the worshipper, a view opposed supra, Ch. 2, at n. 61. See also de Vaux (Sacrifices p. 83ff), especially his assertion: Il n'est pas question, dans ce passage, d'une substitution de la victime à l'offrant, ni question de la vie de l'offrant, il s'agit de la vie de la victime, qui est son sang. . ."

in sacrifice in order to effect, in primitive quasi-magical thought, the production of more abundant life, that is, to make the crops grow and the flocks increase.[79] This primitive notion of the life-principle was taken over by P and put in the context of later ideas of God, as the soverign Creator and Lord of life. Traditionally the blood was sacred to Jahweh as the life-principle; in P the blood had its efficacious power because it was created and given by Jahweh. Although the priest performed the actions for expiation, it was in fact Jahweh who effected it, through the ordained ritual of the blood-offering.[80]

By New Testament times, the commandment of the Law was enough justification for belief and practice. God had given the blood upon the altar to make atonement for their souls. The _Epistle to the Hebrews_ shows that this was accepted without asking how or why: "Under the Law almost everything is purified with blood, and without the shedding of blood, there is no forgiveness of sins."[81]

(c) Conclusion concerning the Rationale of Jewish Sacrifices: Our examination of these two vital points suggests that the idea that the animal died in the offerer's stead is unfounded. In any case, for the

---

[79]James, op. cit., p. 26.

[80]von Rad, op. cit., p. 270.

[81]_Heb_. 9.22. I am indebted to an unpublished article by T. C. G. Thornton on the significance of "Blood" in NT sacrificial contexts, kindly lent to me by Prof. C. F. D. Moule. Thornton contends that the controversy over whether blood meant death or life is not relevant to NT exegesis because it assumes that the Jews had a rationale of sacrifice, which they did not, except for the belief that it had been ordained by God. He supports this position by references to contemporary Jewish and Rabbinic literature. See also James, op. cit., Ch. 3, where it is stated that for the NT writers the atoning efficacy of sacrificial blood was axiomatic. See also Taylor's assertion (op. cit., p. 49): Nowhere in the OT is the rationale of sacrifice explained. The institution is taken for granted as a divine ordinance."

Rabbis and the Jews of New Testament times, sacrifice required no rationale because it was God's ordained means of worship and expiation set forth in the Law and simply to be obeyed. Apart from this, the idea that one offered a gift to God in this way was the only one that had any great influence.

D. Theological Developments and Moral Criticisms

In earlier sections we have already noticed instances in which ancient ritual phrases and practices became invested with new meanings.[82] Sacrificial rites are by their nature conservative, but ideas are more flexible and inevitably change in the course of centuries.[83] The main factor in the transformation of Jewish sacrificial ideas was the developing concept of God's sovereignty, an idea which led to thoroughgoing ethical monotheism, and excluded crude conceptions of what happened when sacrifice was offered. The form of worship remained the same, clinging to ancient tradition, but as theology developed, the attitude of the worshipper was transformed.

An early rewriting of the cult laws in accordance with new concepts of God can be found in Deuteronomy. It is possible that this resulted from the teachings of the prophets,[84] who, long before the Greek philosophers, realised that it was unworthy of God to suppose that he was dependent on or needed sacrifices. It was not Jahweh who got pleasure from the sacrificial

---

[82]E.g., the votive-offering. The ideas that God ate the sacrifice, or smelled the sacrifices, or that costly gifts gained God's favour, or that God could be propitiated by sacrifice have been discussed at the beginning of this chapter.

[83]von Rad, op. cit., p. 252.

[84]See Rowley, op. cit., p. 75. von Rad stands alone in finding another context for Deut; see his Studies in Deuteronomy (London, 1953), p. 69.

feasts but the self-indulgent worshippers; so they might as well eat the flesh of the burnt-offerings as well as the zebachs.[85] God demanded obedience from the people and did not need sacrifices. In accordance with ideas of this sort, Deuteronomy reinterpreted the cultic ceremonies as the offering of fitting tribute to the God from whom all things had been received. The various different rites became, like the Passover, memorials of God's saving acts in Israel's history, and of the special covenant relation which Jahweh had established with Israel. The Exodus from Egypt determined the content of the first-fruits liturgy.[86] Similarly, obedience to the statutes of the Lord was required because he "brought us out of Egypt with a mighty hand and commanded us" to do them.[87] Thus the rituals were filled with thoughts of what Israel owed to God rather than how to extort favours from him. Sacrifice became an opportunity of acknowledging his goodness, and was therefore a time of joy.[88] This contribution to sacrificial thought is important, and joy in God's mercy and goodness never entirely disappeared from the Temple-worship, even when expiatory rites became dominant.[89] But more important is the fact that as early as Deuteronomy attention was directed away from any rationale of sacrifice which supposed that the attitude of God could be changed by gifts. Already sacrifices were regarded as ordained by God to remind

---

[85]See Amos 4.4 and Jer. 7.21: "Add your burnt-offerings to your sacrifices and eat flesh."

[86]Deut. 26.5ff. [87]Ibid., 6.21.

[88]To sacrifice is to "eat before Jahweh," or to "rejoice before Jahweh." See Gray, op. cit., pp. 46-7. Examples of "to eat" and "to rejoice before Jahweh" are found in Deut. 12.12, 18. (Chapter 12 deals with the law of one sanctuary. I have not considered it necessary to discuss this aspect of Deut.'s contribution to the cult.)

[89]Even the Day of Atonement was an occasion of rejoicing, because on that Day, God cleansed Israel of her sins. See Gray, op. cit., p. 321.

his people of his mercy and salvation, the only explanation allowed by later Judaism where the command of God was accepted and no further questions were raised.

Developments in the sacrificial theory of the later Law-books can also be traced in some measure to the influence of the prophets, in that their warnings that Israel was to suffer for her sins paved the way for the realisation that Jahweh was at least a superior God, and eventually that he was the only God, Creator of all things, so sovereign as to be the ultimate source of evil as well as of good, and the cause of judgement, vengeance and expiation. "See now that I, even I, am he, and there is no god beside me; I kill and I make alive; I wound and I heal, and there is none that can deliver out of my hand . . ."[90] God is the one who "avenges the blood of his servants . . . and makes expiation for the land of his people."[91] This is the type of theology which moulded the rituals of P. The idea that man by his own efforts could make adequate satisfaction for his sin was repudiated by stress on the sovereignty of God who alone could effect the expiation of sin and the purification of his people. At the same time, the realisation of God's holiness and power, particularly the realisation that his wrath had caused the exile, led to an increased concern with expiatory rites so as to keep Israel free from such catastrophe again. The wrath of God was not to be treated lightly.[92]

The theological developments we have so far sketched are probably to be attributed to the indirect influence of the prophets. Their direct influence on Jewish thinking about the relationship between morality and sacrifice, is however clear. Several centuries before the Greek philosophers began to insist that morality was more important than the offering of sacrifices, the pre-exilic prophets were preaching this very message. Their attention was drawn to the problem by the sight of rich extortioners making

---

[90] <u>Deut</u>. 32.39. [91] Ibid., 32.43.

[92] This has been discussed earlier in this chapter.

extravagant offerings in the belief that thus they would insure Jahweh's blessing on their dubious enterprises.[93] Against this, the prophets stressed the uselessness of the sacrificial system without moral virtues, and the superiority of justice, mercy and love to all forms of material offering. They did not deny that God required service from his people,[94] but they insisted that Israel was neglecting the one kind of service which God really asked of them.[95] It is only obedience to the moral law, the end of oppression of the poor and acts of loving-kindness that will please or propitiate God. Without efforts to seek justice, he will not even listen to their prayers.[96]

There is considerable dispute in the scholarly world as to whether the prophets were led by their theological and moral criticisms to propose a complete rejection of all cultic practices in favour of a purely spiritual religion.[97] This question is not directly relevant here since in fact the sacrificial system was never rejected in Judaism. The significant point is that the practice of sacrifice, sustained by the idea that it was ordained by God for the good of his people,

---

[93]See, e.g., Amos 4 & 5. Rowley (op. cit., p. 87f) stresses the absence of any intention to reform on the part of those bringing the most costly gifts.

[94]It appears from the Prophets that most of the people were acting on the theory that all God wanted was more and costlier gifts, and that suitable gifts were slain animals. On these grounds, Gray (op. cit., p. 43ff) argues that the polemic of the Prophets supports his view that sacrifices were primarily regarded as gifts, and shows that there is no evidence for Israelite interpretation of sacrifice as communion in prophetic polemic, even though their references are mainly to sacrifices which people ate.

[95]See, e.g., Micah 6.6-8.

[96]Isa. 1.10-17.

[97]For discussion of this question, see the works of Lindblom, Robinson, and Mowinckel listed in the bibliography; also Rowley (op. cit.) and de Vaux (op. cit.).

was tempered by a second almost opposing strand in Jewish thought, namely a long tradition of moral criticism stemming from the teaching of the prophets. Morality was recognised as more important than sacrifice, and sacrifice without morality was seen to be useless. This precluded the idea that the cult worked automatically because the intention of the offerer was recognized as more important than the gift itself. Under its influence the Law itself required confession and restitution before the sacrifice was acceptable.[98]

Particularly interesting is the fact that the Psalms, that part of Hebrew literature most closely associated with the daily cultic worship of the Temple,[99] contain this strand of thought. As hymns accompanying the processions and the sacrificial rites, they gave expression to the meaning implicit in them, but yet we find the recognition that prayer and praise, and especially repentance and confession are really more important.[100] The worshippers are asked to admit that

---

[98] Rowley, op. cit., pp. 82, 86-7, 91. See Lev. 5.5ff and Num. 5.6ff. It is because of this tradition, even in the Law-books, that H. Wheeler Robinson, in his Inspiration and Revelation in the Old Testament (Oxford, 1946), can interpret all sacrifices as analogues to prophetic symbolism, each being a growth from sympathetic magic. The sacrifice had no efficacy unless it was accompanied by the right frame of mind and intention, of which it was the effective and active symbol.

[99] For the place of the Psalms in the cult, see S. O. P. Mowinckel, The Psalms in Israel's Worship (Oxford, 1962). The title of Ps. 100 is "A Psalm for the Thank-offering." Many of the Psalms are obviously connected with processionals, e.g., 24, 42, 122, and 150. For approval of sacrifices, see Ps. 4.5, 5.3, 20.2-3, 27.6, 54.6, 56.12, 66.13-15, 107.22, 116.17-18.

[100] Four Psalms almost reach the level of condemnation of sacrifice: 40, 50, 51 and 69. Mowinckel (op. cit., Vol 2, p. 21) states that there can be no doubt that the Psalmists ranked the hymn of thanksgiving higher than the offering of animals but that the hymn,

they cannot give God anything, for all things belong to him,[101] and obedience to the Law, especially the moral laws,[102] is unequivocally stated to be better than sacrifice for the proper worship of God. The Psalms provided a corrective to the sacrificial worship they accompanied. It is a broken spirit and a contrite heart that God desires, though he also delights in sacrifices rightly offered.[103]

The Wisdom Literature reflects the same moralising tradition, a good example being Ecclesiasticus. Ben Sira exhorts his readers to make worthy offerings,[104] and regards the command to sacrifice as still binding.[105] But at the same time, he claims that the righteous man makes an offering simply by keeping the Law, that almsgiving is a sacrifice of thanksgiving, and atonement can be effected by abstention from

---

rather than excluding, accompanied the sacrifice. The point of the Psalms is that the sacrifice in itself does not reconcile God; it must be accompanied by right intention, etc., before it is acceptable.

[101]Ps. 50.8-15.

[102]Ps. 1, 15, 24, 119, and 40.6-8 provide examples.

[103]Ps. 51.16-19. Mowinckel takes this Psalm as confirmation of his view that the Psalmists were correcting, not repudiating, sacrificial rites. But see H. McKeating, "Divine Forgiveness in the Psalms" (SJT, 1965). In an effort to counter the theory held by many scholars that the final verses were an addition (a theory proposed to account for the apparent contradiction), McKeating suggests that the Psalmist recognises that sacrifices are proper for the expression of praise and thanksgiving, but not a suitable means of requesting divine forgiveness, i.e., he thinks the Psalmist is repudiating expiatory sacrifice but not sacrifices of thanksgiving. Rowley (op. cit., p. 96) suggests that the penitence offered is for sins commited with a high-hand, for which there was no sacrifice, only grace. Neither of these suggestions seem very satisfactory, so I follow Mowinckel.

[104]Eccl. 35.10. See also 8.31 and 14.11.

[105]Ibid., 35.4-5.

wickedness.[106]

It can be shown, then, that all the various types of literature that make up the Old Testament, Law and Prophets, Psalms and Wisdom,[107] have been affected by this tradition. Clearly by the time of the Rabbis, it was integral to Jewish thinking. So, in spite of the fact that sacrifice could not be rejected since it was ordained in the sacred book of the Law,[108] the Rabbis were able to preserve the Jewish religion after the sack of the Temple in 80 A.D. by drawing on this heritage. If Rabbi Joshua felt moved to lament, "Woe to us! for the place wherein the sins of Israel were expiated is destroyed," Rabbi Johanan b. Zakkai was able to reply, "We still have a means of expiation of equal value, viz. the practice of kindness, for it is said, 'For I will have kindness not offering.'"[109] Prophetic teaching, along with the Psalms, gave them scriptural authority for asserting that good deeds, repentance, fasting, prayer and the study of the Law were equivalent to sacrifice.[110] It was axiomatic that God, the Creator, did not need sacrifice,[111] and so

---

[106]Ibid., 35.1-3.

[107]I have not discussed the Histories, but obviously the fact that they reveal the work of a Deuteronomic redactor shows that they were affected by the ideas of that Law-book. In addition, they report activities of prophets who take similar views of the writing prophets, e.g., Samuel.

[108]See Montefiore & Loewe, op. cit., p. 26. Gray (op. cit., p. 51) quotes the following from Rabbi Johanan b. Zakkai: "I have decreed a decree; no man is allowed to transgress my decree; it is written, this is the ordinance of the Law; and that is sufficient reason for performing the ritual."

[109]Montefiore & Loewe, op. cit., pp. 430-1. Quoted by Gray (op. cit., p. 53) and Taylor (op. cit., p. 66).

[110]Montefiore & Loewe, op. cit., p. 230 (with examples given on pp. 25, 27, 118-9, 323, 431, etc.).

[111]Montefiore & Loewe, op. cit., p. 27.

the emphasis was placed on the deprivation of the giver rather than on the acceptance of God: "Master of the universe," prayed Rabbi Shesheth on fast days, "it is revealed before thee that, while the Temple stood, a man sinned and brought sacrifices of which only the fat and blood was offered, and this atoned for him; and now I have sat fasting and my fat and blood has been diminished. May it be thy will that it may be accounted unto me as though I had offered it on the altar, and do thou accept it from me with favour."[112]

It is scarcely surprising that even before the Fall of the Temple, prayer had come to mean more than sacrifice to the Jews of the Diaspora for whom the synagogue was the only normal means of worship. Philo bears witness to the attitude of Hellenised Jews, and shows that, although they revered the Temple-worship, they put more emphasis on prayer as a valid means of worship and in accordance with the prophetic tradition regarded the right frame of mind as more important than any offering.[113]

---

[112]Quoted by Gray, op. cit., p. 49.

[113]In his Philo (Cambridge, Mass., 1947), Wolfson draws attention to the influence of the synagogue in establishing the equal worth of prayer, etc. with sacrifices (p. 242ff). He gives other examples from Aristeas and Enoch. He also shows that Philo himself takes the same position with respect to sacrifice: God does not rejoice in sacrifices even if one offers hecatombs, for all things are his possession and, because he possesses all things, he needs none. Philo did not however reject sacrifice since he recounts going on a pilgrimage to offer sacrifice, but he emphasizes the need for moral purity and the right frame of mind before the sacrifice is valid. Philo's prophetic attitude is instanced by Quod Deus sit immutabilis, where he asks who could survive approaching God without any intention of repenting, and De plantatione, 25, where he insists on justice rather than sacrifice ("God rejoices in altars without fire around which virtues dance."), and ibid., 30, where he reflects on the impossibility of giving God anything except praise; and his criticism of those

Also prior to the loss of the Temple, a similar development had occurred outside orthodox Judaism. According to Philo, the Essenes did not sacrifice, and the Dead Sea Scrolls have revealed the existence of a sect, probably to be identified with the Essenes, which had broken with the Temple and found other more "spiritual" ways of worship.[114] At first sight it might appear that we have here a foreshadowing of the Christian rejection of sacrifice, and in view of the possibility that there were direct contacts between this sect and Christianity, it is necessary to discuss the implications of their ideas.

The most significant passage is: "They shall atone for guilty rebellion and for the sins of unfaithfulness that they may obtain lovingkindness for the land without the flesh of holocausts and the fat

---

who confuse θρησκεία with εὐσεβεία in Περὶ τοῦ τὸ χεῖρον τῶ κρείττονι φιλεῖν ἐπιτίθεσθαι. See also De sacrificantibus, 1.4 etc. Cf. Josephus, Contra Apionem, II.192, where he speaks of worship through virtue. His agreement with Philo suggests that such was the view of most Hellenised Diaspora Jews.

[114]For the following discussion, see J. H. Baumgarten, "Sacrifice and Worship among the Jewish Sectarians of the Dead Sea Scrolls," in HTR (1953). He argues that the attitude towards the Temple and towards sacrifice is consistent with the various Dead Sea Scrolls as well as in the accounts of Philo and Josephus, thus supporting the identity of the Dead Sea Community as an Essene sect. This identity is assumed in my remarks. For discussion of the attitude of the sectarians to the Temple and sacrifice, see also M. Black, The Scrolls and Christian Origins (London, 1961), p. 39ff and Y. Yadin, The Scroll of the War of the Sons of Light against the Sons of Darkness (Oxford, 1962): during the "period of wickedness," sacrifices are not allowed, but substitutes can be found, while the sect looks forward to the time when they will be able to sacrifice in accordance with the laws of the Pentateuch. See also the summary introduction to the Penguin translation by G. Vermes.

of sacrifice. And prayer rightly offered shall be as an acceptable fragrance of righteousness and perfection of way as a delectable freewill offering."[115] All types of sacrifice are thus replaceable. Righteous living is considered capable of procuring God's favour and atonement, and prayer can be regarded as an "offering of the lips."[116]

On closer examination, however, we find that sacrifice is not rejected on principle or in the light of a more "spiritualised" concept of religion. The schism is traced in both the Habakkuk Commentary and the Damascus Document to defilement of the Temple by "the Wicked Priest."[117] In other words the sect had an excessively high standard of ritual purity which they felt had been polluted by the official Jewish hierarchy. There are even a few sacrificial prescriptions in the Damascus Document which anticipate the glorious future when God would enable the proper fulfillment of the Law according to their beliefs.[118] The attitude of the sect is not, therefore, very different from that of orthodox Judaism, since they cling to the belief that the Law should be obeyed, while drawing on the other moralising tradition to provide substitutes when something prevents correct fulfillment.

E. Expiatory Suffering

Meanwhile another tradition had also grown up in Judaism, namely that innocent suffering, such as

---

[115]For quotations from the Dead Sea Scrolls see the Penguin translation by G. Vermes, entitled The Dead Sea Scrolls. This passage will be found on p. 87.

[116]Ibid., pp. 87, 89, 90. The phrase "offering of lips" is found as the LXX version of Hosea 14.3, but this does not explain its use in this Palestinian sect.

[117]See, e.g., ibid., pp. 101, 103, and 240.

[118]Ibid., pp. 109, 110, and 113.

occurred under persecution, was a means of atonement. This is very clearly expressed in one passage from Rabbinic literature: "Beloved are sufferings for they appease like offerings; yea, they are more beloved than offerings, for guilt- and sin-offerings atone only for particular sins, but suffering for all sins."[119]

The earliest example of this kind of thought is to be found in Deutero-Isaiah where the "Servant's" death is given this kind of significance. The "Servant" had been called to perform a special mission for God, but he met opposition and finally death. He believed that God would vindicate him, and after his death, the spectators (maybe his persecutors) reconised that he was wounded for their transgressions and bruised for their iniquities; upon him was the chastisement that made them whole, and with his stripes they were healed. By the will of God he had made himself a sin-offering on their behalf and had borne their iniquities. The victim, instead of being an animal without physical blemish, was a servant of God without moral blemish.[120]

It is noticeable that in the final song about the Servant, where his atoning death is described, it is repeatedly said that it happened according to God's will, that God laid on him the iniquity of all. It is impossible to interpret this death as propitiatory; it is expiatory because God chose to use this method of cleansing the sins of the onlookers. It worked

---

[119]See Montefiore & Loewe, op. cit., pp. 543, 545, and also p. 226: " . . . the martyrdom of Israel at the hands of the Gentiles is an atonement in the world to come."

[120]*Isa.* 42.1-4, 49.1-6, 50.4-9, 52.13-53.12. For discussion of the identity of the Servant, see Rowley, op. cit., p. 103ff; W. Zimmerli & J. Jeremias, *The Servant of God* (London, 1957); H. Wheeler Robinson, *The Cross in the Old Testament* (London, 1955), pp. 65-80. For the efficacy of the Servant's death, see Rowley, op. cit., p. 101ff; Robinson, op. cit., pp. 81-97; M. Hooker, *Jesus and the Servant* (London, 1959), p. 45ff.

exactly like the sin-offerings discussed earlier.

The most important example of the use of this idea is to be found in the Maccabean literature. Under persecution from the Greek kings, the faithful were expected to suffer even death rather than succumb to the temptation to forsake one iota of the Law at the heathen's bidding. Tales of heroism in _II Maccabees_ include theological comment. The martyrs believed that they were suffering because God's wrath had been aroused against Israel's sins. Here was God's punishment; he was disciplining and chastening his people as he had before in the exile. But even though God was angry for a while, he would be reconciled again, particularly through the death of the martyrs. The victims were personally innocent, but died on behalf of the people to stay the wrath of the Almighty.[121]

This idea is carried even further in _IV Maccabees_, where Eleazar prays as he dies, "Be merciful unto thy people and let our punishment be a satisfaction on their behalf. Make my blood their purification and take my soul to ransom their souls."[122] The martyr has become a sacrifice for the purification of the people. God is to effect this purification through the martyr's blood, as he effects expiation through

---

[121]2 _Mac_. 7.30-8 and 6.12-17. For comments, see W. H. C. Frend, _Martyrdom and Persecution in the Early Church_ (Oxford, 1965), p. 45ff and 57; also John Downing, "Jesus and Martyrdom," _JTS_, 1963.

[122]4 _Mac_. 6.28ff: "Be merciful to thy people, and let my punishment be sufficient for their sake. Make my blood an expiation for them, and take my life as a ransom for theirs." (Hadas, trans.) Ibid., 17.20ff: "These, then, having been sanctified by God, are honored not only with this distinction, but also by the fact that because of them our enemies did not prevail over our nation. It was through the blood of these righteous ones, and through the expiation of their death, that divine Providence preserved Israel." (Hadas, trans.) For further discussion, see _infra_, Ch. 10.

the blood of sacrificed animals.

So again in this example from the Jewish literature of the Hellenistic period, the sufferings of the martyrs do not simply propitiate an angry God, even though the wrath of God against sin is seen at work in the persecution they receive and the texts occasionally seem to oscillate towards a propitiatory understanding. The martyrs pray that God will use their sacrifice to cleanse the people, and when He has purified the nation through the instrument of the martyr's sacrifice, He is reconciled. Their suffering is expiatory.

F. Conclusion

So it was that Judiasm was able to develop from a religion in which sacrifice played a most important part to a religion in which sacrifice had no place. Tradition and the words of the ancient Law-books enforced the practice as long as the Temple stood, but for centuries, developments in theology had called the usual interpretations of sacrifice into question. The system was only maintained as it became reinterpreted as God-given for the good of the people, not as a crude means of influencing God. Jewish feasts were reminders of God's saving acts, and sacrifice continued as a recognition of God's goodness and a symbol of the obedience of the worshipper and the community as a whole. But tradition also provided a way out when the sacrificial system was forcibly taken from the nation. For centuries, it had been a commonplace that sacrifice without obedience was useless, that morality was superior, that repentance and vicarious suffering was acceptable to God in place of sacrifice. This tradition is again clearly dependent on the theological beliefs that the people had developed by their experience of his sovereignty, judgement and mercy in the course of history.

It was at this stage of development that Christianity came on the scene. The sacrificial rites and ideas of the Old Testament provided a means of describing Christian worship and the work of Christ on the Cross, and since they were God-given in the book of the Sacred Law, they were regarded as valid precedents for interpreting Christ's death and the Christian cult. The "prophetic moralising" tradition, however, provided justification for a rejection of material sacrifice and the establishment of a purely spiritual cult.

CHAPTER THREE
SUMMARY ANALYSIS OF THE BACKGROUND OF CHRISTIAN SACRIFICIAL IDEAS

It has been convenient to treat Jewish and Greek sacrifices separately, but this has necessitated giving the false impression that until the coming of Christianity, these two cultures hardly met. It will be remembered, however, that Jewish influences were suspected to lie behind the idea of "rational sacrifices" in the *Corpus Hermeticum*,[1] and that Philo represents the influence of Greek philosophy on Judaism. Josephus bears witness to the respect of the Greeks for the "philosophy" of the Jews, and he regards Moses as the source of the Greek philosophical idea of God.[2] The cross-fertilisation of Greek and Jewish ideas must not be overlooked; the process of contact had been going on too long for a hard and fast distinction to be made concerning their respective influences on Christianity. It was in accordance with ideas from both traditions that Christians claimed to offer, and interpreted, their λογικὴ λατρεία.

In this section we have traced in both Greek and Jewish thinkers the movement towards a spiritualising and moralising of sacrifice. We have found similar rejections of abuses and of crude methods of rationalising sacrifice. We have found a reluctance to overturn the accepted practices of each traditional religion (though on rather different grounds). So we have reached the situation that existed when Christianity became the "tertium genus," bridging the traditions and culture of both Jew and Greek, rejecting and assimilating from both. At this time, spiritualising ideas were attractive to both sides, but the traditional cults still flourished.

---

[1]See *supra*, Ch. 1 at n. 25.

[2]Josephus, *Contra Apionem*, II, 164ff and II.167.

This section has also been concerned to analyse the types of sacrifice offered within the framework of each cult, and in conclusion, we may attempt to draw together the types of Jewish and Greek sacrifices, pointing out similarities and differences, so that we can base our subsequent analysis of Christian sacrifices into types on considerations from both backgrounds. In spite of the multiplication of types described in the chapter on Greek sacrifices, we may broadly classify all sacrifices according to the three basic types used in the chapter on the sacrifices of the Old Testament.

1. Communion-sacrifices were to be found in both the Jewish and Greek backgrounds. The Greek θυσίαι are strictly comparable to the Jewish zebachs; in both the worshipper shared in a meal at which the god was considered to be the unseen guest in whose honour the feast was held. Part of the sacrificed animal was offered to the god on the altar. In both the element of praise and thanksgiving to the deity was present. On the other hand, in the Greek tradition there were also communion-sacrifices of a rather different character, in which the worshipper was thought to share in the very substance of the god, who was present in the meat eaten by enthused and frenzied dancers.

2. Gift-sacrifices were also offered in both traditions. The Greek votive-offering was something given to the god as a present, just as the whole-burnt offering in Judaism was an offering to Jahweh. Here, however, the motives of the offering seem to have been a little different. The Greek most often thought of himself as making a bargain with the gods, whereas the Jew thought of himself as giving the highest possible offering of thanksgiving and praise. The holocaust in Judaism was an act of worship offered to their Supreme God, whereas in Greece, the holocaust was offered in fear to propitiate evil spirits, and should be classed with the sin-offerings.

3. In both traditions, sacrifice was thought to deal somehow with the problem of sin, but we find three different ways in which this was supposed to happen.

In the Jewish tradition, sin-offerings were expiatory, a means provided by God for removing the pollution of sin. In the Greek tradition, some sacrifices were intended to avert the spirits who caused evil, to remove the pollution of sin and appease the powers of the underworld; while others were gifts offered to offended "heavenly" deities to placate their anger, whether it was roused by careless neglect or a real moral offence.

When we come to analyse Christian sacrifices, we will firstly be concerned with a broad classification of their spiritual cult into communion-sacrifices, gift-sacrifices, and sin-offerings. We shall then be attempting to decide whether the Jewish or Greek concept of each of these types is relevant to their understanding in Christianity. In this way, we shall find not only that Christian ideas were influenced by the moralising and spiritualising tendency in Judaism and Greek philosophy, but that their own spiritual cult can be understood more fully in the light of the types of sacrifice present in the practices of their predecessors and contemporaries.

SECTION TWO

THE CHRISTIAN SPIRITUAL CULT: ITS DEVELOPMENT AND ITS RELATIONSHIP WITH CONTEMPORARY RELIGIOUS IDEAS

INTRODUCTION TO SECTION TWO

The preceding section was an attempt to outline the contemporary context in which Christian thought about sacrifice developed. In this section, the intention is to show how Christianity rejected, on quite different grounds, both Jewish and pagan sacrifices, and yet, in the development of a cult proudly proclaimed as spiritual and contrasted with the inferior material worship of contemporary religions, in fact assimilated many of the ideas we have outlined.

Ultimately the Christian attitude was affected deeply by the entirely new doctrine that the death of Christ was a sacrifice of a unique character, being both the fulfillment of the Jewish Law and its final abolition; it was also the focus of the sacrificial self-offering of the Christian. At this stage, however, we will not include detailed analysis of Christ's sacrifice, since one of the aims of this work is to consider his sacrifice in the context of a general study of Christian use of sacrificial ideas. Therefore, before turning to an examination of the type of sacrifice offered by Christ, we shall concentrate on the Christian use of sacrificial terminology as a suitable expression for worship, moral life and self-offering in martyrdom. This kind of "spiritual sacrifice" is deeply embedded in the theology of the Eastern Church, and it owed a great deal to the influence of the Jewish and Greek sacrificial ideas we have previously sketched.

So the first chapter of this section will discuss the Christian rejection of the practice of sacrifice, and the second will describe the development of a purely spiritual cult and estimate the extent to which this was dependent on the background cultures we have already discussed. The third chapter of this section will attempt to analyse Christian sacrifices according to the types distinguished earlier in Chapter III. In this way, the main characteristics of Christian sacrificial thought are outlined so as to provide a broader context for discussion of the unifying element in the Christian cult, namely the sacrifice of Christ.

CHAPTER FOUR
THE CHRISTIAN REJECTION OF SACRIFICE

A. The Break with the Jewish Cult

It is a common-place that Christianity began as a sect in Judaism. Its founder, Jesus, appeared as a new prophet with a message for the house of Israel. Judaism, therefore, was the starting-point of Christian ideas.

The reliability of the Gospel accounts of Jesus' life and work is notoriously difficult to determine, but for our purposes, the traditions about him which were current in the early Church are more important, and for these the Gospel narratives are adequate evidence. According to these traditions, Jesus never made any formal repudiation of sacrifice, although he adopted the prophetic attitude that morality was much more important. In the context of Pharisaic Judaism, this took the form of criticism of excessive preoccupation with minute observances of the Law,[1] a preoccupation which only revealed that the Pharisees had failed to understand the prophetic saying, "I desire mercy and not sacrifice;"[2] they were so concerned with outward cleanliness that they neglected inward purity.[3] In the eyes of Jesus, the scribe who said that love of God and of one's neighbour was more important than burnt-offerings and sacrifices, was not far from the kingdom of God,[4] while rigid application of the principle that the right attitude is necessary when sacrificing, meant that a mere quarrel with one's brother rendered a sacrifice invalid.[5] To escape the responsibility of helping aged parents by declaring all the financial support owed them "Corban," that is dedicated to God as a sacrificial gift, was a serious misuse of the sacrificial Law, because it entailed breaking one of the Ten Commandments.[6]

---

[1]*Mt*. 23.23 [2]*Mt*. 9.13; 12.3ff.
[3]*Mk*. 7.1-23; Mt. 23.25-8. [4]*Mk*. 12.33-4.
[5]*Mt*. 5.23-4. [6]*Mk*. 7.9-13.

In other words, Jesus was concerned with abuses of the Law, and this is confirmed by his cleansing of the Temple.[7] This was not a repudiation of Temple-worship, but a protest against turning it into a profitable market-place and corrupt banking-exchange. One saying recorded in the tradition represents Jesus as believing, like his contemporaries, that the Temple was sacred as the special dwelling-place of God,[8] but unlike other people, he drew the consequence that it was a scandal that the house of prayer had been turned into a den of robbers.

Although Jesus is portrayed in the Gospels as having adopted a critical attitude toward Pharisaism and as being himself independent of the minutiae of the Law, he, like the prophets of old, frequented the normal places of worship, the synagogues and the Temple.[9] That he did not out and out repudiate the sacrificial system is indicated by the fact that the early Jerusalem Church, unlike the Qumran community to which it bore some resemblances, did not break with the Temple-worship. The features of the Church recorded in *Acts* include not only the breaking of bread, prayers and communal living, but also daily attendance at the Temple,[10] and it was there that Peter and John cured the lame beggar and roused the ire of the authorities.[11] The Church originally behaved as a community of orthodox Jews, not sectarians, and it was the Jews who threw them out rather than they who rejected Judaism.

There is some evidence that this picture of the primitive Church in *Acts* is Luke's version of the facts, and that really, even though this was the practice of the majority of Jewish converts and remained so until the Fall of the Temple, there was another conflicting point of view in the Jerusalem Church even before the

---

[7]*Mk*. 11.15-9; *Mt*. 21.12-3; *Lk*. 19.45-6; see also *Jn*. 2.13-7.

[8]*Mt*. 23.21.

[9]See *Mk*. 1.23, 6.2; *Mt*. 12.9, 13.54; *Lk*. 4.16.

[10]*Acts* 2.46.

[11]*Ibid*., 3.3.

Gentile mission raised the question of repudiation of the Law. It is likely that Jesus said something about the destruction of the Temple, since the report of the false-witnesses given in the Synoptic Gospels, that Jesus had claimed to destroy this Temple made with hands and in three days build another not made with hands, is given as a piece of actual teaching in John.[12] Whatever Jesus may have meant by such a saying, it seems quite likely that it was taken up by Stephen and the Hellenists, who, by openly opposing the Temple-worship as a form of idolatry and corruption of the Law, brought persecution for blasphemy upon their heads at a time when the still apparently orthodox Apostles were left in peace. The purely negative anti-sacrificial position of Stephen's party did not ultimately have much influence on the development of the Church's attitude to the Jewish sacrificial Law.[13] After the Hellenists had been driven from Jerusalem, the other Christians there remained orthodox in their keeping of the Law and their attendance as faithful Jews at Temple-services. Luke records the tradition that even Paul underwent purificatory rites in the Temple, making the requisite offerings and bearing the expense for this for four others who were under a vow - though it is also reported that this was a deliberate device to prove to the Jerusalem Church that he was still an orthodox Jew.[14]

As Christianity spread outside Jerusalem, the importance of sacrifice naturally decreased. The divorce of the Gentile convert from the obligation to keep the Law, and the certainty that the Gentiles would not have any motivation to make pilgrimages to the Jerusalem Temple, made sacrifice even less important for Christians than for the Diaspora Jews who lived scattered over the Empire. Jesus' "prophetic"

---

[12]See Mk. 14.58, 15.29; Mt. 26.61, 27.40; Jn. 2.19. This probability is supported by C. F. D. Moule in "Sanctuary and Sacrifice in the Church of the New Testament," (JTS, April, 1950), p. 30.

[13]See Additional Note I in Appendix.

[14]Acts 21.23-6.

attitude to sacrifices facilitated the distinction that gradually was made between the moral and ritual requirements of the Law, and the Church modelled its worship on that of the Jewish synagogue rather than the Temple cult.

Not only did Paul free the Gentile convert from obligation to keep the Law, but he also used sacrificial language to describe the efficacy of Christ's death and the Christian life of obedience to God. In the *Epistle to the Hebrews*, this was taken so much further that it amounted to a rejection of Jewish sacrifice *on principle*. The ceremonial Law did not apply to Christians, not because the message of Christ was in conflict with the religion of the Old Testament but because he had so fulfilled it as to make it meaningless. In a sense this is what was done for the ethical Law by the teaching recorded in *Matthew*: although Christ did not come to overthrow the Law, his fulfillment of it was so far-reaching that it ultimately made the Law trivial by comparison with his demands, so that, for example, it is not merely adultery that is condemned but the very heart of the problem, a man's look of lustful desire.[15] In *Hebrews*, a similar approach was made to the sacrificial Law; the system was not condemned but shown to be wanting; ultimately only the death of Christ truly fulfilled the purpose of the Law. The argument of the Epistle theoretically established the principle that Jewish sacrifices must be rejected by Christians not for purely negative reasons (like Stephen), but in the light of a positive Christological reinterpretation of sacrifice. The sacrificial system along with circumcision, observance of the Sabbath and Jewish feast- and fast-days, came to be regarded as part of the Old Dispensation which had been fulfilled and annulled in the New.

The date of this Epistle and the occasion of writing are still in dispute, but the suggestion is attractive that it was written to Jewish Christians who were sorely tempted to renounce their Christian

---

[15]*Mt*. 5.17-48.

faith in the nationalist crisis of the Jewish War.[16] The work cannot have been composed after the Fall of the Temple, since the author could not have failed to mention an event which was such a remarkable confirmation of his argument.[17] But the Epistle is a strong appeal to Jews who were tempted to take up arms in the national cause and defend the Holy City, the Temple and the cult. To these the author argues that literal fulfillment of the sacrificial Law has been annulled by the all-sufficient sacrifice of Christ. The thought of the Epistle is well calculated to ease the conflicts of loyalty which must have arisen for the Christian Jew at that time of national crisis. The Jerusalem Christians fled the city rather than defend it against Rome, so finally proclaiming the split between Christianity and orthodox Judaism.

The Church never went back after this. Events had proved the thesis of the Epistle to the Hebrews and the Fall of the Temple was seen as God's judgement on the Jews for not accepting the truth of Christ. The Epistle of Barnabas reflects the efforts of a Jewish Christian to induce his fellow Jews to forsake ritual observances, arguing, like the Epistle to the Hebrews, that Judaism has found its fulfillment in Christianity,[18] the sacrificial Law having been annulled by the new Law of Jesus Christ in which sacrificial offerings have no place. He interprets the prophetic denunciation of sacrifice as implying that Christians should avoid the mistakes of the Jews and not worry about how to bring material offerings to God;[19] still less

---

[16]See A. Nairne, The Epistle of Priesthood (Edinburgh, 1913) and The Epistle to the Hebrews (Cambridge, 1917). This view is accepted as plausible by C. F. D. Moule, The Birth of the New Testament (London, 1962), p. 44.

[17]H. W. Montefiore, Commentary on Hebrews (London, 1964), p. 3. Also C. Spicq, L'Epitre aux Hébreux (Paris, 1952). He dates the Epistle 67 A.D. (p. 253f).

[18]J. Daniélou, The Theology of Jewish Christianity (London, 1964), p. 35.

[19]Ep. Barn., II.6, 9.

should they indulge in the hopes of the wretched, mistaken Jews that the Temple might be rebuilt, since the Temple-worship is irrelevant to those who understand that God the Creator does not dwell in a Temple made with hands. The author calls for the building of a spiritual temple within Christians.[20]

Both the works we have considered bear the marks of a Christianity still very closely associated with Judaism. Both use a similar exegesis of the Jewish scriptures to show that Christianity is the fulfillment of Judaism,[21] and the problem of the relationship between the Old and New Covenant is argued in a context of positive respect for the Law, a respect which the mainstream of Christian tradition never lost. In contrast to this, the *Epistle to Diognetus* puts Jewish sacrifices on the same level as pagan, and criticises the Jews for their inability to recognise that the Creator of the world cannot be in need of anything, least of all blood, fat and whole-burnt offerings.[22] This position is, of course, the same as that posited earlier for Stephen and the Hellenisers of Jerusalem. However, once Marcion's attempt to reject the Jewish scriptures had been repudiated, Jewish sacrifices were rarely treated as being on the same level as those of other nations, because the Jewish cult had been ordained by God in the Sacred Books of the Law which Christians themselves accepted as inspired scripture. But this position had to be explained in their apologetic, since in the face of the rising influence of the "tertium genus," pagan syncretistic philosophers tended to equate Judaism and Hellenism, in the same way as the Christian author of the *Epistle to Diognetus*, on the grounds that both, unlike Christianity, had

---

[20]Ibid., XVI.

[21]Daniélou, op. cit., p. 98. Detailed correspondences were traced by a Committee of the Oxford Society of Historical Theology and published as *The New Testament in the Apostolic Fathers* (Oxford, 1905).

[22]*Ad Diog.*, III.3-5.

traditional sacrificial practices.[23] Both Celsus and Julian taunted the Christians with deserting Hellenism and failing to accept Judaism properly.[24] So Christians had to construct apologetic specifically for their refusal to practice the Jewish Law while accepting the Jewish scriptures, as well as for their general rejection of all sacrificial practices. It was vital to account for the presence of the sacrificial Law in scripture.

Origen expounded the classic Christian answer to this problem in his reply to Celsus' charges: Jewish sacrifices cannot be dismissed as no different from the cult practices of other nations, simply because they are symbols of spiritual truths;[25] now that the realities have been revealed in Christ, literal observance of the ceremonial Law is over, the proof being the destruction of the Temple a few years after Christ's crucifixion.[26] This summarises the basic treatment of Jewish sacrifices in Christian apologetic. The argument clearly follows the lines already mapped out in the Epistle to the Hebrews, and it depends on the exegetical technique of typology: that is, the Jewish sacrifices are interpreted as prophetic "types" of the reality to be revealed in Christ; now that the revelation has occurred, the symbols of it need no longer be continued.

Julian reveals knowledge of this argument; he quotes the Christian phrase "on our behalf Christ was crucified once for all," and recognises that this

---

[23]Julian, _Against the Galilaeans_ (Loeb ed.) p. 406. Here Julian claims that "the Jews agree with the Gentiles, except that they believe in only one God. . . . All the rest we have in common with them--temples, sanctuaries, altars, purifications, and certain precepts." The differences, he says, are only in trivial matters. See also Origen, _C. Cel._, V.55.

[24]See _infra_, Ch. 4, at n. 62.

[25]_C. Cel._, V.44; IV.31.

[26]_C. Cel._, IV.29; VII.26. _Hom. Lev._, X.1; III.5; IV.10; etc. See also Greg. Naz., _Or._ V.3-4 and Greg. Nys., _Cat. Orat._, XVIII.

was the reason for their assertion that sacrifice has been annulled.[27] But he makes no direct attempt to reply to this position; indeed, it is hard to see how the Christian position could be attacked, except by the sort of scorn of the Cross and of Christ which Julian found no difficulty in supplying. However, he did attempt to undermine the Christian claim that the destruction of the Temple at Jerusalem proved their case. He realised that his own theory that Hellenism and Judaism were the same was threatened by the fact that the Jews did not at that time actually perform sacrifice,[28] and he tried to rectify this and strike a blow at Christianity at the same time by ordering the restoration of the Temple. We know this from the _Orations_ of Gregory of Nazianzus _Against Julian_. Gregory, no doubt correctly, interpreted Julian's move as being in opposition to the Christians rather than on behalf of the Jews, since it would have undercut the Christian argument that the destruction of the Temple showed that literal fulfillment of the sacrificial Law had been brought to an end. No one was more delighted than Gregory when the attempt failed,

---

[27]Julian (ed. cit.), p. 422. According to A. D. Nock, in his _Conversion_ (Oxford, 1933), p. 157, Julian was originally an eager Christian. We know that he was able to study the books of George of Cappadocia, and his writings certainly show that he was acquainted with Christianity and its scriptural exegesis. See _supra_, Ch. 1, n. 70.

[28]When faced with this objection in his treatise, _Against the Galilaeans_, Julian replies that the Jews sacrifice every time they eat since they never eat unconsecrated food and always give first-fruits to their priests. There is nothing recorded in his own writings to show that he knew the reason why the Jews did not perform all sacrifices according to the elaborate Law of the Old Testament. The historians Sozomen, Socrates, and Theodoret relate that Julian summoned the leading Jews and exhorted them to resume their sacrifices. Their reply that they could lawfully sacrifice only in the Temple led him to order its restoration.

thwarted by a providential earthquake which drove many repentant Jews into the Church in fear of the wrath of God to which this natural event bore witness.[29]

Thus, the classic Christian answer to those who accused them of inconsistency in accepting the Jewish scriptures and then not obeying the Law enshrined therein, used typological exegesis to explain the Old Testament sacrifices as prophetic symbols of the perfect sacrifice of Christ, and confirmed this interpretation by appeal to the fact that the Temple had been destroyed so soon after the cricifixion. There was, however, another method used by the Apologists to explain the presence of the sacrificial Law in Scripture; God had instituted the sacrificial Law for the Jews, they claimed, in order to preserve them from idolatry. Justin,[30] for example, argues that the Jews had a tendency to adopt the practices of their neighbours and forsake God. The institution of sacrifice was an attempt to prevent this. The laws relating to circumcision, the feast- and fast-days, the Sabbath, and the sacrifices were all a result of Israel's sins and hardness of heart; her weakness and stubbornness meant that she was not ready to accept a spiritual Law. Exactly the same theory appears in Irenaeus.[31] Sacrifice was ordained to cope with the problem of apostasy, idolatry and "duritia;" the insistence on the faithful fulfillment of the sacrificial precepts was a method of ensuring obedience. The sacrifices were instituted not for God's benefit, but for the good of the worshippers. This theory was certainly based on the sad history of Jewish apostasy portrayed in the Old Testament, and both Justin and Irenaeus found the prophetic criticism of sacrifice an excellent quarry for scriptural support of the idea that God never needed or wanted the sacrifices of the Jews,

---

[29]*Or*. V.3-4.

[30]*E.g.*, Justin, *Dial*., 19, 22, 27, 43, 67, 92.

[31]Irenaeus, *Adv. haer*., IV.14.1,2; IV.15.2; IV.17.1-4. That this was the traditional view of the Church is shown by its reappearance in Greg. Naz., *Or*. XLV.12.

and now the Gentiles alone brought sacrifices which were acceptable.[32]

In Christian literature, the Jewish scriptures were revered, but the Jews themselves were associated with the practice of a material cult based on a literal interpretation of the Law, in contrast to the spiritual worship which was enshrined in the scriptures but hidden in a mystery that only Christians could understand.[33] The Jews were considered to have lost the favour of God when they crucified Christ,[34] and "Judaism" became a term of theological abuse.[35] The break with Judaism was complete, and its sacrificial cult was rejected on principle.

B. The Reaction against Pagan Sacrificial Practices

The sacrificial practices of the Greeks and other inhabitants of the Mediterranean lands did not directly affect Christianity until it had broken loose from the confines of Judaism and was directing its mission specifically to Gentiles. This began to happen as early as Paul's missionary journeys, but at this early stage, Jewish monotheism could still be completely assumed, even in the Gentile mission; for at first it approached mainly "God-fearers" who had already attached themselves to the synagogues without assuming

---

[32]Justin, op. cit., 22, 28, 41, 117; Irenaeus, op. cit., IV.17.1-4.

[33]Greg. Naz. (*Or.* XLI.1; XLIII.43; XLV.11) condemns the Jews for holding their feasts according to the body, in contrast to the Christians who have a spiritual feast. The Jewish Law was a "shadow" of intelligible things.

[34]Origen, *C. Cel.*, IV.32.

[35]Atheism, polytheism, and Judaism are ranked together by Greg. Naz. (*Or.* II.37), and heresies such as Arianism are called the "new Judaism" (*Or.* XXXIV.16, XXXVIII.8, etc.).

the whole burden of the Law and becoming Jewish proselytes.

Within the context of the pagan Empire, Christianity inevitably adopted Jewish polemic against idolatry and reacted strongly against the local cults. Very quickly Greek philosophical criticisms of sacrifice were combined with Jewish arguments. As early as St. Paul's sermon at Athens,[36] traditional Jewish scorn of the worship of idols made of wood, metal or stone by human craftsmen, such as is found in Deutero-Isaiah, is combined with philosophical arguments that God does not dwell in temples made with hands. To the "philosophers" he addressed there, Paul's argument was fully acceptable, and they accepted monotheism happily enough; it was only his preaching of the resurrection which alienated his audience. This common ground between Paul and his educated hearers was no doubt the result of considerable contacts between Jewish and Greek thinkers, such as we saw evidenced in Chapter III. Christianity was heir to the climate of thought produced by these contacts, and used it to good effect. The riot at Ephesus shows that the population realised that the message of the travelling preachers, Paul and Silas, meant the end of their prosperous trade associated with the cult of Diana.[37]

In the Hellenistic world, philosophical ideas had elevated the concept of a Supreme God and reduced the local gods to the rank of δαίμονες. The general acceptance of daemons, good and evil, left Christians with a sometimes unresolved conflict in their attitude to the Greek gods. The idols were nothing; this they understood from Jewish polemic. Yet the power of the evil daemons in the world was obvious, and in the struggle against idolatry and the local cults, the Christian could experience their active opposition. So the Greek gods came to be regarded as evil daemons who had deceived men into thinking they were gods. Justin was one writer who resolved these conflicting ideas: men made the images, which were indeed inanimate and lifeless, and called them gods, though in fact

---

[36] Acts 17.22ff. [37] Ibid., 19.21ff.

they had no power or even real existence. But although they were not in the form of God, they did have the form of wicked daemons who made use of them for their deceptive purposes.[38] Clearly, if this was the status of the Greek gods, they should not be worshipped, and the traditional sacrificial rites were not to be practised under any circumstances.

Christians demonstrated their protest against pagan sacrificial rites in two practical ways: firstly, their refusal to eat idol-meat, that is, meat that had been slaughtered in the course of a sacrifice to the gods; and secondly, by their refusal to offer even a token amount of incense as a show of political loyalty.

The eating of idol-meat was the first problem to arise, especially since much of the meat sold in the markets had been slaughtered at the local temple. According to *Acts* abstention from idol-meat was specifically enjoined by the Apostolic Council which had considered the whole question of how much of the Jewish Law was to be required of Gentile converts.[39] This prohibition held. The *Didache* explicitly identified the eating of meat consecrated to pagan gods with idolatry itself,[40] and when Trypho suggested that there were many who professed faith in Jesus and were considered Christians yet claimed that there was no harm in eating meats sacrificed to idols, Justin replied that they only pretended to be Christians, and his words indicate that he regarded them as heretical.[41]

In spite of the prohibition, Paul found it necessary to argue the case for abstention to his Corinthian

---

[38]Justin, *I Apol*., 9. Celsus (*C. Cel*. VII.62) attributes the same idea to Christians.

[39]*Acts* 15.20. The word εἰδωλοθύτον in *Acts* 15.29 shows that τῶν ἀλισγημάτων τῶν εἰδώλων in verse 20 means idol-meat. The more general problems of the text and the nature of the decree--whether it was simply a food-law or more--do not concern us here.

[40]*Didache*, 6.3.

[41]Justin, *Dial*., 35.

converts,[42] and these arguments became the standard answer to critics; for example, they are used by both Clement and Origen.[43] They are interesting in that they reflect the conflict which we have already found in the Christian attitude to the Greek gods. In the first place, Paul argues on the basis of the non-existence of idols,[44] that Christians are free to eat whatever is offered in the meat-market and accept the hospitality of pagan friends without raising questions of conscience,[45] provided they are ignorant of the source of the meat; if informed, however, they must refuse the meat for the sake of the conscience of the informant[46] who may not have shaken off his pagan ideas so completely and who may therefore be led astray by the sight of fellow-Christians apparently sharing in a communion-sacrifice with the idols.[47] On the other hand, Paul warns against being in fellowship with the daemons,[48] which would be the result of deliberately partaking in a pagan sacrificial festival. In fact, participation in local cult-sacrifices excludes one from the Christian communion-sacrifice, since one cannot be in communion with Christ and the daemons.[49]

If eating meat offered to idols was idolatry still worse was anything that could be regarded as a sacrificial gift, even incense. The authorities soon found that this was a point over which Christians would not compromise, and to persuade a Christian to burn incense to the Emperor's genius was to cause his apostasy. Hence this was used in the law-courts as a test to determine the truth or falsehood of

---

[42] 1 Cor. 8 & 10. See Moule (op. cit., p. 139) for discussion of the problem that Paul does not appeal to the decree or show any knowledge of it.

[43] Clem. Alex., Paed., II.8 and Origen, C. Cel., VIII.24. Both paraphrase and quote Paul's arguments.

[44] 1 Cor. 8.4

[45] Ibid., 10.25, 27.

[46] Ibid., 10.28-9.

[47] Ibid., 8.7-13.

[48] Ibid., 10.20ff.

[49] Ibid., 10.14-29.

information that the accused was a Christian.[50] To the pagan world the Christian's obstinacy over a simple act of loyalty was inexplicable; the philosopher had long since refused to allow that the act conflicted with his theology.[51] But the Christian horror of idolatry, adopted from Judaism, and based on loyalty to a more personal God than the abstract concept of the philosopher, led to an absolute refusal to compromise. Whether the offering was to be made to an idol, a daemon, or even an angel appointed by God himself as an administrator,[52] it did not matter; sacrifice was a means of offering worship and, worship should only be offered to the one true God. A loyalty-oath in the form of religious worship was absolutely refused. Because the Christian would neither accept the traditional cults of the cities and the Empire, nor apparently offered sacrifice as part of his cult, he was ranked with the Epicureans as an atheist, and in the account of the _Martyrdom of Polycarp_ we find all the emotions of the crowd aroused against Polycarp for this very reason. Polycarp is given the sacrifice-test and will not obey,[53] and the reaction is the outcry of the people that he taught many not to sacrifice or worship: "This man is the teacher of Asia, the father of the Christians, the destroyer of our gods."[54] With the power of tradition, instinctive emotion and unreasoned fear of the gods against them, the Christians could gain no fair hearing.

---

[50]Origen (_C. Cel._, II.13): "Christians alone are allowed by the judges even at their last gasp to renounce Christianity and to _sacrifice according to common customs_, and after their oath to dwell at home and live without danger" (trans., H. Chadwick).

[51]Origen, _C. Cel._, V.35, 43; VI.4; VII.44, 46; etc. Origen scorns the philosophers for worshipping the daemons and contrasts the more logical position of the Christian who worshipped only the Supreme Being.

[52]This idea was commonly accepted in Christianity. See, e.g., Origen, _C. Cel._, VII.67-70 & VIII _passim_.

[53]_Mart. Poly._, IV: VIII.2.

[54]_Ibid._, XII.2.

Christian opposition to sacrifice was itself intensified by fear and emotion. Whereas the philosophers had argued against sacrifice by showing how impossible was the notion that gods were fed by sacrifice,[55] Christian teachers, so far from arguing against it, used it to inspire fear in the ordinary convert. Idolatry, they warned, was not merely the most grievous sin and apostasy from God, but it was also highly dangerous; because the daemons were fed by sacrifices, to sacrifice to them was to nourish them and to help increase their strength for evil work in the world. The daemons were represented as greedy for the fat of sacrifices; for the sake of food they deceived men into thinking they were gods and should be worshipped.[56] Origen went so far as to say that in order to exist in the heavy atmosphere that encircled the earth the daemons had to have the nourishment of exhalations, and therefore were always on the lookout for the savour of burnt-sacrifices, blood and incense. He raised the question of thc crimes committed against men by the evil daemons, and regarded those who had sustained them by sacrifice as no less responsible than the daemons who did the crimes. This argument was particularly emphasized by Origen in his _Exhortation to Martyrdom_.[57] It is interesting that Christian apologists and preachers used popular notions in this way to reinforce the dangers of idolatry. It will be remembered that Porphyry also thought that evil daemons thrived on the fat of bloody sacrifices, and used this as an argument for only offering sacrifices in accordance with his vegetarian principle.[58] His writings seem to be the only place in pagan literature where the idea appears, but, by Porphyry's time, it had been current in Christian circles at least since the Apologists. It is tempting to suggest that Porphyry got the idea either directly or indirectly from Christian sources.

---

[55]See _supra_, Ch. 1 at notes 13-16.

[56]See, for example, Athenagoras, _Leg_., 26-7.

[57]_Ex. ad Mart_., 45. See also _C. Cel_., III.28ff; VII.6, 35; VIII.60; etc.

[58]See _supra_, Ch. 1 at n. 46.

Origen's quotations from Celsus' work against the Christians reveal how impossible the ordinary pagan found it to understand the Christian position. Every nation had its traditional religious customs: why did the Christians refuse to keep them?[59] The Christian sect originated in Judaism: why did it not practise the Jewish cult-laws?[60] Why did Greeks forsake their customs for a distorted version of the Jewish national religion?[61] The same point of view was expressed by Julian at a later date.[62] Besides this, the Christian polemic against idols was quite meaningless to Celsus, since no one had ever believed that the statues were gods; they were simply votive-offerings and images of the gods.[63] He found the plea that no one who worshipped God should worship daemons incomprehensible, since the daemons administered the world according to God's will, and it was no dishonour to God to worship his ministers.[64] God was above jealous passions, and in any case to honour his servants was to honour him.[65] The Emperor did not feel slighted if provincial governors were honoured,[66] and it was quite wrong not to thank and honour those who provided the daily needs of life.[67] Celsus summed up: if these idols are nothing, why is it terrible to take part in high festivals? And if they are daemons of some sort, obviously these too belong to God, and we ought to believe them and sacrifice to them according to the

---

[59] C. Cel., V.34, 35. [60] Ibid., V.33.

[61] Ibid., V.41; VII.18.

[62] Julian taunts the Christians with giving up Hellenism and refusing to adopt Judaism properly. He says that the Christians claimed to accept Moses and then refused to obey him; they looked to Abraham but did not imitate him; for in fact Abraham had sacrificed as the Hellenes do, and Moses had ordered sacrifices to the abominable deities who avert evils, as the scapegoat ritual and the sin-offerings prove. Against the Galilaeans (ed. cit.), pp. 402-422.

[63] C. Cel., VII.62. [64] Ibid., VII.67-8.

[65] Ibid., VIII.2. [66] Ibid., VIII.35.

[67] Ibid., VIII.34-5.

laws, and pray that they may be kindly disposed.[68] The final straw for Celsus was that after all these lofty claims to worship only the Supreme God, the Christians in fact excessively honoured this man Jesus, who was dead anyway.[69]

Celsus' views are particularly interesting since they show the characteristic reaction of the educated pagan of that time, and it can be surmised that, to some extent, the Christian development of the idea of a spiritual cult was a deliberate attempt to answer the problem for both convert and opponent that the Christians had no cult of any sort. For Origen, the Christian refusal to worship angels or daemons is argued as the logical outcome of monotheistic philosophy; if God is honoured, all his angels and spirits are favourably disposed as well.[70] So, the Christian absolutely refused to compromise with traditional pagan sacrificial practices, and this was recognised by the opponents of Christianity. The Roman officials used this knowledge to try to eradicate what they regarded as a dangerous new society.

C. Conclusion

Christianity began in Judaism, and so adopted the Jewish opposition to idolatry. Opposition to the many cults of the Empire was absolute and uncompromising, there being no question of Christian converts continuing pagan sacrificial practices. But neither did Christianity retain the national cult of the Jews. Quite early in its history, it broke with Judaism, and gave up the practice of the cult laws of the Old Testament. Both Jewish and pagan sacrifices were rejected on principle.

So Christianity was in the position of having no sacrificial practices that would be recognised as

---

[68]Ibid., VIII.24. [69]Ibid., VIII.4.

[70]Ibid., VIII.64.

such in the Roman world. In place of this, a purely spiritual cult was developed, and in this development we can trace the influence of sacrificial ideas drawn from both the Jewish and Greek backgrounds, even though their practices had been absolutely rejected. In the next chapter, we shall investigate the development and character of this spiritual cult, and trace the background influences which assisted its development.

CHAPTER FIVE
THE ADOPTION OF A SPIRITUAL CULT

A. General

The new religion had no cult; in the eyes of the world, it was atheism. It had broken from its Jewish origins and refused to compromise with the syncretistic religious culture of the Roman Empire. But according to its own account, Christianity, so far from being atheism, was a higher religion; Christians alone faced the practical consequences of the monotheistic ideas of both Greek philosophy and Judaism, and asserted that the Supreme God could only be worshipped by spiritual sacrifices.[1] The spiritual cult was the offering of prayers;[2] the spiritual altar was the mind of faithful Christians; spiritual images of God were the virtues implanted in men by the Logos.[3] The Body of Christ was a spiritual temple,[4] and the Christian people continually celebrated spiritual feasts and fasts by constant prayer and abstention from wickedness.[5] Above all Christ himself was the perfect sacrifice, and he was the High-Priest through whom Christian prayers were offered.[6] The Christians did have a cult, but it was entirely immaterial.

It is along these lines that Origen tried to justify the Christian position in the *Contra Celsum*, and the central importance of the sacrifice of Christ is apparent. His was the perfect sacrifice and the

---

[1]See *C. Cels.*, VI35. Reason should have persuaded the philosophers to stop busying themselves with created things and images, and to ascend above them and present the soul to the Creator. Cf. VI.4; VII.44, 46; and VI.70: God should not be worshipped with flesh and carnal sacrifices but in spirit.

[2]*C. Cels.*, III.81; VII.44, 46 and references under n. 6 *infra*.

[3]*Ibid.*, VIII.17. [4]*Ibid.*, VIII.19.

[5]*Ibid.*, VIII.22ff.

[6]*Ibid.*, I.69; III.34; V.4; VIII.13, 26.

example of which Christian spiritual sacrifices were modelled; he was the High-Priest through whom they were offered. These aspects of the Christian spiritual cult are to be examined in greater detail in later sections; our present discussion concentrates on the nature of the Christian spiritualisation of sacrifice and its probable sources, so as to emphasize the broader context in which the sacrifice of Christ should be studied.

The Christian spiritualisation of sacrifice was radical. In general it meant that only prayer, charity, a life of Christian virtue, and self-offering in martyrdom were reckoned to be suitable sacrifices for the one true God who was in need of nothing but the loyalty and devotion of his creatures. However, certain material offerings survived in the practice of the Church. It is a testimony to the basic Christian viewpoint that even these received spiritual interpretations, and it will be worthwhile to look briefly at this aspect of the Christian cult, and to trace its origins.

The Spiritualisation of Material Offerings in Christian Practice

Certain material offerings were from the beginning part of Christian traditional practice, and the character of these offerings suggests that they may have originated as a result of the Church establishing itself as the New Israel and adopting the customs of the Jewish Diaspora synagogues. It seems to have been in accordance with Jewish ideas that the Church also related these material offerings very closely to their moralising of sacrifice.

The offering of first-fruits is an example. There is considerable evidence that Christians continued this practice for some long time, and the "harvest-festival" even now has a similar function. First-fruits were offered as far as possible according to the laws of the Old Testament; so in the *Didache*, we find that first-fruits of the produce of winepress and threshing-floor, of cattle and sheep, were to be given to the prophets, who were the Christian equivalent of the Levitical priests. This was even carried to the extent that if bread was made or a jar of wine or olive-oil opened, the first-fruits were set aside, and even clothing, money and all possessions were treated in the same manner. But this offering was not a destruction of gifts so as to present them to God. It was support for those working in God's service. Alternatively it was an act of charity, since when there was no prophet in the vicinity, the first-fruits were to be given to the poor. The offering of gifts in kind is associated with the spiritual quality of generosity.[7]

First-fruits are again approved in the Apostolic Tradition of Hippolytus; the Christian was permitted to bring to the altar an assortment of vegetables and fruit, and even flowers, though for some reason cucumber, melon and onions were forbidden.[8] Cheese and olives seem to have been brought frequently. But here the sort of sacrifice involved is different, since after consecration, the gifts were consumed by the participants in the service. A similar communion-meal was permitted in a Christian's home, provided the bishop was asked to break the bread and partake in it. The moment of sacrificial offering was the consecration of the cup of food, an act which made it sacred to God before the worshippers partook of it. The main point of the rite was to render thanks to God and express the gratitude due to him. In this case, the material offering is transformed by its association with the spiritual conception that prayer is the only worthy sacrifice.[9]

At first sight this type of celebration looks like the Jewish custom of saying grace. But there is a difference, since Christian practice apparently required the presence of a bishop, who was equivalent to the Levitical priests under the Old Covenant, whereas the Jews said grace within the family circle

---

[7]Didache, XIII.

[8]Hippolytus, Apostolic Tradition, xxviii (Dix ed., p. 32; Botte ed., p. 78).

[9]See the remarks of H. Lietzmann, Mass and Lord's Supper (Leiden, 1953), pp. 148-51.

at every meal. Since the bishop was the successor of the priest, his consecration prayer[10] contained the words: "that he may minister blamelessly by night and day, that he may unceasingly behold and propitiate thy countenance and offer thee gifts of thy Holy Church." The Church still offered first-fruits, offerings in kind as symbols of praise and thanksgiving, and partook in what was offered as a communion-sacrifice; so the bishop had to replace the priest and be suitable to offer these material sacrifices. But alongside this idea in the prayer appears the petition "that he may please thee in meekness and a pure heart, offering to thee a sweet-smelling savour." The spiritual sacrifice of the bishop's moral purity is associated with his office of presenting the Church's material gifts.

Amongst these offerings in kind must be included the Eucharist, since in our earlier sources it is interpreted as analogous to the sacrifices we have just been considering. In the first place, it was a communion-sacrifice:[11] Paul treats it as comparable to the communion-sacrifices of both Jews and Greeks, and in the *Apostolic Tradition* it appears as a ritual meal in which the worshippers shared bread and wine, just as they shared food in the other rites we have been considering. In the second place, it was a first-fruit offering:[12] this interpretation is found first in the *Didache*, but is particularly developed by Irenaeus, who, because he recognised that this was a literal offering of a sacrifice of material elements, felt called upon to clarify the point that the repudiation of Jewish sacrifices did not mean that offerings in themselves were reproved. Just as there were sacrifices in Judaism, so there were sacrifices in the Church, but the kind of offering had changed. Here he does not give the usual answer that the change was to a spiritual cult. The change was simply that the offerings were now given by grateful children,

---

[10]Hippolytus, op. cit., iii.4.

[11]See *infra*, Ch. 11 A(a) for further discussion.

[12]See *infra*, Ch. 11 A(a) for further discussion.

not slaves. Jews offered a required tithe, but those who had liberty offered everything for their Lord's use with joy and gladness.[13] Christ himself instituted the offering of first-fruits (i.e. the Eucharist), as an expression of gratitude to God.[14] Christians should still bring certain material offerings, not because God needs them, said Irenaeus, but because we need to give them.[15] The Eucharist was, therefore, an offering in kind, though the mainstream of Christian tradition described it as a spiritual sacrifice.

These are not the only cases where a material offering is blended with the idea of spiritual sacrifice. For the _Shepherd of Hermas_, fasting is a sacrifice,[16] as it is in Rabbinic teaching. It is noticeable, however, that in accordance with Christian tradition, fasting is no mere abstention from food, but refraining from wicked deeds and words, serving the Lord with a pure heart and observing his commandments.[17] But although fasting has thus been moralised away, this treatise also suggests that on a fast-day, a Christian should eat only bread and water, then reckon up what he would have spent on food that day and give it to widows, orphans, or anyone else in need.[18] The spiritualising of the fast has not led to abolishing actual observance, but exists alongside it and transforms the act into charity.

In almost every case where we have found the actual offering of material goods, it has been combined with the notion of charity or support of Christian priests. This comes partly from the Jewish Law which made the Levites dependent on the offering of first-fruits, and partly on the "prophetic moralising" tradition that almsgiving was a thank-offering.[19] The Jewish practice of commutation of

---

[13] _Adv. haer._, IV.18.2.
[14] _Ibid._, IV.17.5.
[15] Ibid., IV.18.6; IV.18.5; IV.17.5.
[16] _Hermas_, Sim. V.3.8.
[17] _Ibid._, I.3-5; III.5-6.
[18] Ibid., III.7.
[19] See _supra_, Ch. 1 B; _Eccl_. 35.1-3.

offerings into money meant that financial support of the poor or the apostles and prophets could also be regarded as a sacrifice.[20] Making material offerings to God was thus associated with belief in God's care for the needy, and so the offering of gifts in kind or money was moralised and spiritualised.

All the material offerings made by Christians were to some extent moralised or spiritualised, therefore. Gifts became charity, and communion-sacrifices, as we have already seen, were closely associated with the spiritual sacrifice of prayer, since it was only the prayer of consecration which turned the meal into a sacrifice. So, the Christian material cult was spiritualised by its association with the spiritualising ideas that dominated Christian sacrificial thinking.

B. The Influence of Jewish Traditions on the Christian Spiritual Cult

It is highly probable that Jewish influence contributed to the origin of the material sacrifices we have been discussing. Not only were first-fruits offered in accordance with the Law, but the practice of charity, etc., can be paralleled in Rabbinic and other Jewish literature. The very combination of material offerings with spiritualising or moralising ideas seems to have stemmed from Jewish influence, especially that of the "prophetic moralising" tradition. Indeed, the influence of Jewish traditions cannot be underestimated. The mere fact that the Church retained the Jewish scriptures meant that she had to interpret the same sacred literature as the contemporary synagogue.

Judaism made two particular contributions to Christian thought about the spiritualising of sacrifice which were especially important. The first was

---

[20]See <u>infra</u>, Ch. 5 at n. 21; <u>Phil</u>. 4.18.

the obvious influence of the moralising tradition which stemmed from the prophetic teaching; the second, the influence of the Jewish tradition that martyrdom had expiatory power analogous to that of the sin-offerings. These will be examined in turn.

(a) <u>The Influence of the "Prophetic Moralising" Tradition</u>

In the last chapter we saw that this tradition played a considerable part in the teaching of Jesus, although at this stage it was not accompanied by rejection of sacrifice. It is not therefore surprising to find that, as the Jews faced the loss of the Temple by drawing on this tradition, so the Christians turned to it, after sacrifice had be repudiated on principle, in order to find scriptural backing for their spiritual cult.

The use of this tradition was natural and obvious, not merely because of Christ's teaching, but because steps along this road had already been taken before the rejection of sacrifice. As for the Diaspora Jew, so for the majority of Paul's converts, the Temple cult was remote, and so he followed in the Jewish tradition of regarding acts of charity as a suitable alternative to animal sacrifice. The help the Philippians sent him was a fragrant offering (ὀσμὴ εὐωδίας), a sacrifice acceptable and well-pleasing to God (θυσία δεκτή εὐάρεστος τῷ Θεῷ).[21] A Christian could offer himself to God by living a pure moral life and joining in prayer and praise; by complete obedience and faith, Christians were to present their "bodies as a living sacrifice, holy acceptable to God, which is your spiritual worship.[22] They were to be holy and blameless (ἅγιοι καὶ ἄμωμοι) morally,[23] as the sacrificial victims had been physically.

The <u>Epistle to the Hebrews</u> established the annulment of the Jewish cult, but spoke also of offering a sacrifice of praise, "the fruit of lips which confess

---

[21] <u>Phil</u>. 2.18.
[22] <u>Rom</u>. 12.1.
[23] <u>Eph</u>. 1.4; and of the whole Church, ibid., 5.27.

his name."[24] This language is reminiscent of the Dead Sea Scrolls,[25] but in this case almost certainly came from the LXX version of Hosea 14.3. The origin of the idea must surely be a combination of phrases from the Psalms, where "the praise of my lips" and sacrifices of praise appear alongside each other. The Jewish "prophetic" tradition clearly lies behind the Epistle's advocacy of sacrifices of praise. In the following verse, Hebrews again shows the influence of this tradition, adopting this time the moralising view that just and charitable qualities must be regarded as better than sacrifice: to do good and to share are described as sacrifices that are well-pleasing to God.[26]

As we have seen, the Shepherd of Hermas, in Rabbinic fashion, regards fasting as a sacrifice that is acceptable to God,[27] and combines this with the other Jewish tradition that charity is a sacrificial act by suggesting that on a fast-day the Christian should eat only bread and water, then rèckon up what he would have spent on food that day and give it to widows, orphans or anyone else in need.[28]

In II Clement, to do the will of God,[29] repentance, prayer, fasting and above all charity[30] are means of worship, and by this means, the Christian, instead of sacrificing to dead gods, obtains knowledge of the Father of Truth.[31] The list of suitable offerings is typically Jewish, as well as the polemic against idolatry.

Such lists of suitable "spiritual" sacrifices became tradition in Christianity and need not be instanced further;[32] that originally they came from

---

[24]Heb. 13.15. [25]See supra, Ch. 2 at n. 115.

[26]Heb. 13.16. [27]Hermas, Sim. V.3.8.

[28]Ibid., III.7.

[29]2 Clem., III.4; V.1; X.1.

[30]Ibid., XVI.4. [31]Ibid., III.

[32]It is interesting to find the same things used as "spiritual" sacrifices in the Cappadocians; e.g., Greg. Naz., Or. II.95, Or. XVI.2; Or. XIV.40; Epp. 153 & 223; Greg. Nys., MPG 44/385B, 540A; 46.301, 409.

Jewish ideas cannot be doubted, especially in the generation when most converts came from the synagogue.

In support of both the rejection of actual animal sacrifice, and its replacement by moral qualities, Christian treatises made extensive use of quotations, both from the prophets themselves, and from the *Psalms*; so the weight of scriptural authority helped to justify the "moralising" of sacrifice. In the *Epistle of Barnabas*, for example, *Jeremiah* and *Zechariah* are combined so as to make it plain that, instead of sacrifice, God ordered the Israelites in the desert not to devise evil in their hearts against one another, and to love no false oath.[33] Irenaeus collected together many of the anti-sacrificial passages in the prophets to show that God did not need or want the sacrifices of the Jews,[34] but rather demanded obedience,[35] learning to do good and desist from evil, seeking justice, correcting oppression, and supporting the widow and orphan.[36] Justin used *Malachi* to show that Jewish sacrifices had been rejected and only Gentiles now made acceptable offerings, namely the Eucharist, prayers and thanksgivings; such sacrifices offered by worthy persons were alone perfect and acceptable.[37] He goes on to admit, however, that his Jewish contemporaries also thought that only prayer was an acceptable sacrifice, and interpreted the same

---

[33] *Jer*. 7.22-3 reads: "For in the day that I brought them out of the land of Egypt, I did not speak to your fathers and command them concerning burnt-offerings and sacrifices. But this command I gave them, 'Obey my voice, and I will be your God, and you shall be my people.'" *Ep. Barn*. (II.7,8) paraphrases the above as "This command I gave them," and then uses *Zech*. 8.17.

[34] *Adv. haer*., IV.17.1-4.

[35] *Ibid*., IV.17.1 -- 1 *Kings* 15.22 -- and IV.17.3 -- *Jer*. 7.21.

[36] Ibid., IV.17.1 -- *Isa*. 1.16-17 -- IV.17.3 -- *Isa*. 18.6ff.

[37] Justin, *Dial*., 117.

Malachi passage to mean the prayers of the Diaspora. So, rather backhandedly, he allows the Christian debt to Jewish thought, and recognises that the prophets, though interpreted differently, were in fact a common heritage.

Passages from the Psalms, too, came into constant use. Clement of Rome, in his letter to the Corinthians, brings together Psalms 68(69), 49(50), and 50(51), in order to show that God needs nothing except "confession of him," "sacrifices of praise" and a humble spirit.[38] The same Psalms are found in Irenaeus alongside the prophetic passages already mentioned.[39] The Psalms were of particular value for emphasizing the sacrificial character of repentance, and the use of Psalm 50(51) is especially interesting in this connection. Clement quotes almost the whole of this Psalm, breaking off at verse 17, so that the climax in "The sacrifice acceptable to God is a broken spirit; a broken and a contrite heart, God will not despise."[40] The most interesting instance of the use of this Psalm, however, occurs in the Epistle of Barnabas, where it again appears as the climax to a lengthy passage on sacrifices.[41] This time, however, the first clause of verse 17 is combined with another phrase whose origin is unknown:

> Θυσία τῷ κυρίῳ καρδία συντετριμμένη. ὀσμὴ εὐωδίας τῷ κυρίῳ καρδία δοξάζουσα τὸν πεπλακότα αὐτήν.

The second phrase reproduces the thought of Psalm 68(69) but clearly has been brought into close parallel with the first. This suggests that this combination of phrases may have a liturgical origin, and possibly came into Christian use from the Jewish synagogue worship. Clearly the whole verse, as it stands in Barnabas, would provide excellent justification of "spiritual" sacrifices, and would be highly suitable for liturgical use, expressing as it does the idea that humble repentance is an acceptable sacrifice, and glorification of God a "sweet-smelling savour." The probability of its use by Christians

---

38 1 Clem., LII. 39 Adv. haer., IV.17.1.
40 1 Clem., XVIII. 41 Ep. Barn., II.10.

in a liturgical setting is enhanced by the fact that the two phrases appear again in close association in Clement of Alexandria's *Paedagogus*.[42]

Old Testament texts in the "prophetic moralising" tradition were used throughout our period to justify the Christian spiritualising of sacrifices. It is hardly necessary to document this further, and Origen may serve as a final example. By his time, the New Testament was sufficiently authoritative to be used as scriptural backing for the spiritualising of sacrifices, and the Old Testament tradition was becoming less dominant. Origen does, however, turn to the prophetic texts to argue that God does not need sacrifice but prefers mercy and a humbled spirit.[43] He uses *Isaiah*, *Hosea* and *Psalm* 50(51),[44] that is, the traditional passages; and on the basis of these texts, he concludes that the Law should be interpreted spiritually and not literally obeyed.

(b) *The Expiatory Suffering of the Martyr*

The Christian martyrs went to death with the example of Christ, the perfect martyr, before them. But it is possible that originally the atoning efficacy associated with the death of Christ came from the traditional Jewish association of expiation with the death of martyrs. In any case, the dependence of the theology of Christian martyrdom on Jewish ideas seems to have been established.

This close connection between the theology of the Jewish and Christian martyr need not be argued here in detail.[45] The expectation that the end was imminent and the emphasis on a puritanical rigorism seem to have been common to both. More decisive is the

---

[42]Clem. Alex., *Paed.*, III.90.

[43]*Hom. Lev.*, II.5.

[44]*Isa.* 1.11; *Ps.* 50(51).17; *Hosea* 6.6; *Ps.* 50(51). 19 is also used in *Hom. Lev.*, IV.5 and alluded to in V.3.

[45]For a full treatment of the evidence, see W. H. C. Frend, *Martyrdom and Persecution in the Early Church* (Oxford, 1965), Ch. 1 & 2).

established influence of the Maccabean books on the account of the martyrs at Lyon and Vienne.[46] Similarities of style, vocabulary and ideas have been found, the most obvious being the identification of the mother in the Maccabean story with the slave Blandina. Eleazar is paralleled by Bishop Pothinus, and the martyrs are athletes in an ἀγών. Verbal similarities follow II Maccabees, but the writer imitates the style and rhetoric of IV Maccabees. The Maccabean martyrs go to God and the Christians to their King; all seal their witness in death and gain the crown of immortality. The same literary tradition has been found in the Martyrdom of Polycarp.

This being the case, it is not unreasonable to suggest that the expiatory efficacy attributed to martyrdom came from the Jewish tradition. The Shepherd of Hermas seems to support this, for, while the distinctively Christian idea of imitating the suffering of Christ in martyrdom is absent from this treatise, we do find the idea that "the sins of these have been taken away because they have suffered for the name of the Son of God."[47] In this case the pre-Christian Jewish tradition seems to have been the dominant factor in the attribution of atoning significance to the martyr's death.[48]

The language of Igantius is even more significant. His letters were written on the road to Rome and martyrdom, and he begs the Christians in Rome not to attempt to free him, but to allow him to die willingly for God's sake. He asks them to beseech Christ on his behalf, that he may be found a sacrifice for God (Θεοῦ θυσία).[49] Four times and in three different

---

[46]Ibid., p. 18ff and notes on p. 29. The account is found in Eusebius, Hist. Eccl., V.1. He quotes what is almost certainly a genuine contemporary letter sent by the suffering Churches of Gaul to the Churches of Asia.

[47]Hermas, Sim., IX.28.5.

[48]See Frend, op. cit., p. 197.

[49]Ignatius, Rom. 4.2.

letters, he uses the rare word ἀντίψυχον(ransom),[50] speaking of himself as a ransom for the Christians at Smyrna and Ephesus, for Polycarp and all who obey their bishop. ἀντίψυχον is never found in the New Testament, but occurs twice in IV Maccabees.[51] It has been argued that Ignatius was in fact dependent on IV Maccabees,[52] and certainly the terminology he uses is of Jewish origin. Once he adopts a pagan expression, suggesting that he is to be poured out as a libation,[53] but the idea that his martyr's death was a sacrifice is foreign to pagan religion. His sacrificial death belongs to the Jewish tradition.[54] It is clearly expiatory for the sins of others, and not just for his own; he dies for the Church as the Maccabean martyr had died for Israel.

In the case of Ignatius, it is true that these ideas have been transformed by the desire to imitate Christ by suffering as a martyr. In this, Ignatius is clearly influenced by St. Paul, who regarded the trials he endured for his faith as filling up what was lacking in the sufferings of Christ, and, if we can rely on the traditions in the Pastoral Epistles, looked on his approaching death as a sacrifice.[55] Like Paul, Ignatius wants to suffer with Christ,[56] and "follow the example of the Passion of my God."[57] Ignatius exhorts his readers to be fellow-initiates of the martyred Paul[58] and imitators of Christ.[59] His own death could well be described by the Pauline phrase ἐν Χριστῷ.

---

[50]Eph. 21.1; Smyr. 10.2; Poly. 2.3; 6.1.

[51]IV Mac. 6.27-9; 17.20-2.

[52]See O. Perler, "Das vierte Makkabäerbuch, Ignatius von Antiochen und die ältesten Martyrerberichte," Rivista di archeologia cristiana, IX (1949), pp. 47-72.

[53]Rom. 2.2. Compare the expressions of Paul in Phil. 2.17: "Even if I am to be poured out as a libation on the sacrificial offering of your faith . . ."

[54]See Frend, op. cit., p. 199.

[55]Col. 1.24 and 2 Tim. 4.6.

[56]Smyr. 4.2.

[57]Rom. 6.3.

[58]Eph. 12.2.

[59]Phila. 7.2.

The idea of imitating Christ in fact dominates Christian literature on martyrdom, and it becomes determinative of the ideas expressed. The martyr joins Christ in warfare against the devil and his hosts,[60] and offers a sacrifice of praise to God by the surrender of his life on Christ's behalf.[61] But the idea that the martyr's sacrifice is expiatory never entirely disappears, though it is related closely to the far more efficacious death of Christ which atoned for the sins of the whole world.[62] In fact, the Jewish martyr tradition probably provided the earliest means of interpreting the death of Christ.[63] However, once Christ crucified was considered the one and only sacrifice for the sins of the whole world, the persistence of belief in the atoning efficacy of a Christian's martyrdom is hard to explain unless the idea had already entered Christian thinking independently. The problem of obtaining forgiveness for post-baptismal sins, admittedly, ensured the continuance of the idea that one's own sins could be washed by the Baptism in blood,[64] but the virtue of the martyr's death was still considered to atone not merely for oneself but for many.[65] The problem of the relationship between Christ's atoning death and that of the martyrs will be treated in detail later.[66] The point here is that the Jewish tradition and particularly the traditions about the Maccabees were extremely influential.

---

[60] E.g., Origen, _Ex. mart._, 42; Greg. Nys., MPG 46.781, 704; Greg. Naz., _Or._ IV.67-71, _OR_. V.6, 24ff.

[61] _Mart. Poly._, XIV.1-3.

[62] Origen, _Ex. mart._, 50. See also the interesting description of Stephen's martyrdom in Greg. Nys., MPG 46/712; his death is described in terms reminiscent of the sacrifice of Christ. As a priest, he offered his own body as a sacrifice; his prayer cleansed the sin of his murderers and εξιλεοῦτο for sins.

[63] See Intro. to Sect. III.

[64] Origen, _Ex. mart._, 30; Greg. Naz., _Or._ XXXIX.17.

[65] Origen, _Ex. mart._, 30; Greg. Naz., _Or._ IV.71, _Or._ XI.5; _Or._ XXIV.4.

[66] See _infra_, Ch. 10.

The LXX contained the Second Book of Maccabees, and it was a treasured scripture in the Church. Preachers marvelled at the virtue of martyrs who suffered before the example of Christ and the assurance of his resurrection,[67] and the Maccabean martyrs figure in lists of confessors in Carthage and Syria.[68] They were "prototypes of martyrdom and a source of inspiration to confessors."[69] It is particularly significant that even in late literature, it is the example of the Maccabees which is always quoted alongside Christ;[70] no Christian martyr attained recognition as universal as these heroes of Jewish times or persecution. The sacrificial interpretation of the martyr's death clearly originated in Judaism.

(c) Conclusion

It is clear from our study of these two particular traditions (namely, the "prophetic moralising" tradition and the tradition that the martyr's death was expiatory) that Jewish ideas, besides facilitating the replacement of sacrifice by moral and spiritual qualities, also had a considerable influence on the character of the Christian spiritual cult. The Jewish background was not, however, the only formative influence. There were also many contacts with the Greek philosophical tradition, and the importance of these as sources for Christian ideas must be examined.

C. Contacts with Greek Philosophy

Although, as we have seen, the Christian spiritual cult developed under the influence of certain Jewish

---

[67]See, e.g., Greg. Naz. *Or*. XV on the Maccabean martyrs.

[68]Frend, op. cit., p. 21.

[69]Ibid., p. 20.

[70]Origen, *Ex. mart.*, 22-27; Greg. Naz., *Or*. XV.3: the Maccabees were an "expiation" for the people.

traditions, by the time of Origen, discussion of the subject clearly shows the influence of Greek philosophical ideas concerning the gulf between the purely immaterial Supreme Being and all corporeal existence. The spiritualisation reflects the ideal of the "philosopher's prayer," a life of imitation and contemplation of the divine and separation from the material and earthly. The Greek ethical ideal of ἀπάθεια became the aim of the Christian's self-dedication, even though in some respects it was incompatible with the Christian ethic.

The process by which the God of the Jews was given all the attributes of the philosophical deity of late Greek philosophy began with the Apologists. Throughout our discussion of sacrifice, the point has been implicit if not explicit, that views on sacrificial worship must be directly affected by the concept of God held by those concerned, so that a changing concept of God affected the interpretation of sacrificial rites. It is well known that the Christian adoption of philosophical monotheism raised complicated questions about how to reconcile this concept of God with the facts of revelation on which Christianity rested.[71] However, its effect on Christian attitudes to sacrifice and worship is not so well recognised. On the one hand, it enabled Christians to adopt philosophical criticisms of sacrifice and to apply them with more practical effect since they had in fact ceased to offer sacrifice; on the other hand, it meant that Christians had to take account of these criticisms and answer them when they used sacrificial language themselves.

That God could not conceivably be dependent on sacrifice for food or for any other reason became a commonplace in Christian literature. Often it appears in the Greek form that God, who far transcends the material world, has no need of material gifts, nor does he lack or desire anything, being beyond

---

[71]For a discussion of some of these problems, see M. Pohlenz, Vom Zorne Gottes (Göttingen, 1909).

passions and pleasures;[72] frequently however this is enforced by adding the Jewish argument that, since he is the Creator who in fact possesses all things, it is impossible to give him anything.[73] It is man who needs to worship, not God who receives anything by it.[74] The only thing that God needs is the salvation of his creatures.[75]

That God's integrity could not be undermined by the offering of sacrificial bribes is also found in Christian apologetic, for example, in the _De Monarchia_, a collection from Greek literature of passages which support Christian ideas. (It was attributed to Justin, but is most likely spurious.) In this work, verses are quoted to show that propitiation by libations and incense is impossible, since God will in any case justly deal punishment to all sinners, whether he receives gifts or not.[76] This argument is not unlike the more philosophical one, which was also adopted by Christian philosophers, that sacrifice is useless because God is in any case changeless and therefore cannot be appeased or petitioned. The latter argument obviously came straight from Greek philosophy, being entirely based on the Greek philosophical idea of God. Clement's statement in _Stromatein VII_ uses some phraseology which is identical to that which we found in the Neoplatonists, though we can also detect the influence of the Jewish belief, always assumed in Christianity, that God is the Creator of the world: the Divine nature is not wanting in anything, nor is it fond of pleasure or gain or money, being itself full and affording all things to every creature which is in need; so the Divine nature cannot be propitiated by sacrifices or offerings, not is it allured by them.[77]

---

[72]Aristides, 1; Justin, 1 _Apol_., 10.13; Clem. Alex., _Strom_., VII.14-5.

[73]_Adv. haer_., IV.14.

[74]_Ibid_., IV.14, 17, 18.

[75]Origen, _C. Cels_., VIII.62; cf. Clem. Alex., _Strom_., VII.14.

[76]_De mon_., 4.

[77]Clem. Alex., _Strom_., VII.15.

This type of argument clearly provided useful polemic against sacrifice in general, but it was also bound to raise the question of how to justify Christian spiritual sacrifices. Clearly the Christian interpretation of propitiation, at least, had to be modified. In a later discussion, we shall find how the Christian Platonists, on the basis of the philosophical notion that God must be changeless, rationalised away the emotional aspect of God's wrath which they found so vividly depicted in the Old Testament, interpreting it as simply a means of disciplining mankind.[78] This is reminiscent of Iamblichus and Sallustius who interpreted the wrath of the gods as being a deliberate rejection of their light by men, not a passion of the gods. Just as Iamblĭchus and Sallustius were forced to claim that "appeasement" converts us to the participation in the divine rather than changing the gods in our favour,[79] so Christians were forced to modify their idea of propitiation or else reject it as a means of explaining how sacrifice works. These developments will be examined in greater detail in a later chapter.

The argument that God was changeless and unaffected by sacrifice inevitably affected the Christian rationale of sacrifice. As we have noted, the idea of propitiation had to be modified in the light of it. Some Christian writers were aware of the fact that it raised the question of the point of all sacrifices, material or spiritual. Origen felt bound to answer the question, what was the point of repentance if God's justice was unbending,[80] a problem ignored by the author of the _De Monarchia_. Indeed, he realised that even the possibility of prayer was thrown in doubt; why pray if God's attitude could not be

---

[78]See _infra_, Ch. 8 B & 10 A(c). Also Clem. Alex., _Paed_. I.62ff; Origen, _C. Cels_. IV.71-2; _De princ_. III.1, 10-12.

[79]See _supra_, Ch. 1 C.

[80]_Comm. Rom_. II.1. See _infra_, Ch. 8 at n. 24 for further discussion.

changed by it? He tackled the latter problem in his treatise On Prayer[80a] and answered it by an appeal to the freewill enjoyed by mankind in spite of God's providence and foreknowledge. He justified prayer by appeal to its role in God's dispensation for the universe and the soul; by his prayer, a man reveals his faith and ultimate desire. Origen's discussion is in the philosophical tradition, though he uses scripture to support his case and the argument is twisted to the Christian tradition in which the question was raised. At least his treatment of the subject shows that he was aware of the fact that the Greek concept of God was ultimately incompatible with religious experience, and when adopted by Christianity, had to be reconciled with Christian devotion and the Christian spiritual cult.

Christian writers were particularly concerned that the sacrifices offered should be worthy of God, a concern which we have already found in the Neoplatonists. Justin insists that worship that is worthy of God is not the destruction of his gifts by fire, but thankful use of them for one's own good and for the needy, as well as prayer, praise and thanksgiving for all his gifts.[81] Origen states that God should be worshipped not with blood and carnal sacrifices but in spirit,[82] and ridicules the idea that a God who is known spiritually should be worshipped in a material way.[83] The Supreme God should be worshipped by means of piety and every virtue.[84] Gregory Nazianzen states that only oneself is a worthy gift to God.[85] According to Clement of Alexandria, the achievement of ἀπάθεια, the offering of oneself purified from sin, honouring God by prayer, these are the only sacrifices worthy of God who needs nothing.[86]

[80a]On Prayer, 5.1-10.2.

[81]Justin, 1 Apol., 13. Cf. Clem. Alex., Strom. VII.49.

[82]Origen, C. Cels. VI.70.

[83]Ibid., VII.44. [84]Ibid., VIII.64.

[85]Or. XLII.8.

[86]Strom. VII.14, 31, 33.

It was ἀπάθεια of soul and contemplation of God that Porphyry regarded as the perfection of worship.[87] Now we have found this same ideal in Christian sacrificial thinking. Since God was ἀπαθής, so was Christ; and it was struggling for this ideal of detachment from sin and change that Christians regarded as the means of imitating Christ and offering the ultimate Christian sacrifice.[88] The ideal of ἀπάθεια received its greatest support in the ethics of the later Greek theologians, for whom asceticism had replaced martyrdom, and who understood salvation as the restoration of the image of God in man.[89] Since God was essentially unchangeable and beyond passions, this was the ideal to which they strove, each seeking to offer his pure, ἀπαθής soul to God as a spiritual sacrifice.

It is clear, then, that the character of the Christian spiritual cult was coloured to a considerable extent by the adoption of Greek ethical ideals and the aspirations of the highest Greek piety. The devout aimed at achieving the exalted state of the "philosopher's prayer," a life of imitation and contemplation of the divine and separation from the material, the earthly and the sinful. Like the compilers of the Hermetic Corpus, they strove to offer to God λογικαί, νοεραί or πνευματικαὶ θυσίαι.[90]

So, in the thought of the Christian Platonists, the only worthy offering to God was, ultimately, the ideal of ἀπάθεια and contemplation of the divine; it represented total self-offering. Here they were in agreement with Porphyry. On the other hand, they also

---

[87]See *supra*, Ch. 1 at n. 42.

[88]E.g., Clem. Alex., *Strom*. VII.14, 31, 33, and esp. V.11: Now the sacrifice which is acceptable to God is σώματός τε καὶ τῶν τούτου παθῶν ἀμετανόητος χωρισμός. See E. F. Osborn, *The Philosophy of Clement of Alexandria* (Cambridge, 1957), p. 92ff and 164ff.

[89]E.g., Greg. Nys., MPG 44/364, 45/40-1, 46/285, etc. See J. Daniélou's Introduction to H. Musurillo's translation of some of Gregory's mystical writings in *From Glory to Glory* (New York, 1961).

[90]See *supra*, Ch. 1 at n. 25.

offered sacrifices of praise, prayer and hymns, and claimed that they were offerings suitable for a spiritual deity, whereas Porphyry regarded these as only suitable for a lower grade of gods, the νοητοὶ θεοί.[91] It is interesting that Origen consistently teaches that Christian spiritual sacrifices were offered to the Father through his Son, our High-Priest.[92] This is not unlike the Neoplatonist point, stressed particularly by Iamblichus, that few can attain to proper worship of the Supreme Being, though he can be worshipped through inferior offerings to inferior grades of deity.[93] It must be insisted, however, that the Christians certainly believed that their spiritual offerings went to God himself, whereas the Neoplatonists saw it as a more indirect process, God being affected ultimately by the sacrifices, but the sacrifices being in fact offered to lower powers.

There are a few other interesting contacts between Christian ideas and those expressed by Porphyry. We have already noticed that both regarded bloody sacrifices as a means of strengthening the evil daemons.[94] Porphyry supported the offering of first-fruits and other offerings in kind,[95] as long as animal sacrifice was repudiated, and we have seen that Christian practice in fact followed these lines.[96] Porphyry's theory that animal-sacrifice arose in time of famine is paralleled in Clement's writings where he says he believes sacrifice was an invention of mankind to excuse the eating of flesh.[97] (Clement goes so far as to advise Christians to adopt vegetarianism, though this is not based on the belief in transmigration of souls, as it was in the Pythagorean tradition followed by Porphyry, but is recommended

---

[91]See *supra*, Ch. 1 at n. 41.

[92]See *infra*, Ch. 12 at n. 7.

[93]See *supra*, Ch. 1 at n. 46.

[94]See *supra*, Ch. 4 at n. 57.

[95]See *supra*, Ch. 1 C.

[96]See *supra*, Ch. 5 A.

[97]Clem. Alex., *Strom*. VII.32.

as a discipline and to weaken the sexual appetite.[98]) As late as the Cappadocians we find Christians accusing Greeks of holding sacrificial feasts merely in order to indulge their gluttony, and contrasting the perfect spiritual worship of the Church.[99]

The many contrasts between Porphyry's treatment of sacrifice and the Christian viewpoint were recognised by Eusebius when he quoted long portions of Porphyry's _De Abstinentia_ in his _Praeparatic Evangelica_.[100] In his _Demonstratio Evangelica_,[101] however, he contrasts Porphyry's arguments against animal sacrifice with the sacrificial legislation of the Old Testament, and proceeds to show that the Church's rejection of sacrifice was on quite different grounds from that of Porphyry, namely that the perfect sacrifice of Christ had rendered the old animal sacrifices unnecessary. It will be recalled that Origen also accepted the tradition that lay behind Eusebius' remarks (namely that Jewish sacrifices foreshadowed the sacrifice of Christ), and was therefore careful to draw a distinction between the sacrificial practices of the Jews and of other nations.[102] Such examples serve as a reminder that although Christians could make use of the philosophical tradition to support their position, their rejection rested ultimately on more

---

[98]Ibid., VII.33. This point is interesting since it was clearly not normal Christian practice. Celsus cannot understand why Christians will not give up all meat, like the Pythagoreans, regarding their willingness to eat all meat except idol-meat as a failure to carry the vegetarian principle to its logical conclusion. Origen in answer makes the point that Christians do not abstain because of a belief in transmigration of souls like the Pythagoreans, defends the refusal to eat idol-meat on theological grounds, and adds that they spiritualise abstention to mean abstention from wickedness (VIII.28-30).

[99]E.g., Greg. Naz., _Or_. XXXVIII.6.

[100]_Praep, Evang_. IV.

[101]_Dem. Evang_. I.10.

[102]_C. Cels_. V.44. See _supra_, Ch. 4 at n. 24.

fundamentally and distinctively Christian foundations.

The philosophical insistence on the gulf between the purely immaterial Supreme Being and all corporeal existence should have implied the rejection of material sacrifice. To this extent Christianity took it nearer to its logical conclusion than the philosophers.[103] But in fact both Christianity and Neoplatonism reveal the problem of trying to combine the highest philosophical concept of God with more primitive assumptions about worship. Christianity did repudiate the actual practice of sacrifice and proudly proclaimed a purely spiritual cult, but in regarding martyrdom and certain moral and spiritual qualities as sacrifices, not to mention the death of Christ and the Eucharist, it was in the same position as the later Neoplatonists who sought to defend all the practices of paganism. Both needed to find a rationale of sacrifice. How could the philosophical concept of God be reconciled with the practice of sacrifice? We saw earlier that the Neoplatonists recognised their problem and attempted to solve it by various devices, and we have here noted a few cases where similar conclusions were reached by Christians, especially those in the Platonic tradition. Later discussions will make the Christian position clearer. The basic concern of both philosophies was to offer sacrifices that were worthy of God as they conceived him, and to justify their cult practices as suitable sacrifices. The similarity of their conclusions may be seen in the following passage, quoted from Porphyry by Augustine: "For God, indeed, being the Father of all, is in need of nothing; but for us it is good to adore him by means of justice, charity and other virtues, and thus to make life itself a prayer to

---

[103]See, e.g., C. Cels. III.81: "For without boasting, it is self-evident that nothing better could be conceived than to entrust oneself to the Supreme God and to be dedicated to a doctrine which teaches us to leave everything created and leads us to the Supreme God through the inanimate and living Logos."

him, by inquiring into and imitating his nature. For inquiring purifies us, and imitation deifies us, by moving us nearer to him."[104] The passage could well have been written by an Origenist who applied the words of his master that God was in need of nothing except the salvation of mankind,[105] and thought that this was to be achieved by imitation of Christ, an idea emphasised by the Eastern theory of redemption by θεοποίησις.[106]

D. Distinctive Features of the Christian Spiritual Cult

Yet in spite of the influences we have found stemming from Jewish origins and contact with Greek philosophy, the character of the Christian spiritual cult had certain distinctive features. These were all related to the central position of the sacrifice of Christ, and the distinctive Christian ethic based on ἀγάπη. This is important, for the character of the Christian cult depended not on the mere fact of spiritualisation of material sacrifices, but on the kind of spiritual qualities which replaced the material offerings.

An examination of the similarities and differences in the exegesis of Philo and Origen illuminates this point. Both use the Old Testament as scripture, and both interpret it by the same allegorical technique of exegesis. For Philo, the relationship of the literal and allegorical meanings of scripture is analogous to the relation between body and soul.[107] The spiritual sense of the scriptures must be sought

---

[104]Augustine, Civ. Dei., XIX.23.

[105]Origen, C. Cels., VIII.62.

[106]See infra, Ch. 8, on Athanasius and the two Gregories.

[107]S. G. Sowers, The Hermeneutics of Philo and Hebrews (Zürich, 1965), Ch. 2.

behind the literal meaning of the text, the literal text simply existing as a device to contact slow-witted people who could only contemplate God in human terms.[108] Origen follows Philo when he justifies the presence of the literal sense as a condescending accommodation to the abilities of the simple-minded, and in his skilful removal of anthropomorphisms by allegorical exegesis. The roots of Origen's exposition of scripture according to three meanings, literal, moral, and spiritual also lie in Philo's theory, since he distinguished a number of allegorical senses, for example, psychological and ethical.[109] Philo paved the theoretical way for Christian Platonism.

When we turn to examine how each treated the sacrificial legislation, we find certain differences that are expected. Philo was an orthodox Jew, who in spite of his allegorically achieved spiritualisation of the Law, still believed that it was God's command that it should be observed literally. Origen was in the Christian tradition which saw the Law fulfilled in Christianity, and rejected literal observance on the basis of this belief. For him, the Jewish Law was a symbol of heavenly realities, and once these had been revealed, the Law ceased to apply.

On the other hand, there are striking similarities.[110] Both regard the laws as representing spiritual truths. The ritual purity required for sacrifice is a symbol of moral purity;[111] hymns,

---

[108]Op. cit., p. 26.

[109]Op. cit., p. 32. Sowers distinguishes between two senses of ἠθικῶς and φυσικῶς and gives an example which justifies my using the word "psychological." In fact, the Greek allegorists who used the term meant an allegory describing the true nature of things.

[110]For references, see Table I *infra*. References given there are taken from various works of Philo, but all the examples from Origen are from *Hom. Lev*. The *De victimis* and *De sacrificantibus* of Philo are sections of his *De specialibus legibus*, I.

[111]Philo's allegorisation of the purity of victim and priest reappears in Greg. Naz., *Or*, II.94; the at-

thanksgivings and prayers are regarded as suitable sacrifices. These ideas ultimately came from the Jewish "prophetic" tradition and particularly the Psalms, that is from the common religious background of Origen and Philo. Likewise, both accept the Greek cardinal virtues as suitable spiritual sacrifices, for example, σωφροσύνη, δικαιοσύνη, ὁσιότης; purity of soul is summed up for both in the philosophical ideal of ἀπάθεια. Both work in the atmosphere of Platonic philosophy. Both therefore can produce similar exegesis of the sacrificial legislation; both have similar ideals concerning the sort of spiritual offerings which the literal text represented. They have a common background in the Jewish scriptures and in Platonic philosophy.

But Origen has some additional suggestions concerning the sort of spiritual offerings Christians can make, and concerning the true heavenly realities that lie behind the sacrificial legislation. Origen introduces the Christian virtues of mercy and peace; he speaks of offering a sacrifice by following Christ in martyrdom and charity. He sees the Levitical sacrifices as foreshadowing the perfect self-offering of Christ on the Cross. This allegorisation in terms of the realities of the New Covenant contrasts with Philo's position, a good example of this contrast being their different allegories of the Passover. For Origen, the Passover means Christ, our Passover lamb, the Eucharist, and study of the Divine Word,[112] but for Philo, it represents the journey of the soul from the body and its passions.[113]

A comparison of the "Platonic" schema which they each constructed by means of allegory, is also instructive.[114] In both, the Logos appears as High-Priest of the sacrifices which the Jewish cult symbolised; for both, the sacrifices of the individual soul are the

---

sence of physical blemish is a symbol of perfection of soul.

[112]Comm. Jn. X.11-13.

[113]De spec. leg., II.18.

[114]See Table II infra.

realities under the symbols. But Origen's scheme is quite different because all sacrifices are regarded as types of the sacrifice of Christ.

Besides these differences, Origen had certain arguments for spiritualising sacrifice which Philo did not have.[115] Origen argues firstly from the Fall of the Temple within a few years of the crucifixion,[116] and secondly from the word of scripture, in this case the Epistle to the Hebrews,[117] that literal sacrifices were meant to cease and be replaced by the realities which they symbolised. Both these arguments presuppose the Christological centre of the Christian spiritual cult which is by no means obliterated in Origen's thought by his adoption of the Philonic allegorical method and the ideals of Greek philosophy. Even Alexandrian allegory has been transformed when used by a Christian, simply because of the Christological frame of reference.

These findings may be summarised in the following two tables. The first consists of a fairly arbitrary selection of passages, which serve to indicate the similarities and differences between the respective conclusions of the Jewish and Christian allegorist. The second gives diagrams of their respective "Platonic" schemes.

---

[115]Hom. Lev., X.1 is one of many passages which shows that in general he followed Philo's theories to construct apology for spiritualising sacrifices.

[116]Ibid., X.1; III.5; IV.10.

[117]Ibid., IX.2; X.1; etc. "If anyone reads the whole of the Epistle to the Hebrews . . . he will find how the whole of this part of the Apostle's writing shows that those things written in the Law are types and forms of things that are living and true."

TABLE I

Philo	Origen
Philo accepts sacrifice as part of the Torah.	In the Christian tradition, Origen allows only spiritual sacrifices.
The purity of the victim and priest symbolises the worshipper's purity of soul. _De sacr_. 1; _De vic_. 5.	"Cordis puritas" and "probitas operum" are needed to share in sacrifice. _Hom. Lev_. V.12.
The offering of first-fruits: the best is the soul. _On the Sacr. of Abel and Cain_, 26.	First-fruits; first-fruits of Spirit: symbol of Pentecost. _Hom. Lev_. II.2.
The holocaust=virtue and its divisions: σωθροσύνη, ἀνδρεία, δικαιοσύνη, φρόνησιϛ. Ibid., 25.	Dividing the holocaust= division of scripture--to offer it acc. to diff. levels of understanding. _Hom. Lev_. I.4.
Male-victim=mind (female= αἴσθησιϛ). Ibid.	Male-victim=chastity. _Hom. Lev_. I.5.
Best sacrifice=pure soul, mind purified, perfect in virtue, ψυχή, θεοφιλήϛ. _De vic_. 5.	Each of us is our own holocaust if we renounce everything, take up cross & follow Christ, give body to be burned, have charity and follow martyrdom, etc. _Hom. Lev_. IX.9.
ὕμνοι and εὐχαριστία of the mind suitable sacrifices (no need for voice). _De sacr_.3.	"Hostia orationum." _Hom. Lev_. IX.1.

TABLE I (cont.)

Philo	Origen
Entire soul, full of pure dogmas, rejoicing in divine light, breathing the air of righteousness and virtue. *De som*. 2.10.	Peace- and thank-offering; to praise God in every action, doctrine, speech, "moribus," "disciplina," "Praeceptis." *Hom. Lev*. V.7.
Purity means no disease or πάθος in the soul. *De vic*. 5. Purity of heart vs. weakness of the flesh. *On the Sacr. of Abel & Cain*, 40.	Only when purged of "libido" can one offer sacrifice pleasing to God. Ibid., V.4.
Only a wise man who has not tasted παθῶν and κακίων can share in the feast. Ibid., 33.	

Typical lists used to allegorise sacrifices

ἀρετή, φρόνησις, σωφροσύνη,	hostiam laudis . . .
ἀνδρεία, δικαιοσύνη.	oraticonum . . .
ὁσιότης.	misericordiae . . .
καλοκαγαθία.	pudictiae . . .
ἀρεταί - ἄμωμα ἱερεῖα.	iustitiae . . .
On the Sacr. of Abel & Cain, 12; *De fuga et inv*., 3; *De sacr*., 3, etc.	sanctitatis . . .
	Hom. Lev. IX.1

TABLE II

Platonism and Sacrificial Symbols

Philo	Origen	
Two Temples of God	Heavenly Sacrifice of Christ	
(i) World:	(types)	
High-Priest= ὁ πρωτόγονος θεῖος λόγος	Christian sacrifices	Christ's death on the cross
	(types)	
	Jewish sacrifices	
(ii) λογικὴ ψυχή Priest= ο πρὸς ἀλήθειαν ἄνθρωπος	High-Priest of all sacrifices of New Covenant = Christ, Λόγος	
Jewish priest and traditional sacrifices= copies, visible imitation. (See *De som.*, I.37)	Jewish priests= types	
	(For the above schema, see *Hom. Jos.* II.1, XII.1, XVII.1, XXVI.3. This interpretation is based on an analogy with Origen's treatment of the Eternal Gospel and its relation to the Gospel preached on earth.	

E. Conclusion

In this chapter we have examined some of the influences which played a part in the formation of the Christian spiritual cult. We have found that at first the dominant influence was Jewish, partly because Christianity originated in Judaism, and partly because it retained the Jewish scriptures. Particularly influential were the "prophetic moralising" tradition and the idea that a martyr's death was expiatory. With the Apologists, however, began the process of assimilation of Greek philosophical ideas and ideals. The ascetic ideal embodied the Greek aspiration to απάθεια and this became the supreme Christian self-offering, the ultimate spiritual sacrifice.

All these influences contributed to the character of the Christian spiritual cult, more than to the actual motives for spiritualisation and rejection of material sacrifice. Even in the character of the cult, that is, the sort of spiritual offerings allowed, there is a distinctive Christian element. This distinctive feature is the central place given to Christological considerations. The doctrine of the sacrificial death of Christ made the Church the first society to adopt a truly spiritual cult, and it contributed to the radical spiritualisation of even the few material offerings which survived, the most obvious example being the Eucharist. It gave the whole spiritual cult a central focus, an example to emulate, so raising the virtues of love, mercy and peace to equality with justice, courage and piety. In later sections, this distinctive Christological element in the Christian cult will be examined in relation to the doctrine of Atonement, and in relation to the spiritual sacrifices of the Church; but first we will conclude this section with an analysis of the spiritual cult described in this chapter according to the types of sacrifice already distinguished in Chapter Three.

CHAPTER SIX
THE TYPES OF SACRIFICE OFFERED BY CHRISTIANS

To the enlightened Jew and pagan, the idea of rational and spiritual sacrifice was attractive, but the Church was the first society to insist on almost exclusively spiritual worship. Since, however, this spiritual worship was described in sacrificial terms and owed so much to both contemporary thought and the Jewish scriptures, it is reasonable to classify these spiritual sacrifices according to the types analysed earlier in Chapter Three.

The turning-point in the rejection of literal sacrifices seems to have been the Epistle to the Hebrews; this is therefore a convenient place to begin our investigation into the type of sacrifices offered by Christians. The argument of the Epistle depends on the author's case that the death of Christ was the only possible sacrifice for sin. That offering had been made, and there was no further sacrifice for sin after acceptance of the effects of this one sacrifice in Baptism.[1] Unlike later writers, the author does not suggest that all the material offerings of the Old Covenant are replaced by a spiritual offering of good moral lives, especially not the sin-offerings. Only the death of Christ was a valid sacrifice. Right at the end, however, he does speak of response to the benefits of the sacrificial death of Christ, and this response is described in terms of sacrifices of praise. In other words, although sin-offerings have been annulled by the death of Christ, thank-offerings have not, and the thank-offerings that are acceptable to God are, firstly, praise, "the fruit of lips which confess his name," and secondly, doing good and sharing, the just and charitable qualities that were better than sacrifice in the Jewish "prophetic" tradition.[2]

---

[1]See Heb. 6.4-6.
[2]Ibid., 13, 15, 16.

Similarly in the sermon known as II Clement, the offering of spiritual sacrifices is regarded simply as a repayment made by Christians in gratitude for their salvation through Christ.[3] For this reason even honouring God with the lips is seen to be liable to abuse; the whole heart and mind is needed to offer a worthy sacrifice of thanksgiving to the God who has given so much.[4]

In the Homilies on Leviticus, Origen allegorises the sacrifices "pro peccato" in terms of the sacrifice of Christ, and the sacrifices "pro munere" as the offering of Christians.[5] The gift-sacrifices of worship and thanksgiving are still to be offered by Christians, even though sacrifices for sin have been perfected and annulled by the offering of Christ.

Even the sacrifice of the martyr is not simply expiatory; the language of the Martyrdom of Polycarp, in particular, suggests that the sacrifice was also regarded as the supreme self-offering to God, as an expression of faith and thanksgiving. Polycarp is likened to a noble ram presented from a great flock as a whole-burnt offering acceptable to God, (εἰς προσφοράν, ὁλοκαύτωμα δεκτὸν τῷ Θεῷ ἠτοιμασμένον),[6] and in his prayer he asks to be received in the presence of God among former martyrs as a rich and acceptable sacrifice (ἐν θυσίᾳ πίονι καὶ προσδεκτῇ),[7] prepared by God himself and offered through the High-Priest, Jesus Christ. The sacrifice is nowhere claimed to have expiatory significance; Polycarp offered himself as a thank-offering, a gift-sacrifice, and as he died, by some miracle, the pyre gave off the smell of incense.[8] His death was a supreme act of obedience and worship.

---

[3]2 Clem., I.3, 5; IX.7; XV.2.

[4]Ibid., III.4; IX.10.

[5]Origen, Hom. Lev. II.4 is the only place where he speaks of the offerings of Christians as being pro peccato.

[6]Mart. Pol., XIV.1.

[7]Ibid., XIV.2, 3.

[8]XV.2.

Origen realised that the "holocaust" in the Old Testament meant the highest offering of praise, not an offering of placation as in Greek religion; so his exposition of the Christian holocaust implies the same thing. The Christian's holocaust is himself, and he keeps the sacrifice burning on the altar by renouncing his possessions, taking up his Cross and following Christ; by giving his body to be burned, and following the glory of the martyr, having charity; by loving his brethren, and fighting for justice and truth, even unto death; by dying to all desire of the flesh, as the world is crucified to him, and he to the world.[9] The complete self-offering is a spiritual sacrifice of praise and thanksgiving.

According to Chrysostom, as much as a man is superior to a sheep, so much is Christian sacrifice superior to others, for here one's soul is offered as victim. The most complete offering is the sacrifice of the martyr, the gift of both body and soul completely to God, though voluntary poverty has become an adequate substitute with the end of persecutions. These sacrifices are offerings of devotion and worship acceptable to God, an ὀσμὴ εὐωδίας μεγάλη.[10]

For Chrysostom, martyrdom was a thing of the past, as it was also for the Gregories, who thought of the self-offering in terms of spiritual surrender to God, the monastic ideal, the renouncing of the flesh and of the world. This was likewise an ὁλοκαύτωμα, a living sacrifice of praise. Humility, a contrite heart, the new man recreated in Christ, imitation of the Logos, ultimately oneself freed from sin and passion, such were the only worthy sacrifices of praise to God.[11] By sacrificing the passions, the soul "becomes fragrant throughout her entire life, breathing the myrrh of holiness and an incense variously mixed and compounded of all the virtues; and thus she comes to delight the nostrils of her Spouse (that is, God)

---

[9]Origen, *Hom. Lev.*, IX.9.

[10]Chrysostom, *Hom. Heb.*, XI.

[11]See, e.g., Greg. Naz., *Or.* XVI.2; XL.40; XLII.8; XLV.23; Greg. Nys., MPG 44/388CD, 540A, 897CD, etc.

in an odour of sweetness (ὀσμὴ εὐωδίας)."[12] No one is worthy of God, or of Christ, the victim and priest, unless he has thus made himself a living sacrifice:[13] this is the only worthy sacrifice of praise for salvation.[14]

So, we may say that nearly all the texts imply that the sacrifices Christians offered were not primarily an expiation for sin, but a response of thanksgiving to the perfect sin-offering given by Christ, to use the word of _II Clement_ an ἀντιμισθία. They were gift-sacrifices of praise and thanksgiving, expressed in prayer, in psalms and hymns, in the offering of a life lived according to God's will, in acts of charity and love, in the final self-offering of martyrdom, and its later substitute, monasticism.

Knowing, however, that the idea that martyrdom was expiatory had passed into Christianity from Judaism, is it safe to explain all the spiritual sacrifices Christians could offer for sin, even though the death of Christ had been a full, perfect and sufficient sacrifice for the sins of the whole world?

The _Epistle to the Hebrews_ takes the strict position that since the Son of God has been slain as a sacrifice for sin, no further sacrifice is possible, and once the benefits of his sacrifice have been accepted in Baptism, there is no further opportunity of repentance, mercy and pardon.[15] Origen recognises, however, that this doctrine has caused as much despair as incentive to virtue; the people under the Old Covenant had an advantage in being able to obtain pardon at any time by offering a sacrifice for sin. Since one pardon was clearly inadequate, he allows seven Christian "remissiones peccatorum": Baptism, the suffering of martyrdom, ἐλεημοσύνη, forgiveness of the brethren, conversion of someone else, abundance of charity, and penitence. These he proceeds to equate with the sin-offerings of _Leviticus_, this

---

[12]Greg. Nys., MPG 44956D-957D.

[13]Greg. Naz., _Or._ XX.3.

[14]Greg. Nys., MPG 44/473B.

[15]_Heb._ 6.4-6; 10.26-7.

being the one place where he allegorises sin-offerings in terms of the Christians' sacrifice, rather than the sacrifice of Christ.[16]

In fact Origen's list was entirely in keeping with long-standing Christian tradition. Martyrdom had always been accepted as a means of expiation and within the New Testament we find that love covered a multitude of sins, confession and repentance in prayer could obtain forgiveness, and converting a sinner preserved one's soul from death.[17] The problem of post-baptismal sin haunted the Church, and led both to the establishment of the penitential system and the excessive trust in the virtues of the martyrs which caused so much conflict between confessors and clergy after the great periods of persecution.[18] The _Epistle to the Hebrews_ always raised the problem for the exegete, and Chrysostom was bound to discuss the difficulty in his sermons on the Epistle.[19] He concludes that although the Epistle says there is no second sacrifice, the author does not take away repentance "nor the propitiation which is obtained through repentance." The medicine of repentance, given by the grace of God (compare the idea in Judaism that the expiatory sacrifices were a gift of God), is sufficient to blot out all our sins; it consists in condemnation of our own sins, great humbleness of mind, intense tears and continual prayer, and then amendment of life, almsgiving, not being angry or bearing malice, forgiving everyone else. In other words, repentance, in Chrysostom's

---

[16]Origen, _Hom. Lev._, II.4.

[17]1 _Pet_. 4.6; _James_ 5.16, 19-20. See Polycarp, _Phil_. X.2, and esp. 2 _Clem_. XVI.4. A very similar list to that of Origen is found here.

[18]The problem of readmitting the lapsed was particularly in dispute and was a major factor in the Novatian, Meletian, and Donatist schisms. See Frend, op. cit., and his _The Donatist Church_ (Oxford, 1952). On the problem of post-baptismal sin, see M. F. Wiles, "One Baptism for the Remission of Sins," _CQR_ (1964).

[19]Chrysostom, _Hom. Heb_. XX; IX.

thinking, covers many of the types of sin-offering permitted by Origen.

Since amendment of life and many of the Christian virtues came to have the significance of sin-offerings, the offering of oneself by purifying one's life from sin and passion was sometimes seen as a sin-offering, as well as being the supreme offering of worship. So, in the first place, to mortify one's flesh and please God by one's actions is to present a living sacrifice, sacred and pleasing to God, offering in the body of rational man the worship once offered in the bodies of dumb cattle; but Origen also states that such sacrifices were provided by the mercy of God for those who chance to fall, so that through offering rational sacrifices, the soul may be restored to salvation. The best sacrifice of this kind is martyrdom, then virginity, then refraining from pride, avarice, lying etc.[20] In other words, they are sacrifices by which sin is removed. It is interesting that the sin is actually removed from the life of the former sinner by the action of the grace of God. The principle of the Old Testament that the sin-offering was given by God who alone could expiate sin is completely moralised, the transforming action of God's grace now being described as an expiatory sacrifice.

Further discussion of the type of sacrifice made for sin by Christians is not really possible until after discussion of the sacrificial death of Christ. In order to understand what sort of an offering for sin he made, the place of propitiatory and other related ideas in Christianity will be discussed in the next section. This should also throw light on the type of sin-offerings offered by Christian people, as well as raising the central problem of the relationship between Christ's sacrifice and those of his followers.

Other sacrifices offered by Christians are easily classifiable. As the spiritual sacrifices were a response of gratitude and praise for salvation effected through Christ, so the first-fruit offerings

---

[20] Comm. Rom. IX.1.

were a response of thanksgiving to the Creator. The fellowship-meals and the Eucharist were communion-sacrifices analogous to those of the Jews and the Greeks.[21] This is not to claim that the Eucharist was not more than this; but since it clearly had an intimate relation with the sacrificial death of Christ, full discussion of the types of sacrifice by which it was interpreted will be postponed.

In summary, we may classify Christian sacrifices, taking into account both material and spiritual offerings, as follows:

I. Sacrifices of Praise, Worship and Thanksgiving
(The Jewish type of gift-sacrifice)

(a) First-fruit offerings and other offerings in kind, made in grateful response to the Creator.

(b) The offering of Christian virtues, of prayer and praise, of one's whole life, even to the point of death, in imitation of Christ, and in response to his saving, sacrificial death.

II. Sacrifices of Communion

(a) All fellowship-meals in which the food consumed was consecrated to God. (These seem to have been of the *zebach*/θυσία type).

(b) The Eucharist.

(Both types of communion-sacrifice may be involved in the interpretation of the Eucharist. Detailed discussion will be found in Chapter Eleven.)

III. Sacrifices for Sin
(Analysis into types will be found in Chapter Ten)

---

[21] 1 *Cor*. 10. 16ff.

(a) Baptism, almsgiving, forgiveness of the brethren, conversion of someone else, charity, penitence.

(b) One's own progress in Christian virtue and death to sin.

(c) The expiatory death of the martyr.

Although this summary suggests that Christians offered sacrifices of all the various types, the argument of this chapter will have shown that they were primarily a response of worship and thanksgiving to God, (i.e., predominantly Type I). The most interesting point is that every type was brought into association with the sacrificial death of Christ. The relationship of the Christian's sacrifice to that of his Lord must therefore be discussed, when the latter has been studied.

SECTION III

THE NATURE OF CHRIST'S SACRIFICE

INTRODUCTION TO SECTION THREE

The basic κήρυγμα (preaching message)[1] of the earliest missionaries of the new Christian faith contained both an appeal for repentance with the promise of remission of sins, and the proclamation of the death and resurrection of the Messiah, Jesus. At a very early stage, these elements were connected, so that we find in Paul's message the idea that Christ died for the remission of sins and on behalf of mankind, and the beginnings of theories about the atoning efficacy of his death.[2]

Two elements in the Jewish background seem to have stimulated this development: firstly, the idea that the death of a righteous martyr was expiatory,[3] and secondly, the search for prophecies, which would

---

[1]For the isolation of the _kerygma_ from the NT texts, see C. H. Dodd, _The Apostolic Preaching and its Developments_ (London, 1936).

[2]See ibid., p. 25 where Dodd points out that the earliest kerygma did not state that Christ _died for our sins_. He thinks that it was not merely Pauline theology but was implied by the traditional _kerygma_. Only speculation can suggest when the message of repentance and forgiveness (inherited from Jesus' own teaching) was directly connected with the atoning death of Christ. Morna Hooker, in _Jesus and the Servant_ (London, 1959), p. 117ff, claims that it was purely Pauline.

[3]See John Downing, "Jesus and Martyrdom," _JTS_ (1963); he argues that Jesus himself thought of his death as expiatory in the tradition of Jewish ideas about the atoning efficacy of the martyr's death. His first section states that these ideas were current in Jesus' own day. Whether or not Jesus understood his own death in these terms, the evidence Downing presents, particularly for the modelling of the Passion story on Jewish "martyria," suggests that the church's thinking was formed in this tradition.

account for the unexpected death of the Messiah. Although detailed evidence for the use of *Isaiah* 53 to explain the death of Christ is fairly slim, it still remains probable that the fulfillment of this prophecy enabled the Church to justify his dying the death of a condemned criminal by a method which the Scriptures themselves branded as accursed.[4]

Once the death of Christ was connected with forgiveness of sins and expiation, it was inevitable that actual sacrifice language should be used of it, especially as the Old Covenant came to be regarded as a complete foreshadowing of the New. The whole sacrificial Law was soon understood as an acted prophecy or symbol of the death of Christ, the perfect martyr and sacrificial victim. Christian sacrifices were an imitation of his perfect sacrifice. His death had dealt with the problem of sin and the need for expiation once and for all, and therefore the actual practice of the Jewish cult was no longer necessary.

So far this distinctive element in Christian sacrificial thinking has been, as far as possible, left on one side. We have been concerned with the

---

[4]*Pace* Hooker (op. cit.). Her arguments are impressive, and much of her exegesis is convincing, but it is impossible to believe that the church's search for prophecies did not turn up this passage, and the story of Philip and the eunuch proves that it did. To think that Christ identified himself with a "Servant-figure" is admittedly foolish, since such a figure has only been isolated by modern scholarship. But, considering the elusive nature of references to the OT in the exegesis of the early church, it is dangerous to assume that the atoning aspect of the Servant's death was not ever considered simply because those verses are not quoted in *Acts* 8.32ff. The combination of this prophecy and the idea of the expiatory martyr's death seems to have given rise to the earliest positive explanation of the unexpected death of the Messiah. (I accept her contention that *Isa*. 53 was not applied to the Messiah in the Jewish tradition, as opposed to Jeremias and Zimmerli in *The Servant of God*.)

development of the whole spiritual cult of the Church, and in particular with the influences under which it developed. This plan was adopted so that the sacrifice of Christ could be studied within the broad context of the Church's sacrificial thought, and not simply in terms of its relevance to Atonement theory. Specific examination of the relationship between the Christian cult and Christ's sacrifice will be delayed until the following section; first, we need to establish the nature of his sacrifice in the light of the material we have already assembled.

Since it was particularly as a means of dealing with sin that the sacrifice of Christ was understood, questions of Atonement theory are inevitably raised in discussion of the nature of his sacrifice. But these questions will be tackled, not by making "a priori" assumptions about the rationale of sacrifice, but by enquiring what kind of sin-offering was intended by various thinkers who made use of sacrificial ideas to explain the death of Christ, the analysis being based on the types already distinguished in this study. This particular discussion is undertaken in Chapter Eight. Meanwhile, since the nature of his sin-offering inevitably affects or is affected by Atonement theories, it is proposed to outline in this introduction the theory of Atonement which predominated during this period, and to draw attention to some of the problems involved in regarding the death of Christ as a sacrifice within the context of this theory. In Chapter Seven, we embark on our enquiry into the nature of Christ's sacrifice by considering the effect produced by the application of certain Old Testament "types" to his death on the Cross, this kind of exegesis having provided the earliest method of explaining the connection between his death and atoning sacrifice. Chapter Nine completes our study of the nature of Christ's sacrifice by drawing attention to the various ways it was thought to fulfill the whole of the Old Testament sacrificial Law; this emphasises the fact that his sacrifice was more comprehensive than is generally realised, and also opens the subject of its close relationship with the sacrifices of the

Church, the body of his followers.

The Classic Theory of Atonement

The work of Christ took place in the context of a cosmic drama. The outlook of the early Christian was dualist, not an absolute dualism like Manichaeism, but a dualism qualified by the fact that God was the inevitable victor in the conflict between good and evil.[5] The philosophical problem of the origin of evil if everything was created by God was variously treated, but does not directly concern us here. From the New Testament through to the Cappadocians, the Christian felt himself to be involved in the warfare between God and the devil, good and evil, light and darkness, life and death, righteousness and sin. We have already seen that this conflict was typified in the Christian campaign against idolatry, superstition and magic; the martyr felt himself at war with all these forces of evil when he died for his faith.

In this war, Christ was thought to have already achieved the victory, and his followers were merely

---

[5]For a full discussion of this theory of the atonement, see the original exposition: G. Aulén, Christus Victor (London, 1931). Aulén's main aim was to show that this concept of the atonement had a direct lineage from the NT through the church Fathers to Luther, while Anselm, Abelard, etc., were a by-path; hence he calls it the "classic" theory of atonement. I follow him in regarding this as the basic view of the Fathers, though emphasising further the way in which the dualistic outlook underlay their whole approach to soteriological questions. This dualism, as Aulén points out, must not be regarded as a metaphysical dualism between Finite and Infinite, or between matter and spirit; nor an absolute dualism between God and evil, typical of Zoroastrian and Manichaean teaching, in which evil is treated as an eternal principle opposed to good. Rather, it is between God and the rebellious part of his creation, evil being ultimately subservient to good, though requiring the cosmic action of God in Christ to render it powerless. The dualism is between God and the daemonic forces.

bringing the rout of the opposing principalities and powers to its final conclusion. So, the Fathers understood "the idea of Atonement as a Divine conflict and victory; Christ - 'Christus Victor' - fights against and triumphs over the evil powers of the world, the 'tyrants' under which mankind is in bondage and suffering."[6] 'Christus Victor' conquered death by his resurrection, spiritual blindness by the light of his teaching, and ignorance by his revelation, and all the various aspects of this victory can be described mythologically be reference to defeat of the devil and his angels.[7]

Sacrifice and Ransom in the Context of this Theory of Atonement

According to Aulén, the original expositor of this idea of Atonement in the Fathers, sacrifice is naturally regarded as offered to God, and ransom as the price paid by God to redeem mankind from bondage to the devil.[8] But, how could the death of Christ be both a sacrifice to God and a ransom to the devil? If the conquest of the devil was the basic requirement for dealing with evil, why should sacrifice to God be necessary? How could a ransom offered by God be also a sacrifice to God? Is Aulén's distinction at all valid?

---

[6]Aulén, op. cit., pp. 20-1.

[7]This idea is so widespread in the Fathers that I have not thought it necessary to document it. From the exorcisms of the NT to the spiritual struggles of the man, Antony, against temptation, the same view prevails, and it is difficult to understand why it has so often been disregarded by scholars. That it cannot be explained away, even in Origen, will be argued later (see Ch. 8).

[8]Aulén, op. cit., See his chapter "The Double Aspect of the Drama of the Atonement." His theory that the sacrifice and ransom are part of God's self-reconciliation applies only to the later Greek Fathers, Athanasius and the Cappodocians (see Ch. 8).

In asking the question, "What kind of a sin-offering?" in Chapter Eight, we shall be raising the problem of how the idea of Christ's death as a sacrifice fits into the basic pattern of Atonement thinking we have outlined here. Sacrifice and atonement cannot be explained without reflecting or affecting the writers' concept of God, so that ideas of propitiation or placation must be carefully treated, and their relationship with the Classic theory examined. Sacrifice interpreted in these terms, or as in any sense offered to God, is not apparently consistent with the predominant idea of the effect of Christ's death, which was regarded as a victory over evil. It is with this problem in mind that we approach study of the treatment of Christ's death as a sacrifice.

CHAPTER SEVEN
TYPOLOGICAL INTERPRETATIONS OF CHRIST'S SACRIFICE

We have already briefly mentioned the important role of typological understanding of the Jewish scriptures in facilitating the rejection of material sacrifices. By this method of exegesis, the sacrifices of the Jewish Law were interpreted as symbolic prophecies of the realities revealed in Christ. Sacrifice was rejected, while the scriptures were retained and used to support a spiritual cult.

This method was also most important in the development first of apologetic for the unexpected death of the Messiah and then of a positive doctrine of its atoning efficacy. Both the regular sin-offerings and the great festivals outlined in Chapter Two were interpreted as prophetic "types" of Christ's Passion. This created interplay between the type and its antitype, so that sometimes interpretation of the Old Testament was forced into conformity with the pattern of the Christological fulfillment, and on other occasions, Old Testament concepts determined how the nature of Christ's sacrifice was understood.

There are three particularly good examples of this method of exegesis, and each of these will be examined in turn. It will be noticed that the line between typology and allegory is difficult to draw, and that the authors preferred to frequently pass almost imperceptibly from one to the other.

A. The Day of Atonement and the Red Heifer Ritual

The death of Christ atoned for the sins of mankind. This soon became the basic message and faith of Christianity. One way in which this was expressed was by seeing the ritual of the Jewish Day of Atonement fulfilled in his death. The implications for the Doctrine of the Atonement of regarding Christ's death as any kind of sin-offering will be discussed in the next chapter, but here we may mention some of the ways in which this type was used.

In the Epistle to the Hebrews, this type is used in association with certain others. The author does not, however, make any use of the characteristic scapegoat ritual. What particularly interests him is the action of the High-Priest, who entered the Holy of Holies once a year on this special day in order to perform elaborate blood rituals. Christ is understood to be the true High-Priest who entered heaven once for all, and with his blood purified the consciences of men, as the High-Priest had purified the flesh with the blood of bulls and goats.[1] The expiatory power of the blood is most important, and it is the blood rituals of the daily sin-offerings and of the sacrifices performed on the Day of Atonement, which is emphasised in the Epistle.[2] So the work of Christ is explained in terms of the rituals he is said to have fulfilled: as the blood rituals brought about expiation, so purification from sin is now achieved through the blood of Jesus Christ. This is emphasised by the fact that alongside the expiatory blood rituals is placed the special purificatory rite of the Red Heifer.[3]

This type is found in association with the Day of Atonement elsewhere. The Epistle of Barnabas explains in detail that the scarlet wool used in the Red Heifer ritual is a type of the blood of Christ, and the purificatory rite represents the forgiveness of sins and purification of heart preached by Christian missionaries (as the boys sprinkled the people in the ritual).[4] In this context, there is an amalgam of types of Christ, and, as in the Epistle to the Hebrews, included alongside the Red Heifer, is the

---

[1]Heb. 9.6ff, 23ff; 10.1ff.

[2]Ibid., 9.7, 12-14, 18-22, 25; 10.4, 19.

[3]Ibid., 9.13, 19.

[4]*Ep. Barn.* VIII.1-6.

type of the Day of Atonement;[5] but unlike the *Epistle to the Hebrews*, it is the scapegoat with which the author is concerned. Christ is represented by the scapegoat which is accursed and bears away sins as it is cast out into the desert with scarlet wool around its head (this feature seems to have been transferred from the Red Heifer ritual). The exegesis here is a good example of how the Old Testament was pressed into conformity with its Christological fulfillment, for the ritual of the two goats is made to fit the mocking and crucifixion of Christ, arrayed in his scarlet robe with a crown of thorns on his head amongst which appeared the scarlet wool.[6] Unlike the *Epistle to the Hebrews*, the author does not use the expiatory associations of blood, but he does make it clear that he associates these types with the remission of sins and Atonement accomplished by the death of Christ. One other point in his exegesis depends on the likeness of the two goats in the Day of Atonement ritual; the Jews, he says, will be amazed when they find one just like the one they crucified returning in glory at the Second Coming.

This idea occurs again in Justin's *Dialogue with Trypho*.[7] The two goats represent the two Comings of Christ, one in humiliation and to remove sin, the other in glory. It seems to have become a traditional interpretation.

Origen uses this type a number of times with reference to the work of Christ. He hints at it in his apologetic works, the *De Principiis* and the *Contra Celsum*, and he allegorises it in detail in two different ways in his Homilies on Leviticus.[8] In the

---

[5]It has been suggested that a common Christian Midrash of *Lev*. and *Num*. may lie behind the typological interpretations of *Heb*. and *Ep. Barn*., in both of which the Jewish rites have been so described as to throw into relief their points of contact with the Christian fulfillment. See Daniélou, *The Theology of Jewish Christianity*, p. 97ff.

[6]*Ep. Barn*., VII.6-11. [7]Justin, *Dial*. 40.

[8]*De princ*. II.2.1; *C. Cels*. VII.43; *Hom. Lev*. IX. 4-5; X.2.

next chapter, we shall examine one of these. The other allegorises the two goats as Barabbas and Jesus; Pilate sent off Barabbas alive with the sins of the people on his head, whereas Christ was offered as a sin-offering to cover the sins of those who were to be forgiven.[9]

There were then various ways of interpreting the Day of Atonement ritual so as to show that it was fulfilled in the atoning death of Christ. Whatever the exact picture extracted from the "type," the essential point brought out by each was the belief that the death of Christ had brought about a greater and more lasting Atonement for sin than that achieved by the mechanism of the Old Covenant. How this Atonement was conceived depended on how the sacrifice for sin was interpreted, and this will be the subject of the next chapter. The problem of the relationship between these ideas and the Classic theory outlined in the Introduction to this section, cannot be faced until this question has been decided, so that too will be left for later discussion.

B. The Covenant-sacrifice

In the *Epistle to the Hebrews*, a typological interpretation of the sacrifice which established the Old Covenant appears alongside the types we have already mentioned. The sacrificial death of Christ established a New Covenant; for, just as the special covenant-relation between God and Israel had been established by the sacrifice on Mt. Sinai, so Christ had established a New Covenant-relation with God which replaced the Old, through his sacrifice of himself on the Cross.

Paul had already explicitly taught that the coming of Christ meant the establishment of the New Covenant prophesied by Jeremiah,[10] a Covenant based

---

[9]*Hom. Lev.* X.2. [10]*Jer.* 31.31-4.

on the spirit rather than the letter of the Law and written on the hearts of men not on tables of stone.[11] It is probable that this idea dates from even earlier in the Christian tradition; the shedding of Christ's blood is associated with the establishment of a New Covenant in the traditions concerning Christ's Institution of the Eucharist,[12] and the Eucharist came to be regarded as the characteristic cult-act of the New Covenant established by Christ through his redeeming death.[13]

However, though we frequently find it stated that Christ established a New spiritual Covenant and brought the Old to an end,[14] his death is not often put into explicit typological parallel with the sacrifice on Mt. Sinai, as it is found in the *Epistle to the Hebrews*.[15] The whole argument of the Epistle depends on the exact typological correspondence of the Old and New Covenants, and this includes the method of establishing the Covenant. In place of Moses, Christ is the Mediator of the Covenant, a New Covenant established through his own self-sacrifice.[16] When he had read all the commandments of the Covenant Law, Moses took the blood of sacrificial victims, and half of it he threw against the altar and the other half he threw over the people, so sealing the blood-covenant between the two parties, God and Israel.[17] By the argument of typology, the blood of Christ was

---

[11]2 *Cor*. 3.6, 14; *Gal*. 4.24ff.

[12]*Mk*. 14.24; *Mt*. 26.28; *Lk*. 22.20 (longer text); 1 *Cor*. 11.25.

[13]Eucharistic ideas will be discussed in more detail in the next section; see also Ch. 11.

[14]See e.g., *Ep. Barn*. IV.8; VI.19, and XII-XIV where he proves the Covenant belongs to the Christians and not to the Jews. Justin, *Dial*. 11, 43, 67, etc. Greg. Naz., *Or*. V.27; XIV.14, 27; XVI.11.

[15]For general discussions of the idea of Covenant in *Heb*., see the commentaries, particularly those of Spicq and Montefiore.

[16]*Heb*. 7.22; 8.6; 9.15; 12.24; etc.

[17]*Exod*. 24.6-8; *Heb*. 9.18-20.

efficacious in establishing the New and better Covenant between God and the New Israel; with his own blood, Christ sprinkled the heavenly altar itself. So the author makes the ratification of the New Covenant dependent on the shedding of Christ's blood by using a strict typological parallel with the sacrifice on Sinai.[18]

But blood was also the means of expiation, according to the Law. The problem of the Old Covenant had always been sin, the refusal or failure to obey the Law of God. This failure was inconceivable under the New and better Covenant established in the spirit; and therefore the sacrifice which instituted the New Covenant was also efficacious in finally dealing with the problem of sin. In Jeremiah's prophecy, God promised to remember their sin no more when the New Covenant was established,[19] and it was particularly this aspect that interested the author of this Epistle. The death of Christ had brought about an Atonement of lasting value, superior to that attempted by any of the sin-offerings of the Old Covenant.[20] So the author of *Hebrews* associated the blood of the Covenant with expiatory blood and with various purificatory rites, without distinguishing the different sources of his types; with the typology of the Covenant-sacrifice he intermingled that of the Day of

---

[18] I have not felt it directly relevant to draw attention to the argument in *Heb.* to explain why a Covenant had to be ratified in blood. The Greek word διαθήκη used for Covenant in the LXX and NT means, in secular Greek, "will," and the argument is that the will does not become effective until the testator is dead, i.e., a death is required to bring the will into effect. So the death of Christ was required before Christians could inherit the promises and receive the benefits of the Covenant. See *Heb.* 8.12.

[19] *Jer.* 31.34; see *Heb.* 8.12.

[20] *Heb.* 9.9ff: the sin-offerings dealt with purification of the body and had no effect for purification of conscience. *Heb.* 10.1: they had constantly to be repeated, which proves their ineffectiveness.

Atonement and the regular sin-offerings of Judaism.[21]

The nature of the Covenant-sacrifice was therefore two-fold. Firstly it dealt with the problem of sin, so that this type was closely associated with typological understanding of the Day of Atonement and other sin-offerings; secondly, it established a new relationship with God. This two-fold aspect of the sacrifice of Christ will be found again in some of our later discussions.

C. The Passover-sacrifice

Closely associated with the idea that Christ's sacrifice established the New Covenant is the idea that his death was a new Passover-sacrifice. By means of the Passover, Israel had been saved from Egypt and brought into her special Covenant-relation with God; likewise, Christ had redeemed mankind from the Egypt of sin and death through his sacrifice, and established a New Covenant to replace the Old. Both these types were also applied to the Eucharist, which became the Christian Passover celebration;[22] clearly there was a natural association between them.

The use of the Passover-type is first found in the New Testament. St. Paul says "Christ our Passover is sacrificed,"[23] and he is followed by the

---

[21]See in particular the argument of Ch. 9. In verse 19 he combines with the Covenant-sacrifice the purificatory rite of the Red Heifer (*Num*. 19.1-10) and the requirements for the cleansing of a leper (*Lev*. 14.4-7). Throughout the chapter, allusions are made to the annual purification of sin made during the Day of Atonement as well as other sin-offerings and the Covenant-sacrifice. All are brought into association through the predominant place of blood rituals in each rite, and the author makes no attempt to deal with each type in distinction.

[22]See *infra*, Ch. 11B. [23]1 *Cor*. 5.7.

author of the Gospel according to St. John, whose account of the Passion indicates that Jesus died on the Cross at the same time as the Passover lambs were killed in the Temple.[24]

These typological hints were taken up by the Apologists. Justin uses the idea that the Passover was merely a symbol of Christ's sacrifice in his Dialogue with Trypho. The command to sacrifice the Passover was only temporary, he says, and this is proved by the fact that God would not allow the Paschal lamb to be sacrificed anywhere except in Jerusalem, for he knew there would come a time after Christ's passion when the cult at Jerusalem would be forcibly stopped. The lamb on the spit was roasted in the form of a Cross as a symbol of Christ's passion on the Cross. Believers anoint their homes, that is, themselves, with the blood of Christ, according to the strength of their faith.[25] Later in the Dialogue, he draws attention to more significant aspects of the type. The Paschal blood saved those in Egypt when the first-born were destroyed. Christ was crucified during the Passover feast, and, as the blood of the Passover saved those in Egypt, so the blood of Christ saves those who believe in him. The blood was not really needed in the original Passover to indicate which homes were Israelite, since God would know anyway; the only reason for it was as a sign of the salvation that was to come through Christ.[26]

Over the centuries this type received elaborate development, especially in the Paschal Homilies of the great preachers. The earliest known Paschal Homily is that of Melito (provided the Homily found in a Fourth Century papyrus edited by C. Bonner is rightly attributed to him).[27] The scriptural passage on which

---

[24]Jn. 19.14, 31. [25]Justin, Dial. 40.

[26]Ibid., 111.

[27]P. Nautin, in Trois homélies dans la tradition d'Origène, claims that the Homily is not rightly attributed to Melito. He refers to his Le dossier d'Hippolyte et de Méliton where he gives reasons for disputing such attribution.

the Homily is based on the account of the institution of the Passover in Exodus, the story of which Melito depicts in vivid rhetorical detail.[28] The point of the Homily lies in the parallel between this story and the redemption of mankind by Christ. Melito tells of the Fall of Man and the resultant corruption of his children who lived under the tyranny of sin. Sin and Death are personified and a graphic picture drawn of Man's plight as he was dragged away captive under the shadows of Death.[29] This captivity is typified in the captivity of Israel in Egypt. Israel's escape by means of the Passover had its only "raison d'être" as a prophecy of the redemption of mankind. Israel was guarded by the sacrifice of the sheep, the blood of which stayed the hand of the destroying angel; but the angel only respected the blood because it was the type of Christ and he saw the mystery of the Lord enacted in the sheep.[30] "For, led as a lamb and slaughtered as a sheep, he ransomed us from the ruin of the world as from the land of Egypt, and freed us from slavery of the devil as from the hand of Pharoah . . . .[31] This is he who rescued us from slavery to freedom, from darkness to light, from death to life, from oppression to an eternal kingdom, and made us a new priesthood and a chosen people for ever. He is the Passover of our salvation."[32] Πάσχα, by a false etymology, is

---

[28]Melito, Hom. 11-35. [29]Ibid., 48-56.

[30]Ibid., 30-5. "Such a calamity encompasses Egypt," continues Melito, "and made her suddenly childless. But Israel was guarded by the sacrifice of the sheep, and was baptised by the shed blood . . . O strange and ineffable mystery! The sacrifice of the sheep was found to be the salvation of Israel, and the death of the sheep became the life of the people, and the blood abashed the angel. Tell me, angel, what stayed thy hand . . . the death of the sheep or the type of the Lord . . .? Thou sawest the mystery of the Lord in the sacrifice of the sheep, the type of the Lord in the death of the sheep. Therefore didst thou not smite Israel, but madest Egypt childless" (trans. Bonner).

[31]Ibid., 67. [32]Ibid., 68-9.

connected with suffering, so that it is further shown to be only a prophetic parable of the suffering of the Lamb of God on the Cross. In stating that God instituted the Passover only as a type or parable of the greater salvation that was to come in Christ,[33] Melito is in agreement with his near contemporary, Justin.

Later Paschal Homilies developed this idea with more and more allegorical detail. For example, in the Homily attributed to Hippolytus,[34] the date and time of the feast, the law that the lamb must be completely consumed, the bitter herbs, the haste, the girding of the loins, the wearing of sandals, the carrying of staves, the roasting of the lamb and the fact that no bone was to be broken, all these details of the celebration of the feast are interpreted in terms of the Christian dispensation.[35] But basically it is the same point at issue, that the death of the Paschal lamb freed Israel from Egypt, that the blood kept away the destroying angel, and that these signs were fulfilled in the saving death of Christ.[36]

One interesting detail in the Homily is the idea that the blood applied to the two doorposts represented the blood of Christ applied to both nations, Jews and Gentiles, in Baptism, while the blood on the lintel represented the anointing of the Church which holds the two peoples united under it.[37] Other Homilies in the Origenist tradition interpret this in terms of the

---

[33]See the general discussion of typology and its application to the Passover in ibid., 36-46.

[34]This Homily appears in a collection of Homilies on the Passion ascribed to Chrysostom, but clearly he is not the author. It also appears in another MS attributed to Hippolytus. Most scholars accept this attribution, but Nautin (op. cit.), who edited this Homily, argues in his introduction that in its present form it comes from a much later date, although the preacher used Hippolytus' treatise on the Passion as a source.

[35]Op. cit., 11-42.

[36]Ibid., 1, 2, 4, 6-8.

[37]Ibid., 25.

blood applied to the three parts of the soul,[38] but the basic point as regards the death of Christ is the same, that the Church and Christians are protected by the blood of Christ in the way the Israelites had been by the blood of the lamb.

The occasion of the Homilies is also interesting, since the question is associated with the Paschal controversy. Because Melito was a Quartodeciman, his Homily was preached on Good Friday and so concentrates on the sacrificial death of Christ. The other Homilies are Easter Sermons which rejoice in the salvation that has been wrought and the escape from the Egypt of sin and material pleasures to the life of Christ and the feast he offers with unleavened bread of sincerity and truth. So Gregory of Nazianzus in his Easter Sermon uses the same typology: yesterday the lamb was slaughtered, the Destroyer passed by and we were protected by the precious blood of Christ, but to-day we flee Egypt and no one prevents us from feasting with our God. Yesterday we were crucified with Christ, to-day we rise with him.[39]

"Christ our Passover is sacrificed." This was a theme that constantly recurred in Christian literature.[40] The Christian celebrated the Passover both at Easter time as a memorial of Christ's death, and at all times by feasting with the unleavened bread of sincerity and truth and the bitter herbs of sorrow and repentance.[41] The feast was thus spiritualised by interpreting the sacrifice of the lamb as the sacrifice of Christ, and moralised by being turned into a spiritual sacrifice offered by Christians. It was also associated with the celebration of the Eucharist, but this will be discussed later. The wide use of the Passover-type shows how the sacrifice of Christ

---

[38] Nautin, op. cit., Vol. 2. Here he edits three other pseudo-Chrysostom Homilies. See II.8.

[39] Greg. Naz., _Or_. I.3-4.

[40] It was not confined to the Paschal Homilies by any means, e.g., its use by Origen (see following note) and Chrysostom, _Hom. Heb_. XXVII.

[41] Origen, _C. Cels._, VIII.22-3; _Comm. Jn_. X.13.

was intimately related to the sacrifices offered by Christians, a point which again anticipates later discussions.

Our final task in this context is to consider the implications of the use of this type for understanding the nature of Christ's sacrifice. Although the Passover was called the sacrifice of Jahweh, and Jahweh's "Pesach," none of it was in fact given to God, except after it became a pilgrimage feast, the blood which was poured out at the altar. But Christian interpretation went behind this contemporary ritual to the origins as described in Scripture, and for them the blood ritual was the smearing of the blood on the doorposts to keep away the Destroyer. As we have already seen, the blood was originally "apotropaeic," a means of warding off evil spirits, and in the legend of the Tenth Plague, this aspect of the ritual was retained. Christians interpreted the death of Christ in terms of this earlier saving act of God; so they saw the sending of Christ, like the institution of the feast, as a gift of God to men who were in slavery to sin, death and the devil, the sacrificed lamb as a God-given means of redemption from this enslavement, and the blood of the lamb as the means of averting the evil powers of destruction. In other words, the legend of the institution of the Passover was interpreted quite naturally in terms of the Classic theory of Atonement we have outlined. The blood of Christ, the ransom-price, drives away the devil and his angels, and protects the faithful who are anointed by it. The Passover sacrifice is never thought of as a gift to God, as a sacrifice must be according to Aulen's assumptions. It is rather a sacrifice with averting power, instituted and given by God to keep away the evil daemons. Since the Passover blood was "apotropaeic," it was not unnatural, within the context of contemporary Greek ideas, to think of the blood of Christ, paid as a ransom-price, keeping away the ἀποτρόπαιοι θεοί, the devil and his angels, the ministers of evil with the power of sin and death.

D. Conclusion

Besides these types to which we have given more detailed treatment, others became traditional in Christian literature. The sacrifice of Isaac whereby Abraham gave up his only-begotten son was a type of God sending his only Son to a sacrificial death[42] (though also of the Christian's self-offering in martyrdom[43]). Two others are nearer to allegory, but important since they are so persistent. Rahab's red sign to the invading Israelites, which ensured her safety, was a type of the blood of Christ which saved mankind.[44] Moses holding up his arms was a type of Christ on the Cross; under his outstretched arms Christians were victorious in the war against the devil and his hosts, just as the Israelites were able to conquer as long as Moses did not weary and lay his arms down.[45] These last two clearly fit, like the Passover/Exodus type, into the pattern of the Classic theory of Atonement outlined earlier.

Of the types we have considered, therefore, three are consistent with the concept of Atonement outlined in the Introduction to the section. Of the others, one described the establishment of a new relationship with God which was the result of dealing with the problem of sin, and the other was specifically concerned with dealing with this problem. These, therefore, raise the same problems as the typological application of the sin-offerings to the understanding of Atonement. If the Doctrine of Atonement was basically understood as indicated in the Introduction, how is this consistent

---

[42] _Ep. Barn._ VII.3; Clem. Alex., _Paed._ I.23; Origen, _Hom. Gen._ VIII.6; Greg. Naz., _Or._ I.7; XXVIII.18; _Poem. Dogm._ IX.85; Greg. Nys., _MPG_ 46/601.

[43] Origen, _Hom. Gen._ VIII; Greg. Naz., _Or._ XLIII. 71.

[44] 1 _Clem._ XII.7; Justin, _Dial._ 111; Origen, _Hom. Jos._ III.5.

[45] _Ep. Barn._ XII.2; Justin, _Dial._ 90; Greg. Naz., _Or._ XI.2; Greg. Nys., _MPG_ 44/372A-C.

with the notion of a sacrifice offered to God, and how was it that this sacrifice dealt with sin? The general problem of what kind of sin-offering Christ's death was conceived to be, and how this fitted with the Classic theory of Atonement already outlined, will be the subject of the following chapter.

CHAPTER EIGHT
WHAT KIND OF SACRIFICE FOR SIN DID CHRIST OFFER?

Apart from the use of these special types that we have examined, there was not much reference to the sacrificial aspect of the death of Christ before Origen undertook to allegorise the whole Law in terms of his death, in works such as the *Homilies on Leviticus*. But even though references to sacrifice in particular are rare between the New Testament and Origen, the belief that his blood brought about purification is to be found repeatedly.[1] Whether this came

---

[1]In the NT, the idea of redemption through the blood of Christ is found particularly in the works of Paul, in *Hebrews*, and in the Johannine literature. Examples are too numerous to list. In the Apostolic Fathers, see 1 *Clem*. VII.4, where he refers to the precious blood of Christ poured out for our salvation, and XXI.6, where he says that Christ's blood was given for us; also XLIX.6. Ignatius makes startling use of the idea, e.g., equating the blood of Christ with ἀγάπη (*Tral*. VIII.1 and *Smyrn*. I.i). He speaks of being warmed in the blood of God (*Eph*. I.1) and of belief in the blood of Christ (*Smyrn*. VI.1). He greets the Philadelphians "in the blood of Christ," and makes several references to the blood of Christ which are apparently Eucharistic: drinking the blood of Christ (*Rom*. VII.3), the cup of his blood (*Philad*. IV). Among the Apologists, Justin (*Dial*. 13) alludes to *Heb*. to support his argument that water cannot wash away sin--nor are men made pure by the blood of bulls and goats, but by faith in the blood of Jesus Christ who suffered death for this purpose. In exegesis of *Gen*. 49.10, he refers the expression "washing his robe in the blood of the grape" to the passion of Christ which cleansed those who believe in him by means of blood (1 *Apol*. 32). Clem. Alex. uses the idea that blood is redeeming and lifegiving without further enquiry (*Paed*. II.42, 49,

from viewing his death as the expiatory death of the martyr, or through the application of the Day of Atonement blood rituals, or from full acceptance of a doctrine that his death replaced the sin-offerings of the Old Covenant, it was generally accepted that he died to save from sin, and that his blood was the purifying agent which dealt with man's sin. The power of his atoning blood shed for mankind was proclaimed throughout Christian literature; frequently it seems that scriptural language and the language of confession of faith is reproduced without any attempt to find a rationale. Behind it, however, lay the clear assumption that his death was a sacrifice for sin.

In Chapter III, three types of sin-offerings were distinguished. In Greek religion we found that holocausts were offered to the underworld powers to avert evils, such as plagues and other natural disasters. Offerings were also made to the Ouranian gods to placate their anger and divert the consequent punishment. In Hebrew religion, primitive propitiatory ideas gave way to expiatory sacrifices, a semi-mechanical means provided by God to cope with the problem of sin and ritual impurity.

In which of these ways did the Christians think that the sacrifice of Christ was effective? That it dealt with sin and brought about reconciliation with God was assumed, but how? Was it, for example, by buying off his anger? Clearly these questions raise the problem of the concept of God's nature held by those who claimed that Christ's death was a sacrifice offered for sin. Different answers to our questions are implied in the words of different writers, and some of these will be unravelled in the following discussions, in which we must constantly keep in view both the concept of God and the idea of Atonement involved.

---

etc.), though these appear to be allusions to the Eucharist. The above is far from an exhaustive documentation of the general assumption that blood purifies.

A. The Death of Christ as an Expiatory Sacrifice

The idea that Christ's death was a sacrifice first appears in the New Testament, and here it seems to have been understood as an expiatory sacrifice. This is not, however, generally agreed among New Testament scholars. Discussion of the texts has usually centered round the interpretation of the Old Testament background since consideration of Christ's sacrificial death in the New Testament seems to have been entirely in terms of Old Testament ideas. Following this line of approach, our argument in Chapter II concerning the nature of the Old Testament sin-offerings clearly implies that the New Testament sacrificial language should be interpreted in terms of expiation not propitiation.

Further examination is necessary, however, since the LXX version of the Jewish scriptures is generally more important than the Hebrew for understanding the New Testament; this means that the implications of the translation ἱλάσκεσθαι for l^e^kapper must be ascertained. That this was the Greek word for propitiation is undeniable, but at the same time its use is in line with Hebrew rather than normal Greek usage. It is never construed with God as the object, but does take sin or iniquity as its object.[2] The peculiarities

---

[2]See Gray, Sacrifice in the OT, p. 74; Yerkes, Sacrifice in Greek and Roman Religion, Ch. 9.3; Taylor, Jesus and His Sacrifice, p. 53; and particularly C. H. Dodd, The Bible and the Greeks (Ch. 5) where he argues first that the various other words used to translate l^e^kapper in the LXX give the meaning "to sanctify," "purify" persons or objects, or "to cancel," "purge away," "forgive" sins. Therefore, the meaning of ἱλάσκεσθαι should be similar. Secondly, he sums up the Hebrew words translated by ἱλάσκεσθαι , other than l^e^ kapper; he finds two classes: (i) with a human subject, meaning "to cleanse from sin or defilement," "to expiate"; (ii) with divine subject, meaning "to be gracious," "to have mercy," "to forgive." Dodd concludes that these considerations, plus the use of ἱλασκεσθαι itself, suggest that the LXX translators did not regard

of this use should have been apparent to a Greek reader, the idea of propitiating sin being obviously completely unnatural.

When the passages containing words of this root in the New Testament are examined, it is found that they are most naturally taken to have an expiatory sense rather than a propitiatory. In the *First Epistle of John*,[3] it is explained that love is revealed by the fact that God sent his Son as an ἱλασμὸς περὶ τῶν ἁμαρτιῶν ἡμῶν, and Paul in *Romans*[4] says that God put forth Christ Jesus as an ἱλαστήριον. In both these cases the context shows that here is the idea found in the Old Testament that God provides the means of expiation. Unless these writers thought that God propitiated himself, they must have meant expiation.

These passages taken with the LXX usage, make it all the more likely that the phrase εἰς τὸ ἱλάσκεσθαι τὰς ἁμαρτίας . . . in *Hebrews*[5] should be construed with τὰς αμαρτίας as the direct object of ἱλάσκεσθαι, not as an accusative of respect.[6] The High-Priest, Jesus

---

l^{e}kapper as conveying the sense of propitiating the deity, but the sense of performing an act whereby guilt and sin were removed, and accordingly rendered it ιλασκεσθαι in this sense. In opposition to this, Leon Morris, in *The Apostolic Preaching of the Cross* (London, 1955), challenges Dodd's method, but unconvincingly. He draws attention to the danger of arguing from the range of meaning found for a word by instancing the example of κόσμος which can mean anything from "world" to "ornament." The reason for the choice of a different word may be that, in another context, its meaning is that much different. His main case, however, depends not on linguistics, but on the context; that is, the relation of the word to the idea of the wrath of God (for which, see *infra*).

[3]1 *Jn*. 4.9-10. [4]*Rom*. 3.25. [5]*Heb*. 2.17.

[6]Morris (op. cit.) argues that it was an accusative of respect, not a direct object. He draws attention to the number of times in the NT that the accusative replaces a prepositional construction with little or no change in meaning. To quote two of his examples:

Christ, does not propitiate God, but expiates sin.

This problem cannot, however, be considered in isolation. The New Testament does speak of the wrath of God. Is there then some sense in which God is propitiated?

It has been strongly argued that ὀργή in the writings of St. Paul does not mean the anger of God, at least not in a crude, anthropomorphic sense.[7] In favour of this, it is pointed out that Paul never uses the verb "to be angry" with God as subject, and he only refers to the "wrath" as the "wrath of God" three times. The wrath, it is claimed, is used in an impersonal way, and what Paul means is a process of cause and effect in a morally ordered universe; sin is the cause, wrath the inevitable effect. "Wrath is not an affection of God, but a condition of unregenerate man," as one advocate puts it.[8]

On the other hand, it is argued that the wrath of God is real and serious in the Old and New Testaments not as capricious anger but as a stern reaction of a morally consistent Deity against evil and sin;[9] in this sense it caused the exile, according to the teaching of the prophets, for punishment as well as

---

ἀπορεῖν is followed by περί in _Lk_. 24.4 and _Jn_.13.22--"to be perplexed about"--but in _Acts_ 25.20, it is followed by a simple accusative where the meaning is the same. In one sentence in 2 _Tim_. 4.1, διαμαρτύρεσθαι is followed by both ἐνώπιον plus the genitive and the simple accusative. He admits that there is no exact parallel with ἱλάσκεσθαι , but suggests that, as with the examples given, ἱλάσκεσθαι περί could have become ἱλάσκεσθαι plus the simple accusative. His examples, however, are cases where the verb is intransitive and would not therefore naturally take a simple accusative. In the case of ἱλάσκεσθαι, an accusative was natural, and although the object is a surprising one, it is better to take it as the object than to try to understand it as an accusative of respect.

[7]See in particular C. H. Dodd, _Commentary on Romans_ (London, 1932) and A. T. Hanson, _The Wrath of the Lamb_ (London, 1957).

[8]Hanson, op. cit. [9]Morris, op. cit.

forgiveness comes from God. The prophets had done so well the work of warning against coming judgement that there was no need to specify that it was God's wrath; in any case, five times in the New Testament it is so specified. Judgement is a frequent theme in the Gospels, as it was in the prophets. Therefore, it is argued, the Old Testament rites were in a sense propitiatory, since they dealt with the problem of averting the wrath or judgement of God against sin, and the very fact that the LXX translators and the New Testament writers used the word ἱλάσκεσθαι shows that it was understood that the rites, and the death of Christ, were propitiatory in the sense of turning aside God's wrath.

This side also admits, however, that God himself removes his wrath, and that the rites were ordained by God for the purpose of effecting this. Since it is agreed that sin is the problem, and God is active in dealing with it, we certainly do not have here a crude picture of an angry and capricious deity being bribed to stop an arbitrary punishment by the offering of a sacrifice. Whether we speak of God propitiating himself or of God dealing with the sin that requires his judgement, we are clearly confronted with a totally different conception from placation. The linguistic arguments for interpreting ἱλάσκεσθαι as expiation seem convincing, but the insistence on the reality of God's judgement against sin seems more consistent with both the Old and New Testaments than the view that the wrath was merely a matter of cause and effect. The New Testament in fact, is in the same thought-world as the more advanced position expressed in the Old Testament. God takes sin very seriously, and God judges men for their sin, and will punish them even to the extent of the exile. But God is normally merciful, and "slow to anger"; so he wills to deal with the problem of sin. In fact, he alone can do so. It is God who instituted the expiatory rites of the Old Testament, and it is God who set forth his own Son as an expiation of greater effect. No further rationale was sought, since it was accepted that this was God's ordained means of dealing with the sin of men.

The *Epistle to the Hebrews* illustrates this position very well. The Epistle is a warning to those who were tempted to apostatise; it emphasises the judgement sent by God upon those who rebelled under the Old Covenant and suggests that what Christians have received is so much better that they should expect an even worse punishment for going astray.[10] Our God is a consuming fire,[11] and it is a fearful thing to fall into the hands of the living God.[12] But the Epistle never says that Christ's sacrifice was a means of propitiating the wrath of God. The Old Testament sacrifices and the death of Christ which fulfilled them were a means of dealing with sin, a means of purification, of sanctification.[13] The Epistle accepts without question that the blood was the means and the only means (according to the thought of the Epistle) of obtaining remission and sanctification;[14] no rationale is sought, for this is a presupposition of Jewish sacrificial thought.[15] There is no difference in principle between Old and New Covenants. The difference is in degree: firstly that the blood of bulls and goats could only purify pollution of the flesh, whereas Christ's sacrifice could deal with the conscience of the worshipper, because in it was poured out the more potent blood of one consciously choosing to do God's will;[16] and secondly that, whereas repeated sacrifices were necessary under the Old Covenant, to have one's conscience purified by the blood of Christ's self-offering means that no further

---

[10]See *Heb*. 3.7-4.13; 6.4-12; 10.26-36.

[11]*Ibid*., 12.29. [12]Ibid., 10.31.

[13]Ibid., 1.3; 2/17; 9.9, 13-4, 22, 26; 10.10, 14; 13.11.

[14]Ibid., 9.7, 12-4, 22; 10.4; 13.11.

[15]See E. O. James, *Sacrifice and Sacrament* (London, 1962), p. 73: "The atoning efficacy of blood was axiomatic for the *Epistle to the Hebrews*."

[16]*Heb*. 9.9, 13-4; 10.5-7. That the sacrificial system was only a reminder of sin rather than a freeing from it is found in *Heb*. 10.3 and Philo, *De vita Moysis* III.10.

sacrifice is needed, since he has put away sin by the sacrifice of himself, so perfecting for all time those who have been sanctified.[17] Repeatedly, the work of Christ is described as putting away sin, as cleansing consciences; never is it said that he propitiated God.

The New Testament, then, presents us with the view that the sacrifice of Christ was expiatory and strictly analogous to the sacrifices of the Old Testament. What about the later theologians with which this study is primarily concerned? That the sacrifice of Christ was simply purificatory is found throughout Greek literature on the subject. The blood of Christ is often assumed to purify the heart of the sinner without further explanation, especially in the context of comment on the *Epistle to the Hebrews*. For example, Chrysostom in most of his *Homilies on Hebrews*,[18] follows the Epistle very closely and, except for a few occasions, raises no questions, simply adopting the sacrificial and expiatory language of the author. In fact, the power of the blood of Christ to cleanse from sin is so much assumed in the literature of the Church that its documentation would be tedious.

However, when explanation of this language was sought, the later Greek writers were not satisfied with the simple expiatory view. They tried to account for the fact that sacrifice was the means of dealing with sin, rather than just accepting it as a means given by God and simply to be obeyed, as the Jews and New Testament writers did. So, Origen, as we shall see, explains expiation in terms of the removal

---

[17]*Heb.* 10.2-4; 10.14.

[18]Throughout the Homilies, as in the Epistle, the principle that blood cleanses sin is assumed; the difference between the sacrifice of Christ and the OT sacrifices is seen in terms of purification of the conscience and mind, in contrast to purification of the flesh. Sanctification, purging, purification are the results of Christ's sacrifice for sin. See esp. *Hom.* XV, XVI, XVIII.

of evil powers by means of an aversion sacrifice, and Chrysostom, at times, feels the need to expound the expiatory language of the Epistle to the Hebrews in terms of propitiating the Father so as to obtain forgiveness.[19] In other words, the later Greek Fathers drew on the types of sin-offering found in their Greek background to explain the sacrifices they had inherited from Judaism. For this reason, discussion of the expiatory interpretation of Christ's sacrifice has necessarily been confined to the New Testament, because, as an explanation of Christ's sacrifice, it ceased to be important at a later stage.

B. The Death of Christ as a Sacrifice of Aversion

I do not think that this interpretation of the sacrifice for sin made by Christ on the Cross has ever received investigation. I wish to argue that this was Origen's view, and that it was consistent with his whole soteriological position. To show this, I propose (a) to consider the sense in which Origen uses the idea of propitiation, in order to show that this is not a satisfactory explanation of his rationale of Christ's sacrifice; (b) to examine the context of his treatment of the atoning sacrifice, that is, his general soteriological position; and (c) to discuss his treatment of Christ's sacrifice, in the light of the conclusions reached.

(a) The Wrath of God and Propitiation

Origen is in the same philosophical tradition as Philo, Clement and the Neoplatonists, and therefore, in the light of what has been said already, it is not surprising that he accepts the view that the Supreme Being is not subject to passion, and cannot change. Such anthropomorphisms in the scriptures have to be

---

19 Origen and Chrysostom are discussed later in this chapter.

rationalised. So, confronted by Celsus' criticisms of the concept of God in the Old Testament,[20] he replies that "when we speak of God's wrath, we do not hold that it is an emotional reaction on his part, but something which he uses in order to correct by stern methods those who have committed many terrible sins."[21] He even believes that God created some physical and external evils to purify and educate those who are unwilling to be educated by sound teaching. Origen uses the analogy of the doctor inflicting pain in order to heal and the schoolmaster chastising in order to improve.[22]

Elsewhere he faces the problem of God's repentance in the Old Testament.[23] Origen understands repentance to mean "change one's mind," and he argues that since a supposedly wise man inevitably loses face by "repenting," God can hardly "repent" of a plan he has made, especially as he has foreknowledge of the future. He goes on to explain that while God is not like man, he chooses to appear like man in order to educate his children. Just as we talk baby-language to babies - for a baby cannot be expected to understand adult conversation - so we must think God acts with regard to the human race. When you hear of the anger and wrath of God, you must not think that God suffers the emotions of wrath and anger. "It is a matter of verbal usage for the sake of a child. We put on threatening looks, not because we are angry but for the child's good; if we always show our love and never correct the child, it is the worse for him. It is in this way that God is said to be angry, so as to change and better us."

If God's anger is a means of discipline, reformative rather than retributive, then the concept of propitiation is ridiculous. There is no mercy in

---

[20]Origen, C. Cels. IV.13.71. Celsus complains that God is often said to change, to be angry, or to tell lies.

[21]C. Cels. IV.72 (trans., Chadwick).

[22]Ibid., IV.56.

[23]Homilies on Jeremiah XVIII.6.

letting off a sinner unless punishment has had its effect. A loving father disciplining his children will cease as soon as the child repents and reforms. Elsewhere the same position is reached by a different line of argument.[24] Origen states that God alone is able to be truly just, since he can see the secrets of a man's heart; then he goes on to ask: If God is just, how is this consistent with the remission of sins obtained in Baptism, through penitence or through martyrdom? Is this remission in accordance with true justice, which demands that the evil man receive evil and the good man good? God's justice should demand that he punish evil. At first sight, this appears to open the way for the concept of propitiation, the idea that somehow God's justice is bought off by Baptism, martyrdom etc. But this is not Origen's solution; he gets out of the "impasse" by suggesting that when a man truly repents, he is no longer evil; he is turning to good and is good and deserves good. God deals justice according to his present insight into a man's character, and does not deal retribution for past evil once reform has begun.

So God's justice as well as his wrath is interpreted as bringing salvation through reformative punishment, and in this context, there can be no real sense in which mercy may be bought or wrath propitiated. That Origen certainly did not believe that the sacrifice of Christ changed God from anger to love must be deduced from this, and even more from another passage where the work of chastisement is ascribed to Christ:[25] Christ is judge and administers discipline; the lamb of God takes away sins "by afflictions and evil spirits and dangerous diseases and grievous sicknesses," and through these spiritual

---

[24]Comm. Rom. II.1; II.1. The Latin text suggests that God is obliged to be angry at injustice, but the Greek text (ed. Schérer) does not mention obligation, merely stating that there *is* wrath against injustice. The image of a father disciplining his children is also used in this commentary; see VII.18.

[25]Comm. Jn. I.40-1; VI.37.

healing aids, makes every one ready at the end to receive the goodness of God. In other words, Christ changes man, not the attitude of God.

This theological context of Origen's sacrificial ideas means that his rationale cannot be found in terms of propitiation, but before asserting this with confidence, we must investigate whether Origen uses propitiation language at all, and if so in what sense.

Unfortunately many of the relevant works of Origen survive only in Latin translation, which means that detailed linguistic studies cannot be absolutely relied upon. However as far as one can tell from the Latin version, it does seem, contrary to what might now be expected, that Origen did use words meaning propitiate; but the way in which he uses them suggests that he did not give them their normal sense. For example, Origen describes Christ as "iste qui accedit ad altare ut repropitiet me peccatorem"; the object of the verb is the sinner, not God.[26] Again, Origen asks what it means to "repropitiasse delictum," where sin is the object;[27] and his reply is an indication of how his mind worked on this subject: "If you accept the sinner and by warning, exhortation, teaching, instruction, lead him to repentance, correct his error, amend his vices, and make him such a man that he is converted, God become 'propitius pro delicto' and you are said 'repropitiasse.'" in other words, to propitiate is to change the sinner, to produce a situation in which God can accept him back and forgive him.

Elsewhere Origen speaks of propitiating men to God,[28] and in another text he asks how Christ could have been the Paraclete and the Atonement and the Propitiation, if the power of God, which makes an end to our weaknesses, did not flow over the soul of believers, and was not administered by Jesus, who indeed

---

[26]<u>Hom. Lev</u>. VII.2.

[27]<u>Ibid.</u>, V.4. Compare "ad reproprìtianda peccata," X.2.

[28]<u>Comm. Rom</u>. III.8; the Greek and Latin texts agree.

is prior to it and himself the power of God.[29] In other words, it is through Christ's power to help humanity improve that his work of propitiation is done; it is making men worthy of the Father's forgiveness rather than winning round an angry deity.

When Origen uses the adjective "propitius" or ἵλεως of God, he means "favourably disposed," and he most frequently uses it of the response of God to Christian offerings of virtue. When the Christian is doing God's will, he knows that God is on his side; when he is not, God may discipline him. The adjective does not mean that God's anger with a man has been changed by the placatory offering of an act of charity, for example. When Celsus argues that Christians ought to propitiate the powers of heaven and the powers on earth, Origen replies[30] that they ought to propitiate the one Supreme God and to pray that he may be gracious, propitiating him by piety and every virtue. This is close to the pagan usage, but has the meaning given in this paragraph, rather than reflecting the idea of keeping the gods happy by means of bribes. The demands of the Supreme God are moral and spiritual qualities, and when a man obeys his will, he keeps him on his side.

One context in which propitiation language is used frequently by Origen, is with reference to Christ's High-Priesthood, his mediation with the Father on our behalf.[31] The Son prays to the Father on behalf of his people, but the "repropitiatio" which he offers is in fact the Christians' own gifts of pity, justice, piety, peace;[32] he does not plead the merits of his own sacrifice, but offers the lives of transformed men. He has broken down the middle wall of partition and removed the hostility between God

---

[29]*Comm. Jn.* I.38.

[30]*C. Cels.* VIII.64. Origen seems merely to be taking up Celsus' word, and it probably means no more than "worship" or "pay homage to."

[31]*Hom. Lev.* IX.5-7; *C. Cels.* VIII.13; *Comm. Rom.* III.8.

[32]*Hom. Lev.* IX.6.

and man,[33] but he did this by perfecting man, not by changing God.[34]

In fact, so far from changing God, it was God himself who sent him, because of his love to men, because he loved those who were "alieni et inimici." He was sent so that sinners everywhere would forsake their sin and turn to God.[35] Origen never uses propitiation language in the same context as he speaks of the wrath of God, and certainly never speaks of propitiating his wrath. The nearest he comes to this is in the Commentary on Romans, where he says that because God was just he could not justify the unjust; but because he recognised that man's sin was not entirely his fault, being committed under the tyranny of the devil, he himself sent a mediator who was able to deal with sin and its cause, convert mankind, and so make the just God "propitius" to men in a way that he could not be to sinners.[36] That this work of reconciliation, which Origen is able to describe in rather qualified propitiation language, was accomplished through the blood of Christ,[37] Origen accepts, but how the sacrifice and the blood effected this will be discussed later. For the present, we conclude that propitiation is not used by Origen in the most natural sense, since it is concerned not with changing the attitude of God towards man, but with the conversion of the sinner so that he is made acceptable to a just but loving Father. Christ is God's instrument of discipline and conversion, his way of bringing men back to him. Only in this sense is he a mediator, an advocate, and the "propitiation" for the sins of the whole world.

(b) Origen's soteriology

Origen's ideas on salvation are expressed in a vast range of imagery, for he was untiring as an

---

[33]Comm. Rom. IV.8. [34]Ibid., VIII.4.

[35]Ibid., II.2; IV.10.

[36]Ibid., II.1, 8.

[37]Ibid., IV.8, 12; VIII.4; X.9; etc. Hom. Lev. IX.10.

exegete and as a collector of scriptural passages which applied to any given problem. So with a proof-text for each, Origen collects together in one place[38] all the titles he can find in scripture which express the nature and work of Christ: Light of the World, Resurrection, the Way, the Truth, the Life, the Door and the Shepherd, Christ and King, Teacher and Master, Son, True Vine and Bread, First and Last, Living and Dead, Sword, Servant, Lamb of God, Paraclete, Propitiation, Power, Wisdom, Sanctification, Redemption, Righteousness, Demiurge, Agent of the good God, High-Priest, Rod, Flower, Stone, Logos. These ideas he draws on at random as he discusses Christ's saving work, in Homilies and Commentaries which wander unsystematically from point to point. The only work which is at all systematic is the *De Principiis*; even the *Contra Celsum* takes the form of a commentary on Celsus' anti-Christian arguments, and shows little logical sequence of thought. Yet it seems to the present writer that under this confusing array of ideas, there is a basic pattern to Origen's soteriology, a pattern of conflict between good and evil in which Christ achieves the victory. So this part of our discussion is concerned to argue that Origen *basically* thought of the Atonement in terms of the dualist outlook of the Classic theory described in the Introduction, and that his use of this theory was not an occasional descent to the level of the "simpliciores," an element foreign to his philosophical outlook, as some scholars have thought, but that it is absolutely central to his understanding of salvation.

Most expositors of Origen's thought have regarded his idea of Christ as revealer, educator and enlightenment, that is, as the Logos of God, as his characteristic view of Christ's saving function. That this should be Origen's main account of Christ's work in the *De Principiis* is not surprising,[39] since this was a work dominated by philosophical issues and ideas.

---

[38]*Comm. Jn.* I.22ff.

[39]*De princ.* I.2, 6-8; III.5.8.

It is also prominent in the Commentary on John.[40] As the brightness of God's glory, Christ enlightens the whole creation, and, as the Word, he interprets and presents to the rational creation the secrets of wisdom and the mysteries of knowledge. The Only-Begotten is the Truth, because he embraces in himself, according to the Father's will, the whole reason of all things, which he communicates to each creature in proportion to its worthiness.

This idea is scattered throughout Origen's work, and needs no more detailed exemplification here. As far as our argument is concerned, the interesting thing is that this description of Christ's work fits into the dualist pattern, which we believe lies behind all of Origen's expositions of salvation. Not only is it expressed in the simple opposition of light and darkness, knowledge and ignorance, but it is seen in the context of the war between good and evil, between God and the devil, which is Origen's basic picture of the situation which called for salvation. So Origen can maintain that Christ as Word conquers the opposing powers by reason, "by making war on his enemies by reason and righteousness, so that what is irrational and wicked is destroyed."[41] Right doctrine is a means of conquering sin.[42] The light shines not only on the darkness of men's souls, but has penetrated to where the rulers of this darkness carry on their struggle with the race of men; and shining in darkness the light is pursued by darkness, but not overtaken.[43]

Connected with the idea of Christ as educator, is another important theme of Origen's soteriology, the description of him as the example of obedience which Christians should follow, as the Way. This theme finds expression particularly in the call to martyrdom, which is the culmination of observance of "the entire pattern of living set out in the Gospel."[44] This is

---

[40]E.g., Comm. Jn. I.23-4, 27, 42.

[41]Ibid., II.4.

[42]Comm. Rom. VI.3.

[43]Comm. Jn. II.21.

[44]Exhortation 12. See also Comm. Rom. IV.10; VII.3, 13; C. Cels. VII.17; VIII.44.

closely linked with the idea of illumination which we have already considered, since by following Christ to heaven, especially through martyrdom, men will understand as never before, will learn all secrets and understand all mysteries, and will discover the nature of intelligibles and the beauty of Truth.[45] But again this description of Christ's saving work is part of the picture of the struggle against the devil and his angels, for, above all, "martyrs in Christ despoil with him the principalities and powers and triumph with him, by partaking in his sufferings and the great deeds accomplished in his sufferings - among which is his triumphing over principalities and powers which you will soon see conquered and overcome with shame."[46] Obedience, self-denial and humiliation, death to sin, the spiritualised martyrdom,[47] is likewise an imitation of Christ, part of the educative work of the Saviour, and an incident in the drama of conquering evil and leading to virtue and participation in the divine nature. It was essentially Christ's work to restore what had been corrupted, and deal with the enemy that had caused the corruption.[48]

In the same way, a third predominant theme is part of this whole pattern: Christ brings healing to the morally sick,[49] and resurrection and life to the morally dead.[50] He came into our deadness to deliver mankind from the bondage of corruption.[51] This, too, is part of Christ's conquest of the tyranny of death, sin and the devil, for the devil has the power of death and is the enemy of him who is the life.[52]

So all these various ways of expressing Christ's work have led to the Classic theory of Atonement. The

---

[45]Exhortation 13. [46]Ibid., 42.

[47]Comm. Rom. IX.39; V.8-9; also C. Cels. II.69; De princ. IV.4.4.

[48]De princ. III.5.6.

[49]Comm. Matt. XI.18; C. Cels. VIII.72, III.60.

[50]Comm. Rom. V.1-9.

[51]Comm. Jn. I.25, 28, 35; II.6; X.4.

[52]See Comm. Rom. V.1-9; Comm. Matt. XIII.9; Hom. Jos. VIII.6.

context of soteriological thought is dualistic, and the work of salvation is, first the conquest of the powers of corruption, and then the exaltation of man by a process of healing and education. The conquest of the devil is in fact the most prominent theme of Origen's soteriology. The *De Principiis* spends a chapter on "How the devil and the opposing powers are, according to the scriptures, at war with the human race."[53] The activity of the daemons plays a large role in Origen's arguments with Celsus.[54] The *Homilies on Joshua* are full of warfare against the devil, for Joshua's wars are allegorised as the wars of Christ and his followers against the devil and his angels.[55] In the *Commentary on Romans*,[56] Origen explains the Incarnation and Work of Christ by means of a parable which expresses this soteriological position: there was a just and noble king, who was waging a war against an unjust tyrant, but trying to avoid a violent and bloody conflict, because some of his own men were fighting on the tyrant's side, and he wanted to free them, not destroy them. He adopted the uniform of the tyrant's men, until he managed to persuade them to desert and return to their proper kingdom, and succeeded in binding the "strong man" in fetters, destroying his principalities and powers and carrying off those he held captive. This idea of soteriology appears throughout Origen's work, and cannot be treated "as belonging to a lower theological level," or as "a mere appendage to the philosophically inclined system in which we find the real Origen."[57] It is basic to his whole understand-

---

[53]*De princ.* III.2; also I.5.1; III.3.6; III.5.6.

[54]*C. Cels.* VIII.55-7, etc.; also I.31; VI.43; VII.17; VIII.44, 54.

[55]*Hom. Jos.* XII.1; VII.3-6, 7; IX.4, 5.

[56]*Comm. Rom.* V.10; also V.1, 3, 6, 7, 10; IV.8.

[57]See Aulén, op. cit., p. 54: "Attempts have been made with regard to Origen, as, for instance, by de Faye in his important work on Origen to minimise the importance of this side of his teaching, and to treat it as belonging to a lower theological level, as if

ing of salvation, and is the theory to which he turns to explain all soteriological problems.

The work of Atonement in Origen's thought is, first the worsting of the evil powers, the death and sin which tyrannise over human nature, and then the reconciliation of human nature with God. This scheme underlies all the various images used to describe Christ's saving activity, and also the meaning of propitiation outlined in (a). Before reconciliation is possible, the evil and sin which alienated men from God must be dealt with; then men are acceptable to God.

This description of Christ's work appears as Origen's allegorisation of the Day of Atonement ritual,[58] and with this we may bring together parts (a) and (b). The desert to which the scapegoat was sent, was a place empty of virtues, empty of God, empty of justice, empty of Christ, empty of every

---

it were a mere appendage to the philosophically inclined system in which we find the real Origen. . . In the case of Origen . . . the fact . . . remains that when he speaks directly of the meaning of Christ's work, he adopts the same Classic idea of the Atonement which is common to the Greek Fathers. The fact that even philosophical influence was not able, either in his case or in others, to modify the Classic idea of the Atonement shows how deeply rooted it was in the teaching of the Greek Fathers." It should be apparent by now that I would go even further in repudiation of de Faye, and see the Classic theory as absolutely basic to all of Origen's attempts to express what salvation is. Even Aulén has not realised how central it was to Origen's thought, or he would not have regarded it as something which philosophy might have removed. In any case, Porphyry is at the same level as Origen in thinking that the daemons were fed by animal sacrifices. This may seem crude now, but why should we expect Origen to be more sophisticated than the more sophisticated of contemporary pagan philosophers?

[58]<u>Hom. Lev.</u> IX.4-5.

good thing. The man who led off the scapegoat had to be pure, and he must be understood to represent the Lord himself, our Saviour. Origen draws the parallel between their actions, first pointing out that as the man washed his garments in the evening, so Christ purified the tunic of our flesh and blood, the human nature he had assumed on our behalf. He then interprets his leading away the scapegoat in terms of Colossians 2.15: "he nailed to his Cross the principalities and hostile powers and triumphed over them." This means Origen asserts, that "he fulfilled the lot of the 'apopompaeus' (the LXX word for Azazel) in them, and as the man in readiness led them into the wilderness; thus he led away the spiritual hosts of wickedness and the rulers of the darkness of this world, triumphing over them within himself (in semetipso)." He alone had the power to lead them off to the desert, the empty places of hell. He then returned with his work accomplished, and ascended to heaven, where he was purified more completely at the heavenly altar, that he might present the pledge of our flesh which he took with him in perpetual purity. This then is the "dies propitiationis," when God is propitious to men. When sin has been removed, when the hostile powers have been led out of the way and human nature purified, then reconciliation with God is possible.

This picture of the Atonement seems to have had a fascination for Origen, for he alludes to it in both the De Principiis[59] and the Contra Celsum;[60] the "apopompaeus" is the devil, who is sent off into the desert and averted.[61] So evil was removed by the work

---

[59]De princ. III.2.1.

[60]C. Cels. VI.43.

[61]Chadwick translates: "Further the averter in Leviticus, which the Hebrew text called Azazel, is none other than he. The person upon whom the lot fell had to send him forth in the desert so that he should be a sacrifice to avert evil." This seems to be a misinterpretation of the passage. The lot fell on the goat, not on the person who sent it away, and

of Christ, whose triumphant death accomplished the dismissal of the devil and of human sin. Then human nature was once more acceptable to God, since it had been purified and sanctified in Christ.

(c) Origen's rationale of Christ's sacrifice for sin

Origen has a tendency to argue in a circle: on the one hand the Old Testament laws have their "raison d'être" in the sacrifice of Christ,[62] while on the other, it is in terms of the Old Testament laws that the sacrifice of Christ is to be interpreted.[63] But the reason for this interdependence is that both come from God; it was according to the divine laws that "propitiation" comes through blood.[64] Ultimately Origen recognises that the rationale of both Jewish sacrifice and the sacrifice of Christ is a mystery.[65]

Because of the interdependence of sacrificial interpretations of Christ's death and ways of understanding Old Testament sacrifices, Origen frequently uses Old Testament sacrificial language to describe the death of Christ without attempting to explain further how the sacrifice for sin worked. Consequently in many passages, his view appears to be the expiatory idea found in the Old and New Testaments. Under the Old Covenant, they tried to remove sins by the blood of bullocks and goats, but they could not do it. It

---

Origen knew this perfectly well. The accusative τὸν κλῆρον ἔχοντα should be construed with the ὅν, which refers to the ἀποπομπαῖος, which in this passage is identified with the goat. The devil is dismissed into the desert and averted; as Origen's treatment elsewhere shows, the devil is dispatched with the sins of the people on his head. Origen also recognises that the scapegoat was not sacrificed, so to use the word "sacrifice" in translation is misleading.

62E.g., Hom. Lev. II.5; III.5, 8; IV.8; V.3; X.2; etc. Hom. Jos. II.1; XVII.1; etc. Comm. Jn. I.38; VI. 32; X.11-3; etc.

63Comm. Rom. IV.8, 12; VIII.4; X.9.

64Ibid., III.8.

65Hom. Lev. III.1.

was because they were so ineffectual that the Son of God came in the likeness of sinful flesh and for sin; he condemned sin in the flesh, because he was made a sacrificial victim for sin and was offered for the purging of sin. The whole scripture testifies to this, he claims;[66] he does not question the principle. As we have already seen, the removal of sin was Origen's idea of the means of propitiation; so, as in the New Testament, vocabulary of propitiation is used with an expiatory sense.

Occasionally Origen tries to explain how Christ's sacrifice could remove sin. According to Leviticus, the priests eat the sin-offering: so, says Origen, Christ, who is priest as well as victim, eats the sins of the people. God is a consuming fire. The God of fire consumes human sins; he assumes them, devours them and purges them. Christ thus took upon himself our sins, and like a fire, he ate and assumed them himself.[67] This explanation is pictorial, but not too helpful in providing a rationale of sacrifice. A second explanation depends closely on Old Testament ideas. Christ was a sacrificial offering without blemish; this purity is in a way contagious, so that anyone who touches the flesh of this sacrifice is sanctified.[68] Both these attempts to explain are based on an acceptance of scriptural language and ideas; they emphasise the fact that the sacrifice dealt with sin by removing it, but do not satisfactorily explain how.

Whenever Origen really requires an explanation, he passes over to the Classic theory which we have already found underlying his whole soteriology. For example, "This slain lamb has been made, according to certain hidden reasons, a purification for the whole world; for which, according to the Father's love to man, he submitted to death purchasing us back by his own blood from him who had got us in his power, sold under sin."[69] The sacrifice of the lamb of God is first

---

[66] Comm. Rom. IV.12.
[67] Hom. Lev. V.3.
[68] Ibid., IV.7-8.
[69] Comm. Jn. VI.35.

said, without explanation, to purify; but then his death is interpreted in terms of a ransom given to the devil. In this Commentary (the Commentary on John), Origen frequently confesses himself baffled; but then produces an explanation drawn from the idea of dealing with sin by making an offering to the devil. In one passage, he recognises the difficulties raised by any view that suggests that God demands sacrifices, specifically in relation to the death of the martyrs. "The story (of Jephthah's sacrifice of his daughter) suggests that the Being must be a very cruel one to whom such a sacrifice is offered for the salvation of men; and we require some breadth of mind and some ability to solve the difficulties raised against Providence, to be able to account for such things and to see that they are mysteries and exceed our human nature."[70] Origen is unhappy about the idea that such a sacrifice should be offered to God so as to bring about salvation, and he goes on to solve his puzzle by suggesting that God allows the martyrs to suffer for their faith in order to overthrow the evil powers, instancing as a comparable case, the Gentiles who were said to have offered themselves as victims for the public good. That is, he interprets the martyr's death not as a means of propitiating God, but as God's means of dealing with evil. In other words, the martyr's sacrifice is brought within the dualist scheme of the Classic theory.

If the sacrifice of Christ and of the martyr is reinterpreted as a ransom to the devil, is it still a sacrifice? Aulén maintained that sacrifice was offered to God. But our study has shown that there was a type of sin-offering which if Christianised would exactly fit the situation: the primitive Greek aversion-sacrifice in a Christian context would be a sacrifice offered to the devil to remove the influence of the powers of darkness. Is there any evidence that Origen actually thought of the sacrifice for sin in these terms? I believe there is: namely, his frequent use of pagan stories about men dying for their country to

[70]Ibid., VI.36.

avert plagues and other evils, as an analogy to the death of Christ and of the martyrs. We have already noted one occasion on which he uses this analogy. Elsewhere we find it expressed in greater detail. "He who was crucified quite recently accepted his death willingly for the human race, like those (ἀνάλογον τοῖς ...) who have died for their country to check epidemics of plague, or famines or stormy seas. For it is probable that in the nature of things there are certain mysteries, causes which are hard for the multitude to understand, which are responsible for the fact that one righteous man dying voluntarily for the community may avert the activities of evil daemons by expiation, since it is they who bring about plagues or famines or stormy seas or anything similar."[71] In this passage then, Christ's death is conceived as averting the evil powers. In another passage the same analogy is used, and this time reference to sacrifice is clearer. "But now Christ died for us, and how, since he was the lamb of God, he bore the sins of the world and carried our weaknesses and suffered for us, we have often explained in other places, where we brought as examples accounts that are found in secular histories; for even in them, some persons are said to have driven away pestilences, storms and other such eventualities by throwing themselves into the grip of death, and to have freed their homeland or nation from the destruction of an impending catastrophe. How true these stories are, or what rational explanation they may have, God alone knows. Yet of those of whom these stories are told, not even in fiction is it said that anyone freed the whole world, except Jesus alone, 'who though he was in the form of God, did not think it robbery to be equal with God but emptied himself,' and took the form of a servant and offered a victim for the whole world,

---

[71]*C. Cels.* I.31. The same analogy is used of the death of the martyrs in 1 *Clem*. 55. Philo has to explain why Abraham's sacrifice of Isaac was any different from the surrender of sons by pagan leaders to avert plagues, etc. (*On Abraham* 33). Obviously the example was current in Judeo-Christian literature.

delivering his own blood to the prince of this world, according to the wisdom of God."[72]

The above two important passages have been quoted in full, since together they show that Origen's way of explaining the sacrificial death of Christ and the expiatory power of his blood, is in terms of the offering of a ransom to the devil and the analogy with human sacrifices of aversion, examples of which he found in pagan literature. He is at a loss as to how such sacrifices of aversion work, but basically he feels that the sacrificial death of Christ is only explicable in such terms, while recognising a great difference in degree, for Christ died to save the whole world. The same general position is apparent in Origen's explanation of the New Testament ransom language: Christ gave his soul (ψυχή) as a ransom for many (λύτρον ἀντὶ πολλῶν). To whom did he give it? It could not have been to God; rather it was to the wicked one who had dominion over us until the ψυχή of Jesus was given to him as a ransom for us. But he was deceived; he thought he could master it (the ψυχή) and did not realise that he could not bear the torture of holding it.[73] So the life (ψυχή) offered in sacrifice and the blood shed as an expiation become in the hands of Origen the ransom price given by God to the devil.[74] For it was the Holy Father of Jesus who "spared not

---

[72]Comm. Rom. IV.11.

[73]Comm. Matt. XVI.8.

[74]This is brought into association with Origen's view that the daemons ate the meat and drank the blood of sacrifices (Comm. Rom. IV.11): if they had known (i.e., if the daemons had realised this was the Christ), they would never have crucified the Lord of Majesty, nor would that blood which they drank have quenched not their thirst but their strength, and destroyed their kingdom. For the blood as ransom price, see also Comm. Jn. I.39; Comm. Matt. XIII,8; XII,28. That it was the sacrificial blood, or at least that Origen made no distinction, is obvious by his use of sacrificial language about Christ the victim in this context. See also Comm. Rom. II.14; III.7; IV.8, 12; X.9.

his own Son, but delivered him up for us all," as his lamb, that the lamb of God, who died for every man, might bear away the sin of the world.[75] When Origen is pushed to explain Christ's sacrifice for sin, he turns not to propitiation of God as a rationale; for God himself offered the sacrifice. The sacrifice for sin was a ransom, a sacrifice of aversion, offered to the devil to free mankind from sin for the pure worship of God who was thus reconciled, that is, made "propitius."

It seems clear then that Origen interpreted the death of Christ in terms of sacrifices of aversion, particularly human sacrifices of this kind. The fact that such sacrifices were a rather primitive part of Greek religion does not argue against this. We have already seen that the later Neoplatonists were likewise concerned with such sacrifices, and it is of particular interest that Iamblichus interpreted them as a means of escape from the world of "becoming" and achievement of union with the gods.[76] For Origen, the sacrificial death of Christ gave mankind the means of escape from the domination of the evil powers and of participation in the divine nature.[77]

This exposition of Origen's position shows that Aulén's distinction between sacrifice offered to God and ransom offered to the devil is not valid. Origen's position combines these ideas, and regards both as offered to the devil by God. Sacrifice and ransom are part of the cosmic drama of victory over the opposing evil powers accomplished by God himself on behalf of the human race.

Does this idea of aversion sacrifice appear elsewhere in Christian literature? We have already seen that the idea of Christ's death as Passover sacrifice fits into the Classic theory of Atonement in the same

---

[75] *C. Cels.* VIII.43.

[76] It is interesting that Philo (also in the Platonist tradition) gives two similar reasons for the OT sin-offerings, deliverance from evils and cure of offenses committed by the soul (*De victimis* 4).

[77] *De princ.* IV.4.4: participes divinae naturae.

sort of way. The blood of Christ averted the evil one and protected the faithful. The analogy with pagan deaths to avert plagues etc. had already been made, at least with reference to the death of Christian martyrs, as early as I <u>Clement</u>,[78] this suggests that the use of the analogy was not uncommon as an attempt to account for the problem of how God could demand sacrifice, whether of his Son or of faithful martyrs, before forgiving sins. The answer to the problem was to insist on the fact that God offered the sacrifice to redeem mankind from evil. However, the popular Christian tradition seems to have drawn not only on these ideas, but also, with less theological consistency, on ideas of propitiation, and to these we now turn.

C. <u>The Death of Christ as a Propitiatory Sacrifice</u>

It has already been noted that the normal Greek reader would naturally interpret words of the ιλάσκεσθαι group as meaning propitiate. It was to be expected that the ordinary Church members, untroubled by philosophical reflections on the nature of God, and fresh from paganism with its placatory outlook, would assume that the wrath of God against sin could be propitiated, and that the Christian virtues and rites which were described as spiritual sacrifices would have this effect. There is some evidence that this in fact occurred.

We have seen that Origen modified the meaning of words implying propitiation, and certainly did not think in terms of placating or buying off the anger of God. One of the problems he and his contemporaries faced was the challenge of Marcion's view that in Christ was revealed a God of love, while the God of the Old Testament was a God of justice and wrath, distinct from the Father of Jesus Christ. It was partly in defence

---

[78]1 <u>Clem</u>. 55.

of the Christian retention of the Old Testament and belief in a continuous revelation of the same God, and partly in reply to criticisms of philosophers like Celsus, that Origen rationalised the wrath of God as an expression of love and a simulation of anger for the benefit of mankind. He does recognise, however, that this is contrary to the popular view. "The simpler members of the Church do not imagine that there is another God greater than the Creator, but they do think that God is worse than the cruellest and most unjust of men."[79] This is why Origen had to explain the wrath of God in so many homilies; the popular conception was that God had to be propitiated, and only then would he overlook sin.

For all we have said about Origen's own view, there are some passages where he virtually uses the idea of propitiation in its natural sense, and there can be little doubt, in the case of the homilies, that the majority of the congregation would have understood him to mean this. In the Commentary on Romans, he is forced by the text to treat the question of wrath at some length, and he gives a vivid picture of the consequences of the wrath and judgement of God, even claiming that God does not ever kindle all his wrath, for no one would be able to stand it; it would consume the whole world. The reason he gives for dwelling on the wrath of God is that his hearers might have a better idea of the evils from which the blood of Christ had snatched them.[80] It was by the pouring out of his blood as victim that Christ brought about propitiation, which passes to each believer by way of faith. It is effected through the forgiveness of past sins, which comes through the "repropitio" of the blood of Christ, through God's delaying punishment until the sinner is brought to repentance.[81] The mediation of Christ on behalf of men is explicitly linked in this commentary with the need to satisfy the demands of God's justice; the sacrifice of Christ was in a sense propitiatory,

---

[79] De princ. IV.2.1.
[80] Comm. Rom. IV.11.
[81] Ibid., III.8.

although God himself was its source. This, to some extent, anticipates the view of Athanasius which we shall examine later, and it certainly involves some sense of propitiation, though not at the crude popular level which Origen was concerned to refute in his homilies. Origen's very modifications of propitiatory ideas force us to the conclusion that they were current in the Church and available for modification by his more sophisticated approach.

Origen's reason for rationalising the wrath of God and, to a considerable extent, modifying the concept of propitiation, was simply that he had adopted the theological axioms of Greek idealist philosophy, especially the view that God is changeless. But in a work spuriously attributed to Justin, this concept is explicitly rejected. Plato is not right to censure Homer for showing the gods are changeable, because Homer had a very good reason for this. Those who hope to experience mercy through their prayers and sacrifices must repent of their sins and avoid them in the future, whereas those who believe that God is unchangeable would in no way feel obliged to cease sinning, since in their state of mind they cannot perceive how repentance would help them.[82] The author could only accept the Christian idea of repentance as a sacrifice for sin provided the concept of God allowed the possibility of propitiating him; therefore he rejected the philosophical concept of God. He raised the question for the Christian philosophers: what possible effect can sacrifice have if it does not change God? He saw that the adoption of the Greek philosophical idea of God would undercut Christian spiritual sacrifices as well as the material sacrifices of the pagan - at least according to his conception of how sacrifice worked. In other words, this work supports my contention that at the non-philosophical and popular level, Christians thought about sacrifices for sin in terms of propitiatory sacrifices offered to God to appease his wrath. It is therefore more than likely that where the death of Christ was interpreted as a

---

[82] Exhortation to the Gentiles 25.

sacrifice, it would normally be conceived as a propitiatory sacrifice without questions being raised, in spite of conflict with the Christian belief that he was sent by the Father and revealed the Father.

To leap to the end of our period, the interpretation of God's wrath in the Homilies of John Chrysostom and the Gregories indicates that the simple Christian had always accepted the idea of God's anger and punishment of sin, in spite of the philosophical rationalisations of theologians.[83] That this was associated in the popular view with a propitiatory interpretation of sacrifice may be shown by study of Chrysostom's Homilies on Hebrews, where God's wrath is not studiously rationalised away, but is real and present. The doctrine of Final Judgement plays an important role in his exhortations: maybe now there is a throne of grace, but it is necessary to take advantage of it while it lasts, for later it will be a throne of judgement.[84] Yet, in contrast to this, Chrysostom is sure that the ground of salvation is the love of God, displayed in Christ's concern for mankind and his condescension to us, of which two proofs are available, firstly that he cleansed us of sins and secondly that he did this through himself (δι' ἑαυτοῦ).[85] He took flesh simply out of love for men (διὰ φιλανθρωπίαν μόνον),[86] and it was the Father's love for men that gave up his Son; the present throne of grace is a matter of royal largesse,[87] for though we deserve to be punished, in fact we have been made partakers of endless blessings.[88] Chrysostom never attempts to

---

[83]For discussion, see M. Pohlenz, Vom Zorne Gottes (Göttingen, 1909) and infra, Ch. 10A(c).

[84]Hom. VII. [85]Hom. II.

[86]Hom. V. See also VII & VIII. [87]Hom. VII.

[88]Hom. IX. See also Hom. IV: giving up his Son for the salvation of men was "fitting" for his φιλανθρωπία. In Hom. XXV, Chrysostom suggests that because of his φιλανθρωπία, because he was going to give great grace to me and did not want to seem to do it by grace but as a debtor, he arranged it that a man should first give up his only-begotten son to him at his com-

reconcile the love of God with his wrath and judgement. God in his love sent Christ to save us; but Christ's work consisted in propitiating him, in reconciling us to an angry and hostile God.[89] "He went up with a sacrifice which had power to propitiate the Father."[90] Occasionally Chrysostom, when pressed, shows himself a little uncomfortable at the idea that God had to be propitiated,[91] which proves that the Origenist

---

mand. Hence Abraham offered Isaac. The sacrifice of Isaac was a type of Christ's sacrifice, deliberately enacted to conceal God's grace, to give the impression that it was not a very outstanding thing to do to give up your only son. Chrysostom thus emphasises the love and grace involved in the Father's surrender of his Son for the salvation of the world.

[89]Hom. XVI: "The Son became mediator between the Father and us. The Father willed not to leave us this inheritance, but was wroth against us, and was displeased with us at being estranged from him; he accordingly became mediator between us and him, and won him over." He did it by bringing us words from the Father and adding his death: we should have died, but he died for us and made us worthy of the Covenant. This last statement reminds us of Origen's picture of Christ healing mankind, rather than propitiating God; but Chrysostom uses both ideas without apology. He often speaks of us being estranged and of our need for purification (Hom. III, V, IX), but also of God's enmitv and wrath and the need for propitiation.

[90]Hom. XXIX.

[91]In Hom XXIX, having stated that Christ propitiated the Father, Chrysostom does attempt to correct himself by saying it was not God but the angels who were hostile. Such mitigation of his statements about God's wrath and the need for propitiation are rare, and Chrysostom, unlike Origen, shows no hesitancy in speaking of God's wrath and using propitiatory ideas in the same context. It seems reasonable to conclude that he generally presupposed a propitiatory view of sacrifice but, when pressed, remembered his theological education which questioned the possibility of God's wrath.

rationalisation had become traditional in Eastern theology; but his unquestioning use of the idea in the majority of passages reflects the fact that the common Church members who were his hearers, like the congregation Origen complained about, in fact conceived of Christ's sacrifice as propitiatory, a sacrifice offered to God to appease his anger against sin. "The Father was wroth against us and was displeased with us as being estranged from him; he (Christ) accordingly became mediator between us and him, and won him over."[92]

In Eusebius' Demonstratio Evangelica[93] we find a rationale of Old Testament sacrifices, and thus of their antitype, the sacrifice of Christ, which seems to be the systematisation of popular explanation of the sacrifice of Christ. It is likely that this rationale lies behind the view of Chrysostom we have just examined. Eusebius opens by admitting that Greek philosophers as well as Christians have relinquished sacrifice for a spiritual cult, but he proceeds to argue that the reasons are quite different. Philosophers argue that killing animals is wrong, whereas the Hebrews certainly did not take this line. The sacrifice of Abel was preferred to that of Cain because God was more pleased with animal sacrifice. All the patriarchs sacrificed, and the reason for this was that they realised that a great act of service was needed to cleanse their mortal sins; they thought they owed a ransom for their salvation to the supplier of their life and soul (ζωὴ καὶ ψυχή). They felt there was nothing more precious than their own ψυχή (both the translation "life" and the translation "soul" must be understood during this discussion; in Greek the distinction was not clear); and the only possible alternative was to offer the ψυχή of animals. There was nothing immoral about this because the ψυχή of irrational animals is not really comparable to that of rational and intelligent men. But their blood and the life-force (ψυχή) in their blood, provided a

[92]Hom. XVI.

[93]Dem. Evang. I.10. See also VIII.2 and X.8.

ψυχή to offer in place of their own ψυχή. Eusebius here uses the Leviticus text to justify this claim: the blood is the life (ψυχή) and provides the means of "propitiation"; it is clear that Eusebius understood ἐξιλάσκεσθαι in this sense. The killing of animals gave men an ἀντίψυχον for their own ψυχή. The sacrificer layed his hands on the animal's head to show it was offered in place of his own head. This system, Eusebius continues, was satisfactory as long as there was nothing better to offer, but it was also a prophecy of the better offering that would be made for the cleansing of the whole world, namely the death of Christ. He became the victim who was the substitute offered to God for the life of sinful man; as High-Priest he offered the perfect sacrifice pleasing to the Father, his own body. This is described by Eusebius as λύτρον, ἀντίψυχον, καθάρσιον, ἱλασμός, ἱλαστήριον, ἀπολύτρωσις. In other words, he uses all the vocabulary of ransom, redemption and propitiation of Christ's sacrifice. In another passage,[94] Eusebius seems to think of the ransom price as being paid by God to the devil, but his exposition of sacrifice definitely uses the ransom language of providing a substitute for the offering of life that men should give to propitiate God for their sins. Where Origen and Gregory of Nyssa could not possibly have conceived of the ransom in such terms and explicitly state that the ransom was offered by God to the devil,[95] Eusebius is quite prepared to think of the ransom in terms of the offering of a substitute in sacrifice to God. Aulén's distinction again does not apply.

Eusebius' rationale follows exactly those lines of the rationale of Old Testament sacrifices along substitutionary lines which was refuted in Chapter Two. Does it therefore overturn the position adopted there? This conclusion would be based on an anachronism. I have no statement of this rationale in any literature prior to Eusebius; indeed until about this period

---

[94] Dem. Evan. X.8.

[95] The famous "deception of the devil" in Greg. Nys. is found in MPG 46/605-8.

sacrifice seems to have been assumed without critical discussion or the endeavour to find any rationale or definition. By this time, however, sacrifice was being called in question, not least by the Christian rejection of it. Iamblichus and Sallustius used the idea of offering life to the deity to construct their rationale of the practice; Eusebius was all the more likely to use it because of the *Leviticus* text. A number of factors would make Eusebius' rationale the most natural construction: the *Leviticus* text interpreted in terms of the Greek concept of the soul; the context of an ever-increasing Church with converts from a pagan background in which propitiation was a presupposed understanding of sacrifice; the idea that Christ's life had been sacrificed for the sins of the world, used in conjunction with ransom language, and the similar ideas associated with the martyr's death - ideas which would encourage the assumption that they died as a substitute for mankind. It was natural to think that Christ's life was offered as a substitute for the life of men to propitiate the wrath of God against sin, and there can be little doubt that Eusebius' rationale reflects the attitude of the majority. How this rationale was reconcilable with the goodness and love of God, with his ἀπάθεια and with the fact that God himself saved mankind through Christ, went unexplained; nor was the problem of its consistency with the Classic theory of Atonement faced.

D. Christ's Sin-offering explained in the context of a systematic exposition of Atonement.

Up to the time of Athanasius, there were several aspects of Christian thought about the atoning sacrifice of Christ which were not strictly speaking reconcilable, but which had received no systematic treatment. In the first place, the atoning sacrifice was accepted as a God-given means of dealing with sin in line with the Jewish interpretation of sacrifice. Then, Greek Christians used their own types of sacrifice, namely sacrifices of aversion and of propitiation, to explain how the sacrifices dealt with the problem of sin. Interpretation in terms of the former meant that the sacrifice, like the ransom-price, was given to the devil and was part of the means of overcoming the hosts of wickedness; thus the sacrifice was not an offering to God, but an offering made by God to save men from the power of sin. Interpretation in terms of the latter was inconsistent with the Platonic concept of God accepted by the more sophisticated theologians; it was inconsistent with the belief that God was the source of salvation and the only Being with the power to deal with sin; it raised the difficulty of a conflict between the love and wrath of God; and it was never reconciled with the predominant conception of salvation, namely the rescue of mankind from the power of the evil one.

That the solution found by Athanasius was at any rate latent in the thought of his predecessors must be admitted. But he was the first to give a systematic account of Atonement which reconciled all these views of Christ's sacrifice. When we have examined the nature of this systematic exposition, we shall be able to see how both Origen and Eusebius were reaching towards the same solution, although they never worked it out step by step.

Athanasius' treatment of the sacrifice of Christ must be seen in the context of his whole soteriology. This is therefore outlined first in (a). His use of sacrifice and ransom language is then examined in the course of discussion of his Atonement theory: in (b) it will become apparent that he thought in terms of the Classic "Christus Victor" theory of Atonement, and understood Christ's sacrifice within the framework of this theory as an offering made by God to death; but (c) will show that this dualist mode of thought was subordinated by Athanasius to the concept of God's omnipotence, so that the victory over evil becomes a divine self-reconciliation. In this way, Athanasius employs valuable ideas from both the aversion and propitiation interpretations of Christ's sacrifice, and so resolves the problems involved in using one or the other exclusively.

(a) Athanasius' soteriology

The depth of Athanasius' concern with the problem of Christ's Work can be seen in the fact that he was one of the first to tackle the question "Cur Deus Homo?" His *De Incarnatione* is a systematic treatise on Atonement. In this work, Athanasius is primarily concerned with the restoration of the image of God originally given to Man, but lost in the Fall.[96] Man's disobedience meant that he ceased to participate in the Logos of God, and this led to two serious problems: (i) By loss of the principle of life, the Logos, Man became susceptible to corruption and death. So the Logos took a human body that was capable of dying, and through the offering of that body to death, conquered death; for the body was raised from the dead and clothed in incorruptibility by the living power of the Logos. Athanasius believed that this conquest of death abolished it for all mankind, and that this resurrection recreated humanity, since the indwelling Logos restored in Man the image of God and the eternal life of God.[97] (ii) By squandering his share in the Logos, Man perverted his intellignece, and so turned to idolatry, the worship of the creature instead of the Creator. Although through contemplation of the order ahd harmony of the universe, or attention to the prophets and holy men that God sent, or the attempt to live according to the moral Law revealed to the Jews, men could learn of God, they could not regain proper knowledge of God without participation in the Logos. The only solution was to renew the image of God in men, and this was accomplished by

---

[96]For Athanasius' account of the Creation and Fall, see *De inc.* I-V.

[97]See the exposition in *De inc.* XI-XVI. Athanasius uses this idea in his work against the Arians. Only God could end death; therefore the Logos must have been, not a creature, but God. See, e.g., *C. Ar.* I.44-5, 59-60; II.14, 16, 55, 66-8, 70; III.4, 31, 33, 38, 53.

the Logos dwelling in a man.[98] The basis of Athansius' position was the idea that if Man had not fallen he would have lived as god (ὡς θεός);[99] he summarises the work of Christ by saying that he became human so that we could become divine (Αὐτὸς γὰρ ἐνηνθρώπησεν ἵνα ἡμεῖς θεοποιηθῶμεν).[100]

Only God could restore his own image in Man, so only God could save. This was the vital principle for Athanasius, and it was this that the Christological theories of the Arians undercut. Therefore his fight against the Arians was motivated by soteriological concerns. Never again does he give as full an account of his position as in the De Incarnatione, but behind all his arguments against his opponents, his understanding of salvation can be detected, and developments traced, especially increasing insistence on the idea of θεοποίησις.[101] His soteriology was essentially God-centred, and this basic conviction that the work of salvation could only be performed by God himself spurred him in defence of the essential Godhead of the Son. The Logos is not a creature, but is ὁμοούσιος τῷ Πατρί, because only so is salvation realised and guaranteed.

In his work against the Arians (Contra Arianos), the work of Christ has two aspects: first the removal

---

[98]See the exposition in De inc. XI.XVI. Also C. gent., passim. Against Arius, Athanasius insisted on the importance of the revelation to men of the true nature of God through the Logos, who must therefore be God. See, e.g., C. Ar. I.9, 12, 16, 21, 35, 39, 43, 59, 61; II. 16-7, 22, 24, 54, 80-2; III. 3-7, 11, 14, 16, 46. See also De Syn. 15, 38, 52; and Letters to Serapion I.19. Particularly important is his use of the parable of the sun and its "radiance" to explain the relation of the Father and Son; see C. Ar. I.12, 16, 46-7, 49, 60; II,32-3, 41-2, 53; III.3-6, 13-4, 65.

[99]De inc. IV.6.

[100]Ibid., LIV.3.

[101]For revelation and end of death, see references in notes 97 & 98, supra. For θεοποίησις, see C. Ar. I.37-50; II.41, 47, 53, 61, 65, 70, 75; III.33.

of sin and death, the λύτρωσις, achieved by the acceptance and conquest of sin, human passions (παθή), "the curse," death, and "he who has the power of death, that is the devil";[102] then the θεοποίησις or υἱοποίησις, effected by the resurrection and ascension of sanctified humanity in Christ, to be presented to the Father as a New Creation. This is very similar to the pattern we found in Origen, whereby sin and the devil were first despatched to the wilderness of hell, and then human nature was purified and sanctified so that men could become "participes divinae naturae."

Sin was the problem with which atoning sacrifice was concerned, but as we have outlined Athanasius' soteriology, he seems to have little concern with this, being more anxious about mortality and intellectual perversion.[103] The emphasis in the De Incarnatione is certainly on death, but it must be remembered that in Athanasius' view, death is the result of sin, man's disobedience to God's express command. Athanasius shows a predominant interest in death because it was the curse of sin, the mark of the loss of the divine nature man had had. He even deals with this point, saying that if it had been a case of a mere trespass, repentance could have solved the problem; but man's situation was worse, for the result of sin had been corruption of his nature and loss of grace, and this only the re-creating power of the Logos could restore.[104] In fact in the Contra Arianos, the emphasis does change, and Athanasius speaks a great deal more

---

[102]Heb. 2.14.

[103]This is a common accusation against Athanasius, e.g., Van Harrlem, Incarnatie en verlossing bij Athanasius (Wägeringen, 1961); English summary of pp. 210-211: "Athanasius stresses death rather than the guilt of man. In this respect he is a real Eastern theologian. It is no reason to condemn him. We must see the difference between Athanasius and someone like Anselm against the background of the difference between East and West. The Western and Eastern churches supplement each other."

[104]De inc. VII.

of Christ's work as a redemption from sin and the curse of the Law.[105]

In the context of this picture of what salvation means, how does Athanasius use the ideas of ransom and sacrifice?

(b) Christ's Sacrifice of Aversion in Athanasius

If it were possible to disregard the *Vita Antonii* and concentrate on his doctrinal and argumentative works, it would be tempting to suggest that Athanasius, in contrast to his predecessors (including as we have shown the quite sophisticated Christian philosopher, Origen), had freed himself from the demonology of the populace and found very little satisfaction in the attempt to understand salvation in terms of conflict with the devil. It was not necessary even to mention the power of evil in our summary of his soteriology; in the *Contra Gentes*, an attack on idolatry which discusses the origin of evil, the devil is not mentioned; the few references to the devil might be explained as concessions to traditional Christian language, for salvation is usually treated in other, more distinctivcly Athanasian terms.

This does not mean, however, that Athanasius did not think in terms of the Classic theory of Atonement. One of the principal motifs of his soteriology is the idea of victory over death,[106] sin and ignorance, a major proof of which was the destruction of idolatry which Christianity had effected. The picture of strife between good and evil, life and death, freedom

---

[105]To anyone coming to the *C. Arianos* from the *De incarnatione*, the references to sin are surprisingly frequent. For examples, see *C. Ar*. I.49, 60, 62; II.47, 55-6, 61, 66-8, 70; III.4, 31, 33, 38, 53. This does lessen the force of his argument since only God could cleanse sin; therefore, the Logos must be God, not a creature. See ibid., II.67.

[106]The extent of personification of death is some indication of presence of the same way of thought as the Classic theory. See *De inc*. IV.2; V.2; and possibly VI.2; IX.4; XXI.4; XXII.5; XXVII.2; XXIX.1; etc.

and bondage, knowledge and ignorance is basic to Athanasius' concept of the situation into which Christ came; the context of Christ's work of salvation is still dualistic. This is so even though he defines evil as non-Being, and death's power over man as the return to the non-existence out of which man was created.

This definition of evil must be interpreted in the light of the philosophical tradition of the Platonists, for whom non-Being has some sort of ontological status. There were degrees of Being depending on a thing's participation in True Being; Good was identified with True Being, so inevitably evil belonged to the opposite end of the ontological scale. Thus, in Platonic philosophy, matter, evil and non-Being were equated.[107] For those who accepted this view, the

---

[107]The following quotation from Plotinus illustrates the problem of evil and non-being in Platonic philosophy: "If Being is of this kind, and also that beyond Being, evil can neither be in Being nor in that beyond Being, for they are good. It remains, then, that granted there is evil, it must be in a class of non-beings, existing as a sort of form of non-existence, and it must be found in one of the things which are mingled with non-Being or have some sort of share in it. 'Non-Being' here of course does not mean 'that which is absolutely non-existent,' but only that which is other than Being; not, however, non-Being in the sense of a movement or position with regard to Being, but in the sense of an image of Being or even something less real. This is either the world of sense as a whole and all that is experienced in it or something which comes later than this and is in a way incidental to it, or else its source, or else one of the things which help to complete its distinctive nature. One might arrive at some conception of it by considering it as measurelessness as opposed to measure, the unlimited as opposed to limit, formlessness as opposed to a forming principle, that which is always in need as opposed to self-sufficiency; as something always indefinite, nowhere at rest, affected by everything, insatiable, ut-

material world in which they lived did not really exist, and yet obviously it affected their lives, even as they denied it. Analogously, Athansius maintains that evil is non-existent, and yet his whole attitude reveals his consciousness of being in conflict with the power of evil.[108]

---

ter poverty . . . Just as there is Absolute Good and good as a quality, there must be Absolute Evil and evil which occurs incidentally in something else as a result of the existence of Absolute Evil . . ." (Enn I.8.3; tr. A. H. Armstrong). In Enn. III.6.7, matter is also defined as non-Being. For discussion of the problem, see P. Merlan, From Platonism to Neoplatonism (The Hague, 1953). He reduces the problem to that found throughout Platonic philosophy, namely, that of the relation between the One and the Many.

[108]J. Pelikan, in The Light of the World (New York, 1962), tries to reconcile the apparent conflict in Athanasius' ideas: "According to Athanasius' doctrine [the devils] had no authority or power. For darkness was non-Being, possessing no reality of its own unless someone treated it as though it were real. When Antony recognized this and named the forces of non-being as the unreality they were, the power of divine light prevailed over the darkness to grant salvation to Antony." (The reference is to an incident found in Vita Ant. 10.) There is absolutely no justification in the text for this description of Antony's illumination. The Vita Ant. portrays the activity and deceit of the devils and the temptations to which the devout Christian is subjected; but the emphasis is not on the realisation that these deceits and temptations do not exist, but rather on the victory of Christ over them, a victory in which the Christian can share and whose benefits he can claim for himself in his personal struggle. (See Vita Ant. 5, 24, 27-8, 33, 42, 94.) Athanasius' apparently paradoxical view that evil does not exist (and yet men are involved in warfare against it) must be interpreted in the light of the Plotinus passage quoted in the previous note. Evil is non-Being, and yet there is such a thing as Absolute Evil in which

So, even if evil did not really exist but men had conjured it up in their imaginations, still it had so much power over men now that they were held in bondage, and a bondage from which they could not set themselves free. Athanasius could, therefore, use traditional Christian language about the deceits of the devil and the δαίμονες;[109] and, although he had explained the Fall as man's deliberate act of disobedience to God for which Man is entirely responsible,[110] he could also say it happened συμβουλίᾳ τοῦ διαβόλου.[111] Indeed, in

---

evil things partake. The conclusions of Proclus in his treatise, On the Subsistence of Evil, also throw light on this. Evil has an effective power which is obvious. He therefore describes evil as two-fold: as absolute non-Being, and as being commingled with Being and Good. Evil comes into existence through Good, when it is good for evil to be. The fact that evil, in Neoplatonism, is described as non-Being and yet has a real power for malevolence in the world is admirably brought out by John Hick in Evil and the God of Love (London, 1966), pp. 46-9.

[109]De inc. V.2; VI.5-6; X.4; XII.6; XX.6; etc. C. Ar. II.8, 54-5; Vita Ant. passim.

[110]Athanasius' account of the origin of evil is entirely rationalistic. Man turned away from God and chose the "things nearer to himself" (that is, bodily as distinct from spiritual things) and became corrupted by selfish desires. See C. gent. III-V. Man disobeyed God (De inc. III.4-5; IV.4) and so, emptied of the knowledge of God, began to sink back into non-existence, his natural state (De inc. IV.5-6). Evil does not stem from God; indeed it has no ousia. God could not be the Lord if evil had "a substantive and independent existence" (C. gent. VI); men dreamed it up out of their "lack of the vision of the good" (ibid., VII). See also De inc. XLV and LII on the destruction of idolatry.

[111]De inc. V.1.

the Long Recension of the De Incarnatione,[112] he produces a reason for Christ's death on the Cross which is entirely within the terms of the Classic theory: he died hanging in the air in order to defeat the devil in his own element, so purifying the air and making a way for us through it up to heaven.[113] The Life of Antony is an account of a Christian saint's lifelong battle with the devil and his angels, and in this work Athanasius describes how the powers of evil are fallen angels who do all they can to impede the work of salvation;[114] this description is analogous to his account of the Fall of Man elsewhere, and is based on the principle that God created all things, but certainly did not create anything evil. In this work, Christ is understood to have achieved the overthrow of the evil powers: although they will not admit it, their power, always limited, was destroyed by Christ,[115] and the Christian's part is simply to bring to its conclusion the battle in which victory has already been won. In more theological works, Athanasius does not speak of the devil and daemons but of sin and death, but his concept of Christ's victory is the same; he destroyed death, dispelled ignorance, freed men from idolatry, magic and astrology. The Cross is a trophy, the Gospel

---

[112]Four manuscripts of Athanasius' De inc., discovered between the wars, contain an abbreviated version known as the Short Recension. Study of the relationship between this and the Long Recension which is found in the vast majority of MSS has suggested that both versions originated in the 4th cy. and should probably be attributed to Athanasius himself. The Long Recension seems to be the original, the shorter version apparently being a literary rather than dogmatic revision, motivated solely by the desire to abbreviate. For a detailed discussion of the text of both versions, see G. J. Ryan and R. P. Casey in Studies and Documents XIV; also F. L. Cross, The Study of St. Athanasius (Oxford, 1945).

[113]De inc. XXV.

[114]Vita Ant. 22.

[115]Christ has "deprived [the devils] of their strength" (Vita Ant. 9).

a message of victory.[116]

Athanasius "makes less mention of the devil than almost any of the Fathers";[117] yet his thought moves within the framework of the Classic theory. He constantly uses ransom and sacrifice language. Did he interpret these terms like Origen as the means of averting the power of evil?

Athanasius certainly refrains from using propitiation-language, and his use of sacrifice-language of the death of Christ appears most in the *De Incarnatione*, specifically in contexts concerned with the conquest of death. Christ conquered death by an offering - the offering of his own pure and sinless body; the body was presented to death, and that offering redeemed mankind from the forces of evil and corruption. By surrendering to death the human body which he had taken, as a victim and sacrifice free from blemish, he abolished death for his human brethren.[118] So it was through the sacrifice of his body that he put an end to death; as the *Epistle to the Hebrews* put it, "since then the children are sharers in flesh and blood, he also assumed the same, in order that, through death, he might bring to nought him that has the power of death, that is, the devil, and might rescue those who all their lives were enslaved by fear of death."[119] θυσία is used as a synonym for this death;[120] he was offered as a ransom or substitute (ἀντίψυχον) for all;[121] this was his offering and his sacrifice. Athanasius never mentions God as the recipient of the sacrifice in the *De Incarnatione*. The body is offered to death as a sacrifice.

---

[116] τέλος ἔξει ἡ διαβόλου τυράννις is a typical cry (C. Ar. II.73). τρόπαιον is frequently used of the Cross, e.g., *De inc.* XIX.3; XXIV.4; XXVI.1; XXX.1.

[117] Aulén, *op. cit.*, p. 59.

[118] *De inc.* IX.1.

[119] *Ibid.*, X.4, quoting *Heb.* 2.14ff. The word used for "sacrifice" is θυσία and is used similarly in *De inc.* X.5.

[120] Ibid., XXI.6; XVI.4.

[121] IX.1; XXXVII.7.

In the *Contra Arianos*, sacrifice-language has to a large extent been replaced by ransom-language, although there is a greater concern with Christ's bearing of our sins and weaknesses. We might have expected that where the writer was more concerned with sin he would use more sacrifice-language; but this is not the case with Athanasius. Nor is it the case that, like Origen, he has turned to the idea of a ransom paid to the devil in order to explain his use of sacrifice-language. He never says to whom the ransom was paid, and in any case, in the *Contra Arianos*, he is not concerned with explanation, as he was in the *De Incarnatione*. He seems to use ransom-vocabulary here simply as a traditional means of referring to rescue and salvation from death, sin and "the curse."[122] (ἐλευθερωθέντες is a synonym for λυτρωθέντες in Athanasius' writings.)[123] When explaining the work of Christ, Athanasius uses sacrifice-language, and never resorts to a theory of ransom to the devil to elucidate his meaning, while ransom-language is merely a term of reference taken from traditional Christian expression.

Christ's body was offered to death as a sacrifice. By this sacrificial death mankind was freed from death, sin and "the curse." Clearly Athanasius understands the sacrifice of Christ and the ransom he offered as a means of ridding mankind of the evil powers that dominate his life, in a similar way to Origen. But he never uses analogies and descriptions that could suggest that he consciously thought of the sacrifice as a sacrifice of aversion. Neither sacrifice nor ransom was offered to the devil. In the *Contra Arianos*, the sacrifice is explicitly said to have been offered to God.[124] How is a sacrifice offered to God the means of conquering death?

---

[122] *C. Ar.* I.43, 45, 49-50, 60; II.13-4, 43, 75; III.23, 31, 39. II.52 explains the rescue in terms of a parable, a man's son using a disguise to regain property lost to enemies. Cf. Origen's parable mentioned *supra*, Ch. 8B(b).

[123] *C. Ar.* I.48.

[124] *Ibid.*, I.41.

(c) Propitiation Sacrifice in Athanasius

In our summary of Athanasius' soteriology, it was made quite plain that the act of salvation in his view had to be performed by God himself, and so the Logos had to be of identical nature with the Father. In other words, whatever Athanasius thought of the sacrifice of Christ, he certainly believed it was offered by God himself. Yet he did not resort to the explanation that it was offered as a ransom to the devil, and even said it was offered to the Father. What kind of a sacrifice was it that God offered himself, and how did it solve the needs of mankind, and conquer death and sin?

The sacrifice was the answer to what has been called the "Divine Dilemma."[125] Athanasius describes the situation which called for it in the *De Incarnatione*.[126] God created Man out of nothing and pronounced that if he transgressed his command, he would return to the state of nothingness out of which he came. Man did transgress and it left God in an intolerable position. It was unthinkable that he should go back on his word, and Man, having transgressed, should not die; God could not falsify himself. But it was not worthy of God's goodness that his work should perish, especially in the case of beings which had been endowed with the nature of the Logos himself. It would have been better never to have created them. Repentance would have solved the issue if it had not been for that decree and the corruption of nature that therefore ensued when Man committed sin. The debt to death had to be paid; re-creation of Man's nature was necessary. Somehow God's integrity had to be salvaged while the demands of his love were met. The Incarnation was the solution to this dilemma. The Logos recognised that death held mankind in bonds because it was the penalty for the transgression, and he knew that the decree could not be repealed until it was fulfilled. So in his compassion for mankind

---

[125]By a Religious of C.S.M.V. in translation of the *De inc*. (London, 1963), p. 31.

[126]See esp. VIIIff.

in this helpless position, he himself took a human body just like ours, and he surrendered it to death in place of all, and offered it to the Father. He paid the debt owed by all men, by the death of his own body, then he raised it from the dead, recreating humanity and making it fit for re-acceptance by God. It was a sacrifice to God, an offering to satisfy the demands of his truthfulness. It was a sacrifice made by God himself out of the depths of his love for his creation. God reconciled the world to himself by the sacrifice of Christ, by a life offered to death in fulfillment of his decree.

It is true that Athanasius thinks in the dualist terms of the Classic theory of Atonement, that he can rejoice in the victory over death, the devil and sin just as much as his contemporaries, that salvation for him was redemption from sin, death and "the curse" by the sacrificial offering of Christ. The essential theological value of interpretation in terms of the sacrifice of aversion or simply expiation is preserved, for the sacrifice is recognised to have been made by God on Man's behalf to deal with sin and the powers of evil. But his understanding goes further. The drama of salvation can be described without reference to the devil, because he sees beyond the dualism, not simply by accepting the Christian belief in the ultimate sovereignty of God and the inevitability of his victory over sin, but by seeing that behind the dualism is a subtle conflict in the attitude of God himself, a dilemma posed for God's goodness by the appearance of evil in his creation. This dilemma can only be resolved by a sacrifice offered to God in fulfillment of the demands of his decree, that is, a death died to end all death. Thus Athanasius adopts the idea that Christ died as a substitute or ransom (ἀντίψυχον) for the deserved death of every man,[127] and, in the guise of paying the debt to God's integrity, in fact uses the idea of propitiation in a modified form. Men were liable to judgement under God's decree;

---

[127]See *infra*, Additional Note II.

the Logos received the judgement into himself (εἰς ἑαυτόν).[128] The Logos who was ὁμοούσιος τῷ Πατρί took a body so that he could offer it as a sacrifice to reconcile us with the Father.[129] He ransomed all, on behalf of all ἱλασκόμενος τὰ πρὸς τὸν Θεόν:[130] this phrase is particularly significant since Athanasius rarely uses propitiation language,[131] and here he uses an extraordinary expression. He deliberately has not said that Christ propitiated God, since he of all people could not allow a distinction between God and the Logos; but he has not avoided using the term in relation to God. God did not need to be propitiated; he loved us already. Athanasius would agree with Origen over this. But, in a sense, propitiation was needed and it affected God. No solution to the problem of how Atonement worked could be found by transferring all attention to God's goodness and saying simply that God acted against the opposing forces of evil; God acted with regard to himself, to resolve his dilemma.

---

[128] *C. Ar.* I.60.

[129] *De Dec. Nic. Syn.* 14. See also *Letter to Epictetus* 4 & 6; *Letter to Serapion* I.31; *C. Ar.* II.14, etc., esp. III.6: τὸ γὰρ ἴδιον τῆς τοῦ Πατρὸς οὐσίας ἐστὶν ὁ υἱὸς ἐν ᾧ ἡ κτίσις πρὸς τὸν Θεὸν κατηλάσσετο. οὕτως ἃ εἰργάζετο ὁ υἱός, τού Πατρός ἐστιν ἔργα.

[130] *C. Ar.* II.7ff is a particularly important passage on the High-Priesthood of Christ and his sacrifice offered for mankind. It is in this passage that this phrase occurs. He took a body so as to offer it to the Father and cleanse it from sins with his own blood and raise it from the dead. The passage is similar to Origen in that the relationship with the Father depends on the cleansing of mankind's sin, although, as we have seen, Athanasius' rationale for the sacrifice (i.e., the method of cleansing) is different. The argument of the passage as a whole stresses the idea that the sacrifice was offered by God, to God to reconcile himself.

[131] Apart from quotations of scriptural texts, he uses it only once elsewhere in *C. Ar.* I.64, where ἱλασμός seems to be used merely as one of the traditional titles of Christ.

Only God could pay the debt to his integrity; the sacrifice had to be offered by God himself in a process of self-reconciliation, and, if we may invent the term, self-propitiation.

E. Conclusion

Athanasius' exposition of Atonement brings together the essential elements in the differing types of sin-offerings used to explain the atoning death of Christ. By the restoration of the image of God in Man, the life of Christ purified human nature; the offering of his human body to death finally expiated sin and its consequences, as well as destroying death and the devil. Thus the important elements of the sacrifice of expiation and aversion are retained. At the same time, the payment of the debt to God's truthfulness retains certain aspects of a propitiatory interpretation while avoiding its dangers, especially the danger of denying the involvement of the Father in the reconciliatory work of Christ.

Athanasius was the first to express this divine self-reconciliation explicitly. To some extent it was latent in Greek Christian thought. Those, like Eusebius, who spoke of propitiating God and of Christ freeing us from his wrath, still maintained that God sent his Son, and that his Son revealed him, but the conflict in their position was not apparently resolved prior to Athanasius' systematic account. Likewise Origen, in one commentary,[132] recognises the problem of satisfying the demands of God's justice, so that we might imagine he was recognising, like Athanasius, that self-reconciliation was the ultimate solution; but he goes on to interpret Christ's mediatorial function as a means of delaying God's judgement until men repent and so cease to deserve punishment, rather than in terms of his bearing the judgement owed to men.

---

[132] Origen, Comm. Rom. III.8.

Christians always recogniased the ultimate sovereignty of God and the inevitability of his victory over evil; but few actually believed that the evil powers were subservient to God, and that his victory was a self-reconciliation.

Here I differ with Aulén who originally emphasised the importance of the "Christus Victor" theory of Atonement in the Fathers, and called it the Classic theory. "Because in a measure the hostile powers were regarded as in the service of the will of God, the Judge of all, and the executants of his judgement, . . . the triumph over the opposing powers is regarded as a reconciling of God to himself."[133] It is in discussion of this that he uses the ideas of sacrifice and ransom, claiming, as we have seen, that the ransom is naturally regarded as being paid to the hostile powers under whom men are in bondage while sacrifice is offered to God, and that the two are related because they are both expressions of the act whereby God reconciles himself to himself.[134]

My first difference is that I do not believe this solution was explicit in the thought of the Fathers before Athanasius. Those who understood the sacrifice in terms of propitiation never explicitly reconciled this with their belief that the saving act came from God. Others rationalised away the wrath of God and modified the idea of propitiation.

Secondly, his easy distinction between the ransom and the sacrifice will not do. Those who thought in terms of a propitiatory sacrifice, understood the ransom as the substitution of Christ for men, and never reconciled this with ideas of conquest of the devil and the ransom price offered to redeem men from him. Those who thought of the ransom as the price paid to the devil, interpreted the sacrifice in those terms, and so used the concept of aversion sacrifice to explain Christ's self-offering to the devil to redeem men and avert evil and sin.

---

[133]Aulén, op. cit., pp. 20-1.

[134]Ibid., Ch. on the "Double Aspect of the Drama of the Atonement."

Athanasius' account of Atonement is a rationalisation of the elements of conflicting Christian traditions. We can see that he resolved the problems of use of ideas of propitiation and aversion. Yet he does not basically use sacrifice to understand Atonement; sacrifice language appears merely as a metaphor for the payment of the debt to death. What actually dealt with sin in Athanasius' soteriology was the re-creation of perfect humanity, the θεοποίησις. Once the image of God had been restored in Man, sin and death were inevitably cast out, and this process hardly falls into the categories of sacrificial thought.

Athanasius' systematic reconciliation of the conflicting elements in Christian thought about the Work of Christ in relation to sin, can possibly be seen to lie behind the language used by the Cappadocians, although they never make a clear exposition of this reconciliation. The theological work of Gregory of Nazianzus and the mystical writings of Gregory of Nyssa are permeated by the idea of θεοποίησις, the Work of Christ understood as restoring the image of God in Man by means of the Incarnation. Both, particularly the mystic of Nyssa, are interested in the gradual progress of the individual soul towards the goal of perfection, through increasing participation in the Logos. Gregory of Nyssa does not dwell much on the sacrificial aspect of Christ's Work, though he uses all the traditional Christian types to describe his death, and emphasises the efficacy of his saving blood.[135] On the one hand, he describes the death of Christ almost crudely as a trick played on the devil who thought he was getting a good bargain in return for mankind,[136] and on the other, he says that Christ, by

---

[135]The Passover-type is frequent: e.g., MPG 44/353A-D, 364B. Also Abraham's sacrifice of Isaac: 46/620; and Moses holding up his arms: 44/372A-C. On the blood, see, e.g., 44/353, 364, 424, 604; 45/476, 717. 1156-7, etc.

[136]The deception of the devil and the idea of the "devil's rights" have been discussed so often that I see no need to go into detail here. For the text, see 45/61-9.

the sacrifice of himself, propitiated the Father with his precious blood.[137] For him Christ is priest and mediator who reconciled the world to God; he is also God himself who recreated mankind by taking upon himself a human life and infusing it with the life of God himself.[138] Behind the richness of Gregory's use of scriptural and traditional ideas probably lies a reconciliation of the conflicting elements along the lines of Athanasius' solution.

Gregory Nazianzen, of all the Fathers, makes most use of the idea of Christ's sacrifice, particularly in devotion and preaching, generally as an emotive affirmation of faith rather than as part of a reasoned theological system like that of Athanasius.[139] Christ, as priest, sacrifices himself, as victim, for us, so cleansing the world.[140] In one passage, Gregory explicitly raises the question whether he was offered to God or the devil. He describes the plight of mankind under the tyranny of the devil, and then asks whether the ransom was given to him. His reply concentrates on the ὕβρις involved if it was not merely from God that he received a price, but God himself that he was given, an excessive reward for freeing us from his tyranny. So he faces the problem of why the offering should have been made to God; after all

---

[137]<u>MPG</u> 45/717B. This passage is important since the idea of propitiation is used explicitly in a context describing Christ as priest and victim propitiating God through his sacrificial death. See also 44/1149C-D, where propitiation is again used with reference to the living sacrifice of himself which Christ offered. Propitiation is not explicitly used in 46/612D, but Christ as High-Priest is said to offer a sacrifice to the Father for sin.

[138]These ideas permeate his writings, so that to give detailed references would be tedious.

[139]Note his treatment of Christ's sacrifice in his poems as well as throughout his sermons and epistles.

[140]E.g., <u>Or</u>. XXX.21; XXXIII; XXXVIII.16; etc. Like Greg. Nys., he uses all the traditional types; see esp. his homilies on the Passion, <u>Or</u>. I. XLV.

we were not under his dominion. Clearly, he reasons, the Father accepted it, not asking for it or needing it, but because of the "economy" (οἰκονομία), and the need to sanctify mankind by the humanity of God.[141] His strong affirmation against the idea that the offering was to the devil is surprising when his close relationship with the other Gregory is remembered. But the important point about this passage is that, like Athanasius, he admits the sacrifice was made to God while repudiating the crudest propitiation ideas. God did not need this sacrifice, but it was his method of purifying human nature. Admittedly, Gregory has not explained the "Divine Dilemma" in full, but that this idea lies behind his work is likely.

In contrast to Athanasius, both Gregories use propitiation language quite freely. A constant theme in their writings is the picture of Christ as High-Priest and mediator. But for both of them, as for Athanasius, the real method of removing man's sin was by the sanctification of human nature which occurred when the Logos dwelt on earth as a man, and by the educative process of chastisement and encouragement of the individual soul as it struggles up the path to heaven.

The work of the Gregories sums up nearly every aspect of Christian thought about salvation in the East. More than Athanasius they use all the pictorial language of typology, evocative appeal to offer spiritual sacrifices, brilliant allegory,[142] devotional power, and inspiration for the spiritual life. Behind their comprehensive coverage of all kinds of Christian traditions there seems to lie that systematic exposition of Christ's sacrifice as the payment of the debt to God's honour, first expounded by Athanasius as a consistent summary of the gropings of the centuries.

---

[141] Or. XLV.22.

[142] See esp. Greg. Nys.' mystical interpretations of the Life of Moses and of the Song of Songs.

CHAPTER NINE
THE NATURE OF THE SACRIFICE OFFERED BY CHRIST

The whole of this section so far has been concerned with an analysis of the type of sin-offering made by Christ and how this fits into Atonement theory. That the death of Christ was the Christian sacrifice for sin "par excellence," is obvious. But it was affirmed that the whole of the Old Testament cultus was fulfilled in Christ. Was there any other sense in which Christ offered a sacrifice? Did Greek Christians think that he fulfilled the sacrifices of communion, or of praise and thanksgiving, in any way?

In seeking to answer this question, we have to remember that the analysis of types we have offered in this work was not necessarily conscious in the minds of the writers we have been studying. But, even so, when Christians claimed to imitate the sacrifice of Christ, they did not mean only his sacrifice for sin. In the case of the martyrs, for example, it was certainly Christ's sin-offering they imitated insofar as their death was expiatory, but their martyrdom was also an imitation of Christ's complete self-offering of obedience. The martyr's self-offering, as we have seen, was a holocaust, the supreme sacrifice of praise and worship. Logically, therefore, there must have been a sense in which Christ's sacrifice was one of worship and praise. Is there any evidence that Christians actually believed this?

There certainly is evidence at the end of our period. In Athanasius' thought there were two aspects of Christ's sacrifice. Firstly, there was the offering to death, the sacrifice which paid the debt to God's honour and freed mankind from death, sin and the devil. Then there was the presentation of his pure sinless body to the Father, a sacrifice offered in triumphant worship, as the thank-offering of a perfected humanity and the trophy of the victorious Logos. It was an act of worship offered by means of the achievement of perfect obedience to the will of God, and the reversal of the fatal disobedience of Adam. The High-Priestly function of Christ in heaven was concerned with the sacrificial offering of purified humanity, presented to the Father in the body of the Logos raised from the dead.[1]

This second aspect of Christ's offering is closely linked with the idea of θεοποίησις, the characteristically Athanasian idea of salvation. Humanity ascended to heaven in Christ, who was no mere substitute for men, but the perfect "Platonic" Form of mankind in which men could participate and be incorporated through the Spirit.[2] God accepts him, not in place of us, but because he sees us in him and accepts us through him.[3] By being σύσσωμοι with him, we are transformed εἰς ἄνδρα τέλειον.[4] The presence of the Logos in τὸ ἀνθρώπινον, purified it, sanctified it and made it fit to be offered to the Father as a new and perfect creature.[5]

So we find the two aspects of Christ's sacrifice in Athanasius correspond with the two aspects of his soteriology, outlined in the last chapter. First of all it is a sin-offering, a means of dealing with sin by payment of the debt to death; secondly it is an offering of worship to God in the ascension of perfected humanity to heaven and the life of God himself. We noted before that Origen also had a similar process of salvation, first the removal of sin, death and the evil powers by the sacrifice of aversion, and then the acceptance of purified humanity by God. Is there any evidence that he too understood this as a sacrifice of

---

[1]See esp. C. Ar. II.7ff, a very important passage on the High-Priesthood of Christ. Besides its importance for Athanasian studies, the ascension of Christ to heaven, as our High-Priest representing man to God eternally, became particularly prominent in the later commentaries on Heb., of which a considerable number of fragments are extant (see in particular that of Cyril Alex.). Much of later discussion can be seen in embryo in these ideas of Athanasius.

[2]See infra, Additional Note II.

[3]C. Ar., II.59.

[4]Ibid., II.75.

[5]See e.g., ibid., I.37-45; II.61, 70; etc.

worship, regarding perfect obedience as an offering of praise?

There is one passage in the Homilies on Leviticus where Origen makes exactly this distinction. He regards Christ's sacrifice on earth, that is, his death on the Cross, as a type of his heavenly sacrifice. In one Homily, he claims that the blood of Christ on the heavenly altar cleansed the sin of the heavenly beings, as the shedding of his blood on the Cross purified mankind on earth.[6] But in another, he makes a quite different distinction. The priest offered one bull on the altar as a holocaust "pro munere" and another as a sin-offering which was burned outside the camp. So, interpreting this allegorically, Christ offered a sacrifice on the heavenly altar "non pro peccato sed pro munere," but on earth, that is, outside the camp of heaven, where sin had reigned since Adam, he offered it for sin.[7] In this passage Christ's heavenly sacrifice is explicitly said to be a gift-sacrifice, a sacrifice of praise, worship and thanksgiving. Origen does not state this explicitly elsewhere, but he frequently refers to Christian sacrifices as an imitation of Christ, of martyrdom being a holocaust[8] (which he realised was a sacrifice of praise in the Old Testament, not an aversion sacrifice as in Greek tradition), of perfect obedience and imitation of Christ leading to the holy place,[9] and making the Christian a partaker in the divine sacrifice.[10] At this level, the sacrifice of Christ was the offering of perfect worship and obedience to God, the example for Christians to imitate. We have already seen that most of Christian spiritual sacrifices were sacrifices of praise, and particularly that the martyrdom of Polycarp was seen as the supreme act of worship.[11] Likewise the sacrifice of Christ was one of obedience

---

[6] Hom. Lev. I.3. [7] Ibid., II.3.

[8] Ibid., IX.9.

[9] Ibid., IX.2; XII.4; etc.

[10] Ibid., V.12.

[11] See supra, Ch. 6; also Origen, Ex. mart. 50: the martyr glorifies God by his death.

to God and glorification of him, as well as being the sacrifice which dealt with the problem of Man's sin.

However, this is certainly not the case in all the literature with which we are concerned. In some of the writings, the ascension of perfected humanity to heaven in Christ is not by any means considered a sacrifice of worship. Even in those we have mentioned, it is also part of the process of overcoming sin in human nature and restoring what had been lost through disobedience. So, in the *Epistle to the Hebrews*, Christ's achievement of obedience and his offering of his body in sacrifice were the means of purifying mankind, and nowhere is it suggested that this was the culmination of Man's worship of God.[12] At the other end of our period, the Gregories adopted Athanasius' ideas of θεοποίησις and the ascension of Man to God in Christ, but rarely did they describe Christ's offering of perfected humanity to the Father as a sacrifice of worship. When they spoke of Christian spiritual sacrifices being an imitation of Christ, they meant it in the sense of an imitation of his obedience and sinlessness, but they were shy of the idea that the obedience of Christ, who was God, was a sacrifice of praise to God. Gregory of Nyssa does speak on one occasion of Christ offering "his man" to the Father and drawing up with it the whole human race, but the sacrifice language is not unambiguous.[13]

So not all of the authors with whom we have been concerned, thought that Christ's sacrifice was a sacrifice of praise and worship. Still less is there any evidence that they thought that he offered any sort of communion sacrifice. Of course, the relationship between his sacrificial death and the Eucharist is a subtle one, and the Eucharist, as we shall see, was a communion-sacrifice. But his sacrifice, considered apart from the Church's cult-memorial of it, certainly was in no sense a communion-sacrifice.

So when the affirmation was made that the whole Law was fulfilled in Christ, this apparently did not

---

[12] *Heb.* 10.5-14, etc.

[13] *MPG* 46/628.

mean that his sacrifice was in some sense the fulfillment of all the types of sacrifice found in the Old Testament. To suppose that this statement implied this, would be to imagine the early Christians applying an analysis of the Old Testament cult such as we have made. It is true that Origen recognised distinctions of the kind we have used, but in general what we have been studying is a largely unconscious use of the sacrificial types inherited from their background religions. Besides this, the affirmation that all the Law was fulfilled in Christ, did not necessarily mean in his sacrificial death only; it meant within the New Covenant established by his sacrifice, including the life of his Body, the Church. The interrelation of Christ's sacrifice and the sacrifices of the Christians was very close, and to more detailed study of this, we shall turn in the following section.

In summary of our present section, we may say that the sacrifice of Christ was first and foremost God's way of dealing with sin, although, as we have seen, this was variously understood. It overshadowed all the other sacrifices for sin Christians might offer. In a sense, it was also the offering of supreme human worship and obedience. Usually, however, the broad distinction found in the _Epistle to the Hebrews_ applied: Christ had offered _the_ sin-offering, and the sacrifices offered by Christians were predominantly a response of praise and thanksgiving for this once for all saving act.[14]

---

[14]See _supra_, Ch. 6.

SECTION FOUR

THE RELATION BETWEEN CHRIST'S SACRIFICE AND THE SPIRITUAL SACRIFICES OFFERED BY CHRISTIANS

INTRODUCTION TO SECTION FOUR

So far we have discussed background influences on the formation of the Christians' spiritual cult and considered the nature of their sacrifices by analysis into current types; then, again by using analysis based on background types, we have considered the problems for Atonement theory of regarding the death of Christ as a sacrifice. It remains to try to indicate how the sacrifices of Christians were related to the sacrifice of their Lord and Master, especially since we have claimed that Christ's sacrifice was the focus of the whole spiritual cult of the Church.

In an earlier discussion, a broad distinction was made between the two: the sacrifice of Christ, we said, was the final, supreme and sufficient sin-offering, and the sacrifices offered by Christians were a response of praise and thanksgiving for that act of salvation. But this broad distinction is not satisfactory. We have already mentioned that Christians sought in their sacrifices to imitate the perfect self-offering of Christ; but how was it possible for Christians to imitate Christ's sacrifice, if the nature of their respective sacrifices was quite different? We have noticed earlier that Christians did offer certain sacrifices for sin, though we did not go further in our analysis of them; but how could Christians offer sacrifices for sin at all if Christ had already offered the full, perfect and sufficient sacrifice for the sins of the whole world?

Since the broad distinction suggested clearly does not apply with exactitude, this section is devoted to an examination of the complex and intimate relation that existed between Christ's sacrificial work and the sacrifices offered by the Church. In the first chapter, Christian sin-offerings are analysed, and the problem of their relationship with the death of Christ is discussed. In the second, we examine the nature of the characteristic Christian sacrifice, the Eucharist, which had a particularly close relationship with the sacrificial death of Christ while being a sacrifice offered by the Christians themselves. Finally, Chapter Twelve presents a brief summary of the complex relationship between the whole spiritual cult of the Church and the sacrificial activity of the perfect High-Priest, its founder.

CHAPTER TEN
MARTYRDOM AND OTHER CHRISTIAN SIN-OFFERINGS IN RELATION TO THE SACRIFICE OF CHRIST

In our earlier analysis of Christian spiritual sacrifices we noticed that certain sacrifices were not analysable as sacrifices of praise and thanksgiving, but were clearly regarded as sin-offerings.[1] Among these were repentance and almsgiving, works of penance and, above all, martyrdom. In this chapter, we are concerned to ask what type of sin-offerings these were, sacrifices of expiation, aversion or propitiation; and then to ask how it was possible that Christians could offer sacrifices for sin at all if Christ had already made the one perfect and sufficient sacrifice for the sins of the whole world. In both cases, martyrdom will inevitably dominate the discussion, since it raises in an extreme form the question of the relation of Christian sin-offerings to the sacrifice of Christ.

A. Analysis of Christian Sin-offerings into Types

(a) The Expiatory Sacrifice of the Martyr

We have seen that the death of Christ in the New Testament was an *expiatory* sacrifice for sin. St. Paul's use of the idea of expiatory suffering is mostly in close association with the death of Christ; for example, his desire to "complete what is lacking in Christ's afflictions."[2] This suggests that the martyr's suffering, where it appears in his writings, is expiatory as in the Jewish tradition, and exactly analogous to the type of sin-offering made by Christ.

However, Ignatius' language is less easily explained. We have already noticed that the character-

---

[1]See *supra*, Ch. 6. [2]*Col*. 1.24.

istic word he uses is ἀντίψυχον.[3] What did he mean by this? It is clear that he used it of the martyr's sacrificial death which he was himself about to die,[4] but how did he think this sacrifice worked? Ignatius himself offers no passages which can explain his understanding of the word, but since he seems to have used it in a similar way to IV Maccabees, and may possibly have known that work, it will be possible to throw light on his understanding of it by looking more closely at its meaning there.[5] In Chapter II, the Maccabees' concept of suffering for the sins of the nation was explained as being expiatory like the Old Testament sacrifices, without much discussion. For our present purposes, however, it is necessary to look more closely at the contexts in which IV Maccabees uses the idea of sacri-

---

[3]See supra, Ch. 5B9b); Eph. 21.1; Smyrn. 10.2; Pol. 2.3, 6.1.

[4]Lightfoot in his commentary does not regard ἀντίψυχον as necessarily a reference to Ignatius' martyrdom; but it seems most likely, in view of other passages in Ignatius, that he did mean his vicarious martyr's death, esp. if the connection with 4 Mac. is valid. Lightfoot was not aware of the possibility of such a connection.

[5]It has been argued, on the basis of similarities in vocabulary, style and content, that Ignatius was directly dependent on 4 Mac. See O. Perler, "Das vierte Makkabäerbuch, Ignatius von Antiochen und die ältesten Martyrerberichte," in Rivista di archeologia cristiana (1949). He also argues that 4 Mac. influenced 1 Clem., the Martyrdom of Polycarp, and the account of the martyrs at Vienne. There is no reason why this should not be so if 4 Mac. is dated prior to the Fall of the Temple in 70 A.D. (see M. Hadas, The Third and Fourth Books of the Maccabees; the same date is assumed by Perler and by Frend in his Martyrdom and Persecution in the Early Church). However, it should be noted that some would date the book in the 2nd cy. A.D. In discussing ἀντίψυχον, one of the contacts of vocabulary, Perler points out that Ignatius ignores λύτρον and ἀντίλυτρον and similar words which appear in the NT and uses instead ἀντίψυχον, which is a very rare word.

ficial ranson or substitution, since many passages seem to imply a propitiatory understanding.

Two passages are particularly important for this discussion,[6] and in both, it is God who produces the expiatory effect of the martyr's sacrifice. In one passage, God is said to have sanctified the martyrs, so making them suitably pure to be sacrificial victims. It was through the blood of these righteous ones and the expiation-ἱλαστήριον- of their death, that the land was purified and divine providence preserved Israel. In this context they are said to have been made an ἀντίψυχον for the sin of the nation. In the other passage, the martyr prays that God will be merciful and accept his punishment for the sake of his people, that he will make his blood an expiation and take his life as an ἀντίψυχον for theirs.

Taking these two passages together, it is clear that God was thought to be the source of the expiation, the agent who used the blood of the martyrs to cleanse the people. But the persecution was the result of his divine wrath against the sins of the people, just as the exile had been centuries earlier. The martyrs hoped to bring the effects of the divine wrath to an end by putting themselves in the position in which God could use the offering of their faith and lives to expiate the sin of the nation. The martyr's life was laid down for the sake of the people, as God's means of purifying the nation and ending the need to punish it for its sin. The life was offered in exchange for the life of the sinner who should have suffered in punishment, and in a sense it was offered to God. But it was also a life hallowed and purified by God in order to bring about expiation. It was not straightforwardly offered as a placatory sacrifice to win round a crudely offended deity, but it was a willing self-sacrifice offered in accordance with the will and purpose of a Providence which used this way to save the people. Admittedly, the life of the martyr was offered to God as a ransom and substitute for the life of the

---

[6]4 Mac. 17.20-22 & 6.28-9. For the text, see supra, Ch. 2, n. 122.

sinner; but this idea of substitution does not simply imply that a propitiatory theory of sacrifice is involved here, even though the texts sometimes suggest this. As we have already seen, the language of ransom or substitution tended to be interpreted in terms of the idea of sacrifice used by a particular author; on the one hand, Origen links Christ's aversion sacrifice with the idea of a ransom offered to the devil, while on the other hand, Eusebius rationalised sacrifice as the offering of a ransom or substitute for one's own life to propitiate the wrath of God.[7] In the IV Maccabees passages, we must see the substitution as linked with an expiatory sacrifice, offered so that God could use this method of purifying the sins of those for whom the sacrifice was offered. The general outlook of the passages indicates this, and appeal to the use of ἱλαστήριον, (noted above), does not undermine this argument. ἱλαστήριον must be understood in an expiatory sense as in the New Testament.

If we are right to interpret Ignatius in the light of the IV Maccabees passages, it is chiefly in expiatory terms that we must understand his sacrifice. He was sanctified and offered as a ransom so that God could use this method of expiating the sin of the Church. His martyr's death was understood in terms of the Jewish tradition as an expiatory sacrifice, efficacious for the purification of the sins of those for whom he suffered and died.

To some extent, the idea that the martyr's suffering was expiatory persisted throughout our period. Through his death, the martyr could obtain forgiveness of his own sins at least; his death was a Baptism in blood, which could replace Baptism in water if he were still a catechumen, or expiate his post-baptismal sins if he was a Baptised Christian.[8] Besides this, at any

---

[7]See *supra*, Ch. 8B-C.

[8]Cyril of Jerusalem, *Cat. Orat*. III.10: There is no salvation without baptism, except that martyrs receive the Kingdom without water; Origen, *In Matt. Comm. Ser*. 30: while there is no remission of sins without baptism, we have been given a baptism in blood.

rate in popular devotion, the martyr or confessor was supposed to be able to mediate forgiveness to others, and this idea may well have been based on the same tradition as that which led Ignatius to believe that his martyr's death could expiate the sins of the Church.[9] However, the Church officially repudiated this view when faced by the claims of confessors that they were able to readmit the lapsed wholesale to full communion, without the discipline of penance normally required.[10] Nevertheless, this tradition did not entirely disappear; Gregory of Nyssa in a sermon on Stephen, suggests that, as a priest, he offered his own body in sacrifice and obtained forgiveness for his murderers.[11] In most of our period, however, the predominant interpretation of the martyr's sacrifice was in terms of aversion sacrifices.

(b) Martyrdom as Aversion Sacrifice

As Origen explained the death of Christ by using the analogy of human sacrifices offered in Greek tradition to avert evils, so *I Clement* used the same analogy to describe the sacrifice of the martyr.[12] The tradition of Christianity was that the martyr shared in Christ's warfare against the devil and his angels; it was in fear of worshipping the daemons and entering into idolatrous communion with them that the martyrs refused to offer sacrifice, a fact which shows that they thought of their opposition to idolatry and the devil in quite literal terms.[13] It was the Adversary

---

[9]That this was part of the continuous tradition from Jewish martyr-theology is implied by Frend, op. cit., p. 364.

[10]The conflict between the Confessors and the hierarchy over this is apparent, not only in the churches of North Africa where, in spite of Cyprian's early success in solving the problem, it led eventually to the Donatist schism, but also in the church in Egypt where it was one important cause of the Meletian schism.

[11]*MPG* 46/712. [12]*I Clement* 45.

[13]For the martyrs' opposition to idolatry, see *supra*, Ch. 4B.

or the Anti-Christ which caused the persecutions in the hope of persuading Christians to apostatise. The surest way of overcoming the devil was to confess God and die for him.[14] In the person of the suffering martyr, his body wracked from endless tortures, "Christ accomplished most glorious things, utterly defeating the adversary . . ."[15] Blandina is described as "a small, weak, despised woman who had put on Christ, the great invincible champion and in bout after bout defeated her adversary, and through conflict had won the crown of immortality."[16]

These examples are sufficient to show that the martyr's conflict with authority and paganism was conceived in the dualist framework that lay behind the Classic theory, and that the martyr was regarded as participating in the battle against the devil in which Christ had been victorious on the Cross. The martyr was in Christ and Christ was in the martyr, as he braved the tortures of war with the opposing forces.

The martyr's sacrifice has to be seen then in the context of this same dualist picture, and it would not be surprising to find that, like the death of the greatest martyr, Christ, his sacrifice should be interpreted as a means of averting the evil daemons. Clement's use of the analogy with the death of patriotic pagan citizens to avert plague etc., suggests that this was the kind of terms in which the sacrifice could be understood. Origen's _Exhortation to Martyrdom_ confirms this, which is hardly surprising, since we found he was the chief exponent of the aversion sacrifice as a means of understanding the atoning death of Christ. Origen exhorts his readers to persevere in the war against the daemons, insisting that idolatry is the only alternative to martyrdom.[17] He describes as the

---

[14]See the _Martyrdom of Polycarp_, esp. XVII.1; the account of the Martyrs at Vienne in Eusebius, _Eccl. Hist_. V.1; and Origen, _C. Cels_. VII.17, VIII.44. For discussion, see Frend, op. cit., p. 15ff.

[15]Eusebius, op. cit., V.1.23.

[16]Ibid., V.1.42.

[17]Origen, _Exhortation_ 32ff and _passim_.

rewards of martyrdom, the attaining of sinlessness and the bliss of heaven.[18] But he also describes the atoning value of the martyr's sacrifice,[19] and sets before him the joy of imitating and participating in the sufferings of Christ.[20] The work of the martyr in Christ consists in despoiling with him the principalities and powers and triumphing with him, by partaking in his sufferings and the great deeds accomplished in his sufferings.[21] For "it may be that as we have been purchased by the precious blood of Jesus . . ., so some will be ransomed by the precious blood of martyrs . . ."[22] The martyr's sacrifice is exactly analogous to the sacrifice of Christ and therefore to be interpreted as the same kind of sacrifice - that is, in the case of Origen, as a sacrifice offered as a ransom to avert the power of the evil one, as part of the warfare against the devil in which Christ had already won the ultimate victory. Like Christ, the martyr glorified God simply by his willing self-sacrifice to the cause of dealing with the sin and evil of the world.[23]

The tradition that the Christians fought the daemons in their self-oblation in martyrdom continued throughout our period, and is expressed by Gregory of Nazianzus very forcibly when he accuses Julian of having promised a few Christians to the daemons as a sacrifice.[24] But by this later period, actual martyrdom for the faith was rare, and it had largely been replaced by the idea of complete devotion of one's life

---

[18]Ibid., 14ff.

[19]Ibid., 30. Cf. Comm. Jn. VI32ff: The OT sacrifices were types of the sacrifice of the martyrs as well as of Christ. See also Comm. Rom. II.14.

[20]Ibid., 12ff.

[21]Ibid., 42; cf. Comm. Jn. VI.36.

[22]Ibid., 50. [23]Ibid.

[24]Greg. Naz., Or. V.26. On the martyrs' fight against the devil, see Or. XXIV.10, 18-19 and Or. XV; Greg. Nys., In S. Steph., MPG 46/704, 712; In 40 Mart. MPG 46/780.

to the service of God in the acceptance of voluntary poverty and monasticism. This, too, was part of the warfare against the devil, since every successful refusal to succumb to temptation was a reverse for the forces of evil. This idea is particularly graphically expressed in Athanasius' account of Antony's constant confrontations with the opposing powers. Overcoming one's personal sin was part of this process of averting the evil power, as well as being a spiritual sacrifice of praise and worship offered to God.[25]

(c) Christian Propitiatory Sacrifices

Although, as Eusebius makes clear, persecutions were occasionally regarded as produced by the wrath of God against the Church,[26] and although the martyr's death was regarded as a sacrifice both to expiate sin and to present himself to God as a complete self-offering, yet the idea of propitiating God by means of martyrdom is rarely expressed. Rather martyrdom was popularly conceived as following Christ to the final extremity in the war against the devil and sin, confessing a God on whose side they fought, not trying to win round an offended deity whose wrath was displayed in the hostility of the imperial government.

That Christian sacrifices for sin, like penance and almsgiving, voluntary poverty and other Christian virtues, were regarded as propitiatory is, however, clear. When Chrysostom is faced with Hebrews' uncompromising statement that after Baptism there is no further sacrifice for sins, he replies that the author does not take away repentance, nor "the propitiation which is obtained through repentance."[27] Although in one passage Chrysostom says that this medicine is given to us by the grace of God,[28] in another, he exhorts

---

[25]Besides Athanasius' Vita Antonii, see Greg. Naz., Or. XI.4-7; Greg. Nys., De perf., MPG 46/252ff., esp. 260-1; and De inst. Chr., MPG 46/288ff, esp. 300-1.

[26]E.G., Eusebius, op. cit., VIII.1.

[27]Hom. Heb. XX.

[28]Ibid., IX. In this homily he defines repentance as condemnation of one's own sins, intense tears, con-

his hearers to wipe away their sins and amend their lives, for "we must first cleanse ourselves and then God cleanses us."[29] God will only give the cleansing power of his grace after men have repented and amended their lives; these efforts are required to propitiate him before his grace is vouchsafed to men.

In a sense, however, this idea of propitiating God by repentance has received transformation in the same way as Origen's idea of propitiation. Genuine repentance is not an arbitrary gift given to God to try to buy off his anger; it is part of the process of reformation. This is seen clearly in a sermon of Gregory of Nazianzus.[30] He is concerned with a demonstration of divine anger that had recently occurred in the form of a hailstorm which ruined all the crops and caused extensive damage. That this had been caused by an offended providence in punishment of the sins of the community, he does not doubt. His sermon is a call to his hearers to search out the cause, the local sin that had brought down on their heads the wrath of God. He speaks of this display of divine wrath in Origenist terms as a chastisement for the good of the people, not an emotional reaction of hostility. He warns the people not to feel cosy in God's love thinking no harm will come to them. God's love is punishment, training, education, correction.[31] Gregory tells the congregation to learn their lesson. To prevent further plagues, they should recognise that they had sinned, that God was angry, and they should repent and reform; they should die with Christ so that they could rise again to his perfection.[32] In this context, he does not hesitate to use the vocabulary of propitiation, of prayer for mercy, of pleading that God will not give them up for ever, but chastise them in his goodness not in anger.[33] He exhorts his hearers to propitiate God

---

tinual prayers, etc., followed by amendment of life, almsgiving, not being angry, forgiving others, etc. This is similar to Origen's list of possible Christian sacrifices for sin.

[29]Hom. Heb. XII. [30]Or. XVI.

[31]See Or. XVI.6. [32]Ibid., 11. [33]Ibid., 12.

with ὁλοκαυτώματα and θυσίαι, to spare no efforts which could make God merciful.[34] That we have here the idea of propitiating God's wrath is clear, though certain elements of Christian tradition have considerably modified the cruder placatory version. Firstly, God's wrath is not arbitrary, but associated with just punishment for moral sin; it is rationalised according to the "discipline" view of Origen. Secondly, what is offered to placate this wrath is not a gift to gratify the supposed tastes of God, but a real answer to the reason for the wrath, namely repentance and the endeavor to reform. The spiritual sacrifices offered to propitiate the God of the Christians are the virtues, the absence of which caused the righteous anger of God.

We shall find that it is in this later period that ideas of propitiation enter discussion of the meaning of the Eucharist,[35] as well as the Homilies of Chrysostom and Gregory of Nazianzus. We saw earlier that these ideas had probably always had a place in popular theology, in spite of Origen's influence. The existence of these ideas in Christianity must be largely attributed to the association of the Jewish prophetic tradition of God's wrath against sin with the pagan idea of propitiating the gods by means of sacrifice. The pagan ideas have been very much modified by being brought into relation with the concept of God as the Righteous Judge and the ultimate means of salvation, by an interpretation of his anger in terms of love, and by the spiritualising of the sacrifices offered to propitiate him. It is perhaps of considerable significance that even though Christians thought God had to be propitiated for moral sins by moral reformation, the bloody sacrifice of the martyr was not regarded as propitiatory, but as partaking in God's warfare against the presence of evil in the world.

(d) Conclusion

We have found evidence for the use of each of the

---

[34]Ibid., 13.

[35]This will be discussed further in the following chapter.

various types of sin-offering outlined in our background study, to explain the sacrifices which Christians were able to offer for their personal sins and for the sins of others. As in the case of the supreme sacrifice for sin offered by Christ, interpretation of these sin-offerings developed from simple acceptance of expiatory significance in the New Testament and the earlier part of our period, to the later adoption of more detailed explanations which used the notions of aversion and propitiation. So the types used to explain Christian sin-offerings are parallel to those used of the perfect sacrifice offered by Christ for the sins of the whole world; each type is used of both Christian sacrifices and the sacrifice of Christ by the same authors, the development of the use of the various types being exactly concurrent. For example, it is in the works of Origen that aversion sacrifices are used to explain Christ's death and the deaths of the martyrs, and it is in the later, less sophisticated works of Chrysostom that propitiation ideas are so prominently used of both Christ's sacrifice and Christian works of penance.

Since the same types of sacrifice are used to interpret both the Church's spiritual sin-offerings and Christ's perfect and sufficient sacrifice for the sins of men, our second question is raised the more acutely: how was it possible for Christians to offer sacrifices for sin when Christ had already made the one and only sufficient sacrifice for all?

B. The Relationship of Christian Sin-offerings to the All-sufficient Sacrifice of Christ

One reason why it was possible for Christians to offer sacrifices for sin in spite of belief in the all-sufficiency of the death of Christ was mentioned in Chapter V: it was only in Baptism that a man received the benefits of Christ's sacrifice, and thereafter he was expected to sin no more. So inevitably post-baptismal sin became a major problem for the Church. This does, of course, imply some qualification of the sufficiency of Christ's sacrifice; it was sufficient for the sins of all mankind in their unredeemed state, but once the benefits had been accepted, it could no longer atone for sins caused by the weakness of Christians in living up to their ideals, and their failure to embody the character of the new creation in Christ which they were supposed to have become. Origen recognised that without some means of atoning for post-baptismal sin, men were doomed to despair,[36] and the problem led inevitably to the establishment of the penitential system.

Both martyrdom and the propitiatory sin-offerings could deal with this problem. As a second Baptism in blood, martyrdom was a particularly efficacious means of wiping out one's personal post-baptismal sins: and the propitiatory offerings of repentance and works of penance were clearly intended as additional sacrifices to God to propitiate him for sins committed after the benefits of Christ's sacrifice had been received.

Indeed, this was the only real connection between Christ's sacrifice and Christian propitiatory offerings, for in no sense were they an imitation of or participation in Christ's sacrifice. The relationship between Christ's sacrifice and martyrdom, on the other hand, was much more intimate. "Allow me to imitate the Passion of my God," begged Ignatius, as he went to Rome to suffer martyrdom.[37] Throughout our period, imitation of Christ was most important. To follow the path of his humility and endurance, his love and chastity, his sinlessness, was the ethical ideal which for centuries found its ultimate consummation in martyrdom, and, at the end of our period when persecutions had largely ceased and the Church was dominant, in voluntary poverty and monasticism.[38] We have already noticed

---

[36]Origen, Hom. Lev. II.4. [37]Rom. VI.3.

[38]Clem. Alex., Strom. IV, On Martyrdom, concentrates on the martyr's attainment of scorn of death, of sinlessness and passionlessness in imitation of God: IV.4. 9. 16, 22-3. In the works of the two Gregories, the imitation of Christ is particularly pro-

that this imitation of Christ was the height of spiritual worship and a sacrifice of praise and thanksgiving; it became an effort to imitate and participate in Christ's sacrificial gift of perfected humanity to the Father. The Christian shared in his sufferings, becoming like him in his death.[39] But, this imitation of Christ was also an imitation of his sacrificial self-offering for the sins of men. Expiatory martyrdom imitated the expiatory sacrifice offered by Christ, though it was a mere reflection of that all-embracing sacrifice for sin. The ultimate aim of the monk's ethical strivings and the martyr's self-offering to death became a participation in the battle Christ had in principle won on the Cross against evil in all its forms. It was an imitation of his aversion sacrifice, his offering himself as a ransom to the devil.

But we have already gone beyond language of imitation. The Christian aim was to participate in the saving work of Christ. The Church felt a sense of call to carry on Christ's work as his Body on earth, and this is why imitation of Christ's all-sufficient sacrifice was possible. It was not an independent sacrifice for sin which the martyr offered; it did not conflict with the claim that Christ's sacrifice was perfect. It was an entering into Christ's own sacrificial work. It was not merely a practical means of dealing with post-baptismal sin, but a self-offering intimately related to Christ's sacrifice as an imitation of and participation in it.

---

minent; see Greg. Naz., *Or.* XV. and Greg. Nys. *In. S. Steph.*, *MPG* 46/704, 712. Greg. Naz. speaks of the Christian priest imitating the priesthood of Christ (*Or.* II.54, 73) and frequently of the Christian's aim to imitate Christ: e.g., *Or.* XI.6; XIV.4, 15, 25-6; XVII.9; XXIV.2; XXXVIII.18. Greg. Nys. uses this idea specifically in the *De perf.*, where he defines perfection as imitation of the divine nature (*MPG* 46/252-285), concentrating particularly on the imitation of the divine qualities of Christ, the perfect man, and his achievement of sinlessness through temptation (46/272,277).

[39] *Phil.* 3.10.

It is in these terms that Paul's difficult expression in his Epistle to the Colossians must be understood: "Now I rejoice in my sufferings for your sake, and in my flesh I complete what is lacking in Christ's afflictions for the sake of his Body the Church, of which I have become a minister."[40] This verse highlights the problem with which we are concerned; how can anything be lacking in Christ's sufferings if his sacrifice was a full, perfect and sufficient sacrifice for the sins of the whole world? Actually, there is no explicit inconsistency in Paul's writings, since he, unlike the author of the Epistle to the Hebrews, never definitely states the all-sufficiency of Christ's sacrifice for sin; however, it is very surprising that he should dare to imply that there was anything lacking in Christ's sufferings for the Church in view of his insistence that only faith in the blood of Christ is necessary for salvation. How then is this verse to be understood? The word Paul actually uses is ὑστερήματα, and a suggestion that goes a long way to explaining the problem is that while the death of Christ was really sufficient, there was at least a small part left over which his followers could play in the redemption of the world, namely to suffer in the drive to spread the Gospel of salvation to all mankind. Christ himself had warned the disciples that they would be persecuted for his sake, and for Paul, this is part of the joy of discipleship, that the minister of Christ enters into afflictions, like his Master, for the sake of establishing his Body, the Church. But for Paul it is more than that. It is so much a partaking of the Lord's own sufferings that the disciple can feel he contributes to the saving effect of the Lord's passion by accepting afflictions as Christ did for the sake of preaching the Gospel and building the Church. Within the context of Pauline ideas, this text must be treated as his expression of gratitude for the privilege, not only of dying to sin with Christ in Baptism, but also of participating in Christ's sufferings for the redemption of the world.

---

[40] Col. 1.24.

That this idea of sharing in Christ's sufferings remained part of the Christian martyr-tradition is shown by the language of the accounts of martyrdom. Christ works in and through the martyr, and the martyr not only imitates, but "puts on Christ."[41] Origen naturally speaks of partaking in Christ's sufferings,[42] and Chrysostom of having communion in his sufferings.[43]

In summary, we may say that all the Christian sin-offerings were concerned with the problem of post-baptismal sin; that the propitiatory offerings were solely concerned with this, while the expiatory and aversion sacrifice of the martyr and the monk was an actual entering into Christ's work of salvation. The Christian, in the latter case, did not offer a different sacrifice, but fought the powers of evil and sin with Christ, by conquering personal temptation, by suffering for the spread of the Gospel and by dying for his faith. This is how it was possible for the Church to put the sacrifice of Christ in the center of its spiritual cult and call upon Christians to imitate it, even though they maintained that his sacrifice had been all-sufficient for dealing with the problem of the sin of mankind. The Christian not only responded to Christ's sin-offering by giving spiritual sacrifices of praise and thanksgiving, but also participated in his sacrificial work by imitating his self-offering for the sin of the world.

C. Conclusion

Since, as we have seen, the martyr's sacrifice was consistently regarded as an imitation of Christ's sacrifice, the type of sacrifice whereby it was understood must be significant also for understanding his

---

[41] Eusebius, op. cit., V.1, 20, 42.

[42] E.g., Exhortation, 42.

[43] E.g., Hom. Heb. XXXIII.

sacrifice. The martyr's death never appears as a propitiatory sacrifice in the documents representing the Greek Church tradition, but is consistently regarded as a sharing in Christ's battle with the powers of evil and, as such, is often explicitly interpreted as a sacrifice or ransom offered to avert the power of the devil and his hosts. In the light of this finding, we may conclude that the aversion sacrifice was not used only by Origen to understand Christ's sacrifice, but was far more common than has so far appeared; in fact, we suggest that it was more important than the propitiatory view of his death, though the latter certainly was not absent from popular theology and clearly predominated at the end of our period.

This chapter has shown clearly that Christ's sacrifice was the focus of the Christian spiritual cult; the ultimate Christian sacrifice was an imitation of and participation in his sacrifice, by living a life and dying a death that was worthy of his example and assisted in his work of salvation. In the next chapter, we shall find that the central act of Christian worship was also intimately bound up with the sacrificial death of Christ.

CHAPTER ELEVEN
THE SACRIFICE OF THE EUCHARIST

We have already mentioned several times that the characteristic cult-act of the Christian religious society was the fellowship-meal of the Eucharist. Malachi had prophesied that a pure sacrifice would be offered in every place and God's name would be honoured among the Gentiles,[1] and this text was frequently applied to the Eucharist. It provided proof that the Eucharistic sacrifice had replaced the sacrifices of the Jews for the author of the *Didache*, Justin, Irenaeus, Tertullian and Hippolytus. This fact is sufficient to show that the Eucharist was consistently regarded as a sacrifice. But in what sense was it a sacrifice? What kind of sacrifice was presupposed in the belief and action of the Church? Does our analysis into types throw any light on developing ideas about the Eucharist?

It is particularly important to examine these questions, since failure to distinguish the types of sacrifice involved has led to some confusion. Lietzmann's analysis of the various liturgies in *Messe und Herrenmahl* certainly did make use of some distinctions between kinds of sacrifice.[2] On the other hand, in *The Shape of the Liturgy*, Dix confused certain types, assuming that the Eucharist was only a fully sacrificial action as something offered to God in adoration, thanksgiving, petition and propitiation,[3] while regarding the communion as not strictly a part of the sacrifice.[4] Clearly analysis needs to be more careful, in the light of our study so far. The first part of this chapter is therefore devoted to an examination of

---

[1] *Malachi* 1.11.14.

[2] See, e.g., his treatment of the liturgies of Hippolytus and Serapion.

[3] See *infra*, Ch. 11 at n. 17.

[4] See *infra*, Ch. 11 at n. 41.

the use of different types of sacrifice to understand the Eucharist.

One of the main reasons why the nature of the Eucharistic sacrifice is so difficult to grasp is its close relationship with the sacrificial death of Christ. It was a sacrifice in its own right, offered to God by the Christian Church, and yet at the same time it came to be regarded as a sacrifice only insofar as it was a memorial or re-enactment of Christ's sacrifice. This intimate relationship will be examined in the second part of this chapter.

A. Analysis of the Eucharist into Types

In our analysis of the Christian spiritual cult in Chapter VI, we classified the Eucharist under communion-sacrifices, and suggested that both types of communion-sacrifice distinguished in Chapter III may have been involved in the interpretation of the Eucharist. Communion-sacrifices are therefore discussed first. But our other main categories of sacrifice were also used of the Eucharist; so we go on to consider the Eucharist as a gift-sacrifice of praise and thanksgiving, and as a sin-offering. We may also note here that two of the typological motifs used of Christ's sacrifice (discussed in Chapter VII), were applied to the Eucharist as well, namely, the Passover and the Covenant-sacrifice. These "types" will be treated incidentally in this analysis, but are clearly important in considering the relationship between the Eucharist and Christ's sacrifice.

(a) The Eucharist as a Communion-Sacrifice

Although it is possible to make conjectures about the primitive Eucharistic celebrations from later sources, the earliest discussion of the sacrificial significance of this central Christian cult-act appears in the writings of Paul. Paul quite clearly regards the Eucharist as a communion-sacrifice of the zebach/θυσία type.

Paul discusses the Eucharist in only one Epistle, and here it is raised in the first place by the problem of whether or not it is permissible to eat idol-meat.[5] As we have already seen, Paul rules on this problem that if a Christian does not know whether the meat has been offered to idols or not, he need raise no question of conscience, but if he takes part in what is obviously a religious festival, or if he knows that his pagan host at a dinner-party has offered the meat in sacrifice, then he is committing the sin of apostasy. This is because, by joining in the meal, he allows himself to be in communion with the daemons. The pagan religious festivals of communion are parallel to the Christian sacrificial meal, and it is impossible to enter into communion with both Christ and the daemons. Jewish sacrifices make the worshippers "sharers in the altar" and pagan sacrifices establish communion with the daemons; the Christian meal likewise establishes sacrificial communion with the Lord.

In this passage, Paul also emphasizes that it is one loaf of which all partake, and in the following chapter, it is the unity implied by communion in the one loaf that is his main point. He has now turned to the problem of divisions and splinter-groups in the Church. The Church is one Body, and it shares in one loaf. Unity is implicit in the meal of fellowship. In the second passage, Paul also emphasizes the dangers of eating the bread unworthily. His insistence on the need for purity in those who partake is an additional indication that Paul regarded the Eucharist as a communion-sacrifice, a zebach, for which ritual purity was required.[6]

---

[5]1 _Cor_. 10. Ch. 11 also discusses the Eucharist, but in a different context.

[6]Ritual purity was required of all OT sacrifices except the sin-offering, but it is clear that Paul means a sacrifice in which the worshippers partook, i.e., he must mean a _zebach_. The Greek _thusia_, which, as we have seen, was parallel to the _zebach_, also required ritual purity.

Paul's discussion therefore shows unambiguously that he regarded the Eucharist as exactly analogous to the Jewish and Greek communion-sacrifices in which the worshippers shared in a fellowship-meal with the god. Purity was required of those who partook of this sacred meal, because they were eating in the presence of the deity. This interpretation of the Eucharist probably arose from the primitive Christian belief that it was a foretaste of the eschatological feast of heaven, at which the Risen Lord was present in fellowship with his disciples.[7] Perhaps the Aramaic prayer "Maranatha" was primarily a request that the Lord come and share the feast with them, as the unseen host.[8]

---

[7]Dix (op. cit.) and Lietzmann (op. cit.) argue that the Eucharist was the continuation of the *haburah* meals of fellowship which the disciples had enjoyed during Jesus' life; the risen Christ continued to be present with them. Insofar as this depends on the *haburah*-theory of Eucharistic origins, it is open to dispute, but the presence of the Risen Lord in fellowship at the Eucharist seems to be expressed in Luke's post-resurrection narrative of the meal at Emmaus, where the Lord is recognized by the characteristic action of blessing and breaking bread (*Lk*. 24.30-1). The eschatological character of the Eucharist seems to be assured. In the parables of our Lord, the image of the feast is used of the establishment of the Messianic Kingdom, and the feeding-stories seem to have been understood as anticipations of the feast of the Kingdom. Luke introduces a "feast parable" with the words: "Blessed is he that eats bread in the Kingdom of God" (*Lk*. 14.15), and his account of the Last Supper contains strongly eschatological sayings (*Lk*. 22.16, 18). The analogous cult-meal of the Qumran community seems also to have been an anticipation of the Messianic feast. See K. G. Kuhn, *The Lord's Supper and the Communal Meal at Qumran* (London, 1958).

[8]Paul preserves the Aramaic phrase in 1 *Cor*. 16. 22.

But even in Paul's treatment of the Eucharist another communion-element is present, and it is this which predominates in later understanding of the Eucharist. Because the communicants eat the bread and wine which represents the body and blood of Christ, they are partaking in supernatural food, spiritual food; they are participating in Christ himself. In the New Testament, this idea is most forcibly expressed in the discussion found in John 6, but it is already present in this passage of St. Paul. Our problem is whether this form of communion is to be regarded as sacrificial, because, if so, the only background type that could possibly throw light on it, is the "Dionysiac" type of sacrifice in which the worshippers partook of the nature of the god himself. This conclusion would force us to accept the theories of some scholars that the Eucharist underwent a drastic change when it was Hellenised; that Paul was responsible for turning it into something analogous to the pagan mysteries; and that the traditions of the Last Supper were moulded into an aetiological myth to explain the Christian mystery.[9]

---

[9]Bultmann (Theology of the New Testament, I, p. 148ff) thinks that Paul follows a development that had already occurred in Hellenistic Christianity. He regards the re-enactment of Christ's death in the symbols of bread and wine as influenced by the mystery-cult drama of the dying and rising god, and assumes a "Dionysiac" type of communion in his interpretation of Paul's discussion of communion-sacrifices. This follows the lines of others who have differentiated between two kinds of Eucharist in the NT, distinguishing the primitive "breaking of bread" from the sacramental mystery found in Paul. The most notable exposition of this theory is Lietzmann's Messe und Herrenmahl, but unlike Bultmann, he regarded Paul as the author of the new interpretation. By such scholars, the Hellenistic mystery religions are regarded as the background for such new developments in the Christian cult-act, and the Institution narrative is considered to be a later invention--an aetiological cult-myth.

It seems most likely from Paul's discussion of it that in origin the idea of spiritual food being imparted in the Eucharist was not sacrificial, and not to be associated with the theophagy type of sacrifice. His treatment of the Eucharistic elements follows analogies in Jewish history and religion, not Hellenistic forms. The Eucharistic elements are supernatural food, like the manna and the water provided by God when the Israelites were in the wilderness. Just as the Christian has been delivered by Christ, then baptised, and now eats supernatural food and drink, so the Jew had been delivered from Egypt, had been baptized by the crossing of the Red Sea, and had eaten the supernatural food of the manna and drunk supernatural water provided by the Rock (which, Paul says, was Christ). Paul's point is that when the Israelites in such an analogous situation worshipped idols, God had been provoked to jealousy, and he warns that so it will be for the Christian who consciously partakes in communion festivals with the daemons; but the importance of this passage for our argument, is that Jewish "types" are used to describe the supernatural food of the Eucharist.

So far, in Paul's discussion, the supernatural food and drink of which the manna and Rock were "types," had not been identified with the body and blood of Christ, and there are no grounds for thinking that the idea of supernatural food came from the Greek "Dionysiac" type of sacrifice. But, in his discussion of the communion-sacrifices, Paul does speak of participation in the blood of Christ and in the body of Christ, and this has led some scholars to assume that the communion with the daemons implies communion in the deity by theophagy.[10] This assumption is almost certainly mistaken.[11] In the first place, Paul uses

---

[10]See Bultmann, loc. cit.

[11]I find that Rawlinson, in his essay entitled "Corpus Christi," in Bell and Diesmann (ed.), Mysterium Christi (London, 1930), p. 229, states that Paul's allusion is not to the mysteries but to the εἰδωλόθυτα, i.e., the normal pagan sacrifices. My following argument shows this in greater detail.

not only the analogy of the pagan communion-sacrifices, but also the Jewish idea that those who sacrificed were in communion with the "altar" (a synonym for God, commonly used in contemporary Judaism to avoid unworthy reference to the transcendent deity); this indicates that it is the zebach/θυσία type of sacrifice to which he is referring. Secondly, Paul's other passage, where he stresses the unity of the loaf, suggests not a sacrificial communion of the "Dionysiac" type in which the individual is empowered by participation in the nature of the god, but a fellowship-meal in which the Church shares the bread which unites it as the Body of Christ, the bread being a symbol of the unity of Christ's Body. The presence of the Risen Christ at the fellowship-meal, symbolised by the bread which, according to tradition, he had prophetically identified with his body,[12] is also his presence in his Body, the Church. So, a distinctively Pauline idea is involved, not a transformation of the fellowship-meal into a "Dionysiac" type of mystery.

Nevertheless, it is impossible to deny that Paul has taken steps in his discussion which imply not merely communion in supernatural food within the context of a zebach/θυσία communion-sacrifice, but actual participation in the body and blood of Christ. This

---

[12]Whatever the actual words of Jesus at the Last Supper (a problem too involved to tackle here), it is easier to suppose that his actions over the bread and the wine were prophetic symbols of some kind, than that he drew the Johannine conclusion that the disciples were actually to eat his body and drink his blood. It is possible that he intended the symbols to be interpreted as a prophecy of his vicarious death, as the traditions imply, but, in the light of the eschatological setting, I incline to the view that they were rather a symbolic guarantee of his presence with them at the Messianic feast when God would have triumphed and vindicated him in spite of death. This would naturally lead to the kind of eschatological fellowship-meal with the Risen Christ which seems to have been the character of the primitive Eucharist.

is taken even further in the Gospel of John. Are we then to suppose that John was influenced by "Dionysiac" rites, even if, as we have argued, Paul was not?

John's discussion comes in the context of the story of the Feeding of the Five Thousand,[13] and the sole theme of his treatment is spiritual feeding. Jesus is depicted as telling the people not to labour for food that perishes, but for food that endures to eternal life;he indicates that this food is given by the Son of Man. "I am the bread of life," he is represented as saying; he, like the manna, is bread from heaven. But whereas the Hebrews ate the manna and died, he who eats the living bread that came down from heaven will live for ever. A man has no life unless he eats the flesh of the Son of Man and drinks his blood; but if he does, he receives eternal life. He who partakes of this spiritual food abides in Christ, and shares in his life, which is eternal.

Is this discussion influenced by the "Dionysiac" concept of communion-sacrifice? Direct influence seems highly improbable. As in Paul's discussion, the analogy is Jewish, the manna; besides this, there is no sacrificial reference of any kind, as there certainly was in Paul. On the other hand, the parallels between Johannine thought and the Corpus Hermeticum suggest that he was in contact with Hellenistic ideas.[14] Has he then been influenced by the idea of theophagy in a communion-sacrifice? Two points tend to suggest that he was not. Firstly, there is very little evidence for theophagy-communion in the Hellenistic period; initiation into the Dionysiac religion was, of course, frequent, but nothing seems to have been made of the distinctive theophagy element.[15] Secondly, it is only to contacts with spiritualised Hellenistic religious ideas that the evidence points; and there is no mention

---

[13]John 6.

[14]See C. H. Dodd, The Interpretation of the Fourth Gospel (Cambridge, 1953), pp. 10-53.

[15]See A. D. Nock, Early Gentile Christianity in its Hellenistic Background (New York, 1964), pp. 73-4, 114-5.

of a spiritualised theophagy in Philo or the Hermetic Corpus or the other literature which apparently influenced the author of John's Gospel.[16] John's position seems to have been the logical outcome of the realisation that the bread and wine which Jesus had identified with his body and blood were, in fact, consumed by the worshippers as supernatural food, of which God's gift of the manna in the wilderness had long been regarded as the "type." The "cannibalistic" scandal which resulted from John's daring statement of the consequences of Christian belief and action, was acceptable to neither Jew nor Greek.

It seems then that there was no direct influence of "Dionysiac" sacrificial ideas in the New Testament. At this stage, the spiritual feeding ideas which were associated with the Eucharist, were apparently distinct from any sacrificial analogy applied to understanding of the meal. In fact, John merely carries further the ideas already expressed in the Synoptic Gospels,[17]

---

[16]See Dodd, op. cit., p. 339, n. 1.

[17]That the feeding stories in the Synoptics are Eucharistic in implication is shown by the description of Christ performing the characteristically Eucharistic actions over the bread (and the fishes, which were also an early Eucharistic symbol); the words used for "blessing" and "giving thanks" in the two different versions are the same terms found in the Institution stories. The clue to the implication of the stories for understanding the Eucharist is found in the story of the Feeding of the Five Thousand, where in Mk and Lk Jesus, after telling the disciples to feed the multitude and receiving the reply that to buy food for so many was impractical, then uses what little they had available, so demonstrating that he, the Christ, is sufficient to feed all. The effect of this conversation with the disciples is heightened in Mt when Christ says, "They have no need to go away. You feed them." The miracle story is a foreshadowing of the spiritual food of the Eucharist in which the worshippers have communion with Christ and feed on him

where the Feeding Stories are interpreted as prophetic symbols that Christ alone is sufficient to feed mankind; for man shall not live by bread alone but by every word that proceeds from the mouth of God, and Christ gives, and even is, the Word of God. John underlines these ideas by restating them in the vocabulary of spiritual food which imparts the eternal life of God to the worshipper through participation in the body and blood of Christ. These ideas are not to be regarded as sacrificial in origin, or as implying sacrificial-communion of the "Dionysiac" type.

In the New Testament, then, we have found two distinct communion-ideas. The first is sacrificial; it is a reinterpretation of the fellowship-meal with the Risen Christ as a zebach/θυσία type of sacrifice. The second is not sacrificial in origin; it emphasizes the communicants' personal participation in the spiritual food of Christ's body and blood. The presence of both these ideas as distinct communion-elements is also found in the Didache. In this work, the Eucharist is explicitly called a θυσία in one passage;[18] in the other section which seems to refer to the Eucharist, both communion-elements seem to be present in the prayers which apparently accompanied the rite.[19] As

---

spiritually, through the distribution of the bread of God by the disciples. This interpretation is not specifically drawn out in the Synoptics, but the implication of their accounts is there in hints which are explicit in Jn's version.

[18]Didache XIV. θυσία may simply be a general term for sacrifice (see above for Greg. Naz.'s use of it in the sense of sacrificial gift). But our discussion shows that the Eucharistic sacrifice was understood as a communion-sacrifice in the Didache.

[19]Ibid., IX-X. It has been contended that these chapters refer not to the Eucharist proper but to the Agapé. I do not intend to enter into this debate here because, even if this were so the ideas expressed in these prayers appear elsewhere as Eucharistic. The gathering of the scattered grains of corn is not only reminiscent of Paul's treatment of the unity of the

in Paul, the unity of the Church is likened to the unity of the loaf, the second part of the prayer over the bread asking that, as the bread has been made into one loaf from many scattered grains of corn, so the Church may be gathered into the Kingdom from the far corners of the earth. The θυσία is the fellowship-meal in which the whole church is eschatologically united in the presence of God. Again, as in Paul, purity is required of the worshippers who are to take part in the "zebach"; in the very context where the Eucharist is called a θυσία, appears an exhortation to confess before the sacrifice, for if the sacrifice is to be pure it must be offered by those who are pure. Clearly, a communion-sacrifice of the zebach/θυσία type is involved in the interpretation of the Eucharist in the Didache. But at the same time, Johannine ideas predominate in the prayers, which give thanks for the ζωή and γνῶσις imparted to men through Jesus Christ, and also for the spiritual food given "through thy Son." This spiritual feeding idea is not, however, associated with the sacrificial element of the Eucharist; the ideas appear in quite different passages,[20] and there is no suggestion that the Eucharist was thought to be a communion-sacrifice of the "Dionysiac" type. The Didache, then, shows the same position as the major dimensions found in the New Testament.

With Ignatius, it gets more difficult to state without qualification that the spiritual feeding idea is not interpreted as a communion-sacrifice. Like John and the Didache, he refers to the body and blood of Christ as spiritual food, equating them with the Eucharistic cup. In line with the Jewish "moralising" tradition, he can even speak of faith and love as the flesh and blood of Christ, so showing that the spiritual implications are important to him; but, as an

---

loaf, but is reproduced in the liturgy described by Serapion at the end of our period. Other ideas are Johannine, and were assumed by later writers to belong rightly to the Eucharist.

[20]The sacrificial ideas appear in Ch. XIV, and the Johannine spiritual feeding ideas in IX and X.

anti-Gnostic argument, he also insists on the literalness of the sacramental eating and drinking of Christ's body and blood, just as John had done. The Eucharistic elements are the medicine of immortality.[21] Ignatius never uses the word θυσία of the Eucharist, but he frequently concentrates attention on the altar where it was celebrated, showing no doubt that he thought it was a sacrifice of some sort.[22] Does his spiritual feeding language imply more than that of John and the Didache? Does he go further towards understanding the Eucharist as a communion-sacrifice of the "Dionysiac" type? The one hint that might be interpreted in this way is his expression Παύλου συμμύσται,[23] a phrase obviously suggestive of initiates into mystery-cults; very shortly after this, he speaks of the Eucharist. But this is not sufficient evidence for his acceptance of the idea that the Eucharist was a theophagy of the "Dionysiac" type. The distinctive thing about the mysteries in general, was not a communion-sacrifice of this type, but a secret, sacred drama portraying the dying and rising god, and it was as the re-enactment of Christ's passion that the analogy between the Eucharist and the mysteries came to be generally accepted. So this is not evidence for the use of the "Dionysiac" communion idea in interpreting the sacrifice of the Eucharist.

The same is true of Justin's suggestion that the Mithraic mysteries were analogous to the Eucharist. He explains in I Apology[24] that Christians have been taught to regard the food which has been made the

---

[21]Eph. 20, where the phrase φάρμακον ἀθανασίας is used. For other references see Rom. 7, where Ignatius says that he wants the bread of God, which is the flesh of Christ, and as drink, his blood, which is ἀγάπη ἄφθαρτος. Compare this with Tral. 8, which says that faith is the flesh of the Lord and love the blood of Jesus Christ. See also the reference to the one cup which is ἕνωσις τοῦ αἵματος αὐτοῦ in a plea for unity in Phil. 4.

[22]Esp. Phil. 4. [23]Eph. 12.2.

[24]I Apol. 65-6.

Eucharist by prayer, as the flesh and blood of Jesus who was made flesh for our salvation; then he explicitly accuses the daemons of imitating the Eucharist in the Mithraic mysteries, and continues "for you can know or learn that bread and a cup of water are among the rites administered to the initiated, with certain prayers." Little is really known about the Mithraic rites, but there does not seem to have been a rite in which the believers thought that they were taking in the nature of the deity himself through a communion-sacrifice. It has been conjectured that the bread should be connected with Mithras' slaying of a bull from which corn proceeded; but the evidence is slim and does not necessarily imply a "Dionysiac" communion in Mithras.[25] The analogies with current mystery-religions do not therefore provide any irrefutable evidence that Christian writers were influenced by pagan theophagy-sacrifices.

There is, however, one passage where a direct comparison is made between the Dionysiac rites and Christianity. Does this give us any grounds for maintaining that Christians were influenced in their interpretation of the Eucharist by theophagy-rites? This reference to Dionysus appears not in a popular work, but in Clement of Alexandria;[26] it refers not to a contemporary rite, but to the literary work which preserved Dionysiac religion in its most arresting form - Euripides' play, The Bacchae; the analogy is applied not to the Eucharist, but to the Christian life as a whole; and there is no reference at all to the theophagy-rites in the Dionysiac-cult, only to the inspired frenzy of the worshippers dancing on the mountain. There does not therefore seem any grounds for maintaining direct influence of Dionysiac-communion

---

[25]See Nock, op. cit., p. 76, where he mentions Loisy's conjecture about the Mithraic communion from the single piece of evidence provided by Justin, and emphasizes the severe lack of evidence concerning Mithraism.

[26]Clem. Alex., Protr. XII.188ff. For discussion, see Nock, op. cit., p. 139.

sacrifices on the Christian Eucharist.

But, as we have already seen, from the earliest time the Eucharist was regarded as a communion-sacrifice in the sense of a zebach/θυσία fellowship-meal with the deity; and with it was associated the "type" of the manna and a belief that spiritual food was imparted to the communicants so that they assumed something of the life and character of Jesus Christ. Both these ideas are found in later Greek Christian literature; but, while the idea that the Eucharist is a communion-sacrifice never dies, the second interpretation of the nature of the communion comes to predominate. Consequently, the two communion ideas are conflated, and the Eucharist becomes a communion-sacrifice in which the communion is a participation in the life of the deity through consuming the spiritual food of Christ's body and blood.

This situation inevitably led to a diminishing of the importance of the fellowship-communion of the whole Church by comparison with the individual's communion in the spiritual life of the Risen Christ. This situation is particularly clear in the treatment given to the Eucharistic communion by the Alexandrians. For both Clement and Origen, the bodily feeding on the elements becomes a symbol of spiritual feeding on the Word, which is then equated with intellectual and moral nourishment found particularly in scripture, right doctrine and mystical contemplation.[27] When the sacrament is received in the right frame of mind, it feeds both body and soul, nourishing both parts of the composite being, Man;[28] but Origen quite explicitly states that, without spiritual awareness, participation in the communion-sacrifice has no effect, the food just passing through the material body like any other.[29] The spiritual food which brings immortality to those who

---

[27]Clem. Alex., Strom. V.10.66.

[28]Paed. II.2.20. For general discussions of the Eucharist as spiritual food, see I.6.3ff and Strom. IV.25.161; also Origen, Hom. Jer., 19.13 and In Mt. Comm. Ser. 85.

[29]Origen, Comm. Matt. XI.14.

partake with faith, cannot be eaten by unworthy persons, since it depends on spiritual participation in the Divine Word.[30] The fact that the Eucharist can be eaten to one's condemnation (a fact well illustrated by the Last Supper, of which the disciples all partook for their salvation, except Judas who partook for his condemnation), is interpreted by Origen to mean that the Word which brings salvation to the soul which is basically healthy, may be a stimulant to worse evil if given to a sick soul.[31] The purity needed for communion has thus been completely moralised, and divorced from its origin as a requirement in a zebach/θυσία sacrifice. Here we do not have a fellowship-meal symbolising the unity of the Church with Christ, but a rite which has been so individualised and spiritualised as to reach the point where the congregation and the material elements are hardly necessary for the individual's consumption of spiritual nourishment. In fact, Origen takes this so far that it is not always clear whether he intends a reference to the Eucharist or not. Although it was generally accepted that the Eucharist was a memorial of Christ's death, Origen's exegesis of offering the "memorial portion" makes no direct mention of it, even in a context involving the eating of sacrifices; Origen interprets the whole passage in terms of meditating on and memorising Holy Scripture.[32] On the other hand, elsewhere the "memorial portion" is explicitly understood as the Eucharist, though even in this context offering bread to the Lord is interpreted as having knowledge of sacred doctrines.[33] It is possible, therefore, that the Eucharist was alluded to in the earlier passage as well. Origen clearly believed that what he received in the Eucharistic com-

---

[30]Ibid. This is how Origen explains "he who eats this bread will live forever." For other references to the effect of the Eucharist being to impart immortality, see Ignatius (<u>supra</u>) and Clem. Alex., <u>Quis Dives Salvetur</u> 23.4.

[31]<u>Comm. Jn</u>. 32.24.309ff.

[32]<u>Hom. Lev</u>. IV.9.

[33]<u>Ibid</u>., XIII.3.

munion, was the Word of God which enlightens the ignorance of the world. The communion-sacrifice has thus been intellectualised as well as individualised, and the fellowship-meal uniting the Church as communion with the Risen Christ, is completely submerged.

For the later Greek writers, the communion-idea became an essential part of the θεοποίησιϛ . By eating his flesh and drinking his blood, "we become Christ-bearers, since his body and blood are distributed throughout our limbs. So as the blessed Peter expressed it, we are made partakers of the divine nature."[34] In the Eucharist, Christians share in the sufferings and Godhead of Christ,[35] and are united with him in one body and one flesh.[36]

So the communion-sacrifice of the Eucharist comes to be predominantly interpreted along lines deriving from the concept of spiritual feeding. The Eucharistic prayer attributed to Serapion asks that God's Word will transform the bread and wine into the body and blood of the Word and Truth, so that it can be a medicine of life.[37] As we have seen, this idea was not sacrificial in origin, but because it was associated with a rite that was already understood as a communion-sacrifice of the zebach/θυσία type, it became the predominant way of interpreting the communion involved in the rite.

Nevertheless, the original fellowship-meal type of interpretation can still be found in some of the relevant documents, or at least survivals of it. In Irenaeus and the _Apostolic Tradition_ of Hippolytus, the Eucharist is understood as being strictly analogous to the other material offerings brought by Christians, that is, as a first-fruit offering which was consumed as sacred food in a zebach/θυσία type of fellowship-meal; it will be recalled that such offerings were shown to be communion-sacrifices of this type in an

---

[34]Cyr. Jer., _Cat. Or._ IV.3.

[35]Greg. Naz., _Or._ IV.52; XL.31.

[36]Chrysostom, _Hom. Matt._ 82.5.

[37]My source for the text has been Litzmann, op. cit., p. 152ff and trans., Dix. op. cit., p. 163ff.

earlier chapter,[38] and the Eucharist was associated with them in that discussion. In these works, the spiritual feeding idea is far less prominent than elsewhere, though Irenaeus does regard the elements as conferring resurrection on bodies nourished by the body of Christ.[39] A survival of the fellowship-meal communion is found in Serapion's adaptation of the prayer in the Didache; God is to unite the Church through this rite, as the bread has been formed out of grain that was scattered over the mountains. This prayer has nothing to do with the spiritual feeding of the individual soul, but is concerned with the fellowship-communion of the Church in the bread which represents its unity. Another survival of the original zebach/θυσία type of communion-sacrifice is the insistence found throughout our period on the need for purity in order to partake in the sacrifice. Generally speaking, however, the communion-sacrifice idea is conflated with the notion of spiritual communion in the body and blood of Christ, and the two different ideas no longer appear distinct.

Enough evidence has been produced to show how basic and important the communion-sacrifice type was for interpretation of the sacrificial character of the distinctive Christian cult-act, the Eucharist. Two types of communion were involved in the interpretation of the communion-sacrifice, the first, the zebach/θυσία type of sacrifice, and the second the idea of spiritual feeding. Since the spiritual feeding involved consuming the body and blood of Jesus Christ in symbolic form, there were clear analogies with the "Dionysiac" type of theophagy sacrifice, but we have found no evidence at all for the view that the Christian Eucharist was directly influenced by this type of sacrifice. Be that as it may, communion understood in the terms we have described became the most important way in which the Eucharist was understood in the East, and, because of its association with the zebach/θυσία type of sacrifice, it must be regarded as sacrificial. Dix's assumption that the communion was not part of the

---

[38]See supra, Ch. 5.A.
[39]See infra, at n. 53.

sacrifice cannot be accepted, at least with respect to the Greek tradition. He cited one occasion where Augustine associates the act of communion with the sacrificial action, and suggested that it should be regarded as exceptional; but clearly it should be accepted as a statement of what had long been implied in Christian thought.[40] The Eucharist was a communion-sacrifice of the zebach/θυσία type, in which the communion was reinterpreted as a participation in the body and blood of Christ, whereby the communicants were endowed with his eternal life. It did not seem anomalous that a single rite should express both the fellowship and unity of the Church with her Risen Lord and the spiritual nourishment of the individual who thus received the immortal life of God, even though, as we have argued, these ideas were in origin, distinct.

In Chapters One and Two, attention was drawn to the fact that the zebach and the θυσία were also sacrifices of praise and thanksgiving to the God with whom the worshippers were in fellowship. This element was present in the Eucharist from the earliest times for which we have evidence. However, more than a mere offering of thanks in communion came to be involved, since the Eucharist became the actual offering of a gift-sacrifice to God as the supreme act of Christian worship. To this development we must now turn.

(b) The Eucharist as a Thank-offering

The word "eucharist" means thanksgiving, and this seems to have been an important element in the rite from the beginning. The earliest Eucharist seems to have been celebrated in an atmosphere of eschatological expectation and joy as an anticipation of the Messianic feast. This would inevitably be accompanied by the offering of praise and thanksgiving to the God who was to fulfill all his promises. The use of the word ευχαριστία, however, seems to have originated in the Jewish practice of saying grace before a meal. In the Pauline account of the Institution of the Eucharist, the Marcan Feeding of the Four Thousand, and the

---

[40]See Dix, op. cit., p. 241, n. 2; he refers to Augustine's De civ. X.6.

Johannine Feeding of the Multitude, ευχαριστήσαϛ is found instead of ευλογήσαϛ, the word used of Christ's action over the bread in the Marcan and Matthaean accounts of the Last Supper and the other Feeding stories. In a Jewish context, ευλογεῖν meant "to say grace over a meal," and this was probably replaced by ευχαριστεῖν in order to clarify what was meant for Gentile Christians.[41] In later Eucharistic traditions, this simple grace before a meal was retained in general thanksgiving prayers for all God's mercies including the creation and preservation of the world; and to this was added specific thanksgiving for the revelation imparted through Christ, and the spiritual food of his body and blood, of which the worshippers were about to partake.

Besides this, the tradition that the Eucharist was the Christian Passover meant that it was analogous to the Jewish Passover in being a thankful celebration of God's past great act of deliverance from sin and death. It was also, like the Jewish Passover, an anticipation of the future eschatological deliverance that God was to bring to fulfillment.[42]

We have already mentioned that the thanksgiving element was naturally present in the Eucharist, once the fellowship-meal was interpreted as a zebach/θυσία type of communion-sacrifice, and its apparent origin in the saying of grace before a meal suggests that

---

[41]The institution accounts are found in Mk. 14. 17-25; Mt. 26.20-9; Lk. 22.14.20; and 1 Cor. 11.23-9. For the view that εὐχαριστήσαϛ represents a Hellenising of εὐλογήσαϛ, see J. Jeremias, The Eucharistic Words of Jesus (Oxford, 1955), p. 119: "In secular Greek εὐλογεῖν means predominantly 'to praise or glorify someone,' and is used with a peraonal or impersonal object. The meaning 'to bless,' as well as the technical meaning 'to say Grace' . . . is a Semitism, as is also the omission of the object. . . The substitution of εὐχαριστήσαϛ for εὐλογήσαϛ in the parallel texts of 1 Cor. 11.24, Lk. 22.19a, is a Graecising of the Semitism."

[42]However, see Additional Note III, infra.

originally it had no independent, sacrificial significance. However, the offering of the elements on the altar soon became a gift-sacrifice in its own right, especially as it was regarded as a first-fruit offering. The thanksgiving was then associated with the gift-sacrifice, the perfect thank-offering which gave Christians the right to join in the very worship of heaven.

Justin bears witness to the fact that for him the Eucharist was a sacrifice of thanksgiving, though the thanksgivings remain linked with the communion-sacrifice. In I Apology,[43] he gives an account of Eucharistic practices as he knew them, and it is clear that the thanksgiving-prayers were of primary importance. After various preliminaries, bread and a cup containing wine mixed with water are given to the president of the ceremony, who takes them and offers praise and glory to the Father of all, through the name of the Son and of the Holy Spirit, and recites lengthy prayers of thanksgiving to God. At the end of the prayers, the bread and wine are distributed and all present partake.

In a passage in the Dialogue with Trypho,[44] the emphasis is even more strongly on the thanksgiving element in the Eucharist. Justin is concerned to defend the Christian exegesis of the Malachi prophecy, which, as we have already mentioned, was traditionally understood as fulfilled in the Eucharistic sacrifice. Since he needs to confute the Jewish interpretation that it referred to the offering of prayers in the Dispersion, he pointedly draws attention to the anti-Jewish context in which the passage occurs. His only other argument is a rather weak one: whereas "there is not one single race of men among whom prayers and thanksgivings are not offered to the Father and Creator of the universe in the name of the crucified Jesus," the Jewish Dispersion does not extend "from the rising of the sun to the going down thereof." It is particularly interesting that with reference to the central issue, he is forced to agree with the Jews that prayers

---

[43] 1 Apol. 65-6. [44] Dial. 117.

and thanksgivings offered by worthy persons are the only perfect and acceptable sacrifices to God. Thus, he not only claims that Isaiah and the other prophets indicate that at the Second Coming, there will only be true spiritual praises and thanksgivings and no bloody sacrifices,[45] but, he even tends to subordinate the Eucharistic elements to the sacrifices of prayer and praise that are alone perfect and acceptable: "The Christians," he explains, "were instructed to offer only such prayers, even at their thanksgiving for their food, both liquid and solid, whereby the passion which the Son of God endured for us is commemorated."[46] The tendency to spiritualise sacrifice which we have already examined makes even the Eucharistic elements secondary to the prayers of thanksgiving. Justin's Eucharist is primarily a sacrifice of worship and thanksgiving, the partaking in spiritual food being subordinate to the spiritual offering of thanks and praise in the prayers which accompanied the offering of the elements at the altar.

However, Justin spoke of prayers "at the thanksgiving for their food," and the origin of the thanksgiving as a grace before a meal, or part of the communion-sacrifice is not obscured. It is from the tradition of thanksgiving for God's gift of food that the idea of interpreting the Eucharist as an offering of first-fruits must be derived, though, once established, it clearly indicated that the elements were offered to God as a gift-sacrifice, independently of the communion-sacrifice. The two types of sacrifice were never completely sundered, but the thanksgiving became quite clearly an offering and a sacrifice in its own right, not merely the thanksgiving implied in a communion-sacrifice. The thanksgiving did, of course, retain the ideas that originated in the grace before meals, and concentrated on gratitude for the gifts of food, both material and spiritual. But the offering of the elements on the altar began to have other sacrificial significance, being an actual gift-sacrifice offered in gratitude for salvation in Christ,

---

[45]Ibid., 118. [46]Ibid., 117.

as well as for creation and preservation.

The association of the Eucharist with the offering of first-fruits is found first in the *Didache*, which provides clear evidence of the developments just mentioned. As we have already seen, it is clear from this work that the Christian community continued the Jewish practice of offering first-fruits,[47] and it is immediately after discussion of these that a description of the Eucharist is found which shows it was analogous to the first-fruit offerings.[48] It was thus a gift-sacrifice, independent of the communion-sacrifice. In the thanksgiving prayers found elsewhere,[49] thanks for the creation, for food and drink, and above all for the spiritual food and drink and eternal life granted through God's Son, are found alongside prayers of specific thanksgiving for the revelation imparted to the faithful by Jesus Christ. The simple grace before meals has become a much more general thanksgiving for all God's mercies, though retaining thanks for food and spiritual communion, while the analogy with the first-fruit offering indicates that the thanksgiving is associated with a gift-sacrifice, the offering of the Eucharistic elements to God prior to their consumption by the communicants.

This is true also of the liturgy given in the *Apostolic Tradition* of Hippolytus. The bread and wine are presented as a thank-offering of which the Church then partakes, so receiving spiritual food, the type of sacrifice being analogous to other material offerings which Christians could make, namely, first-fruits of every kind and the cult-meals at which the bishop was present to consecrate the food then consumed as holy by the individuals present.[50] In all these sacrifices, the fellowship-meal was preceded by a gift-sacrifice of the elements which were to provide the food for the communion-sacrifice.

---

[47] *Didache* XIII. [48] Ibid., XIV.

[49] *Ibid.*, IX-X.

[50] See Dix ed., sect. xxviii; Botte ed., 31-2. See the discussion in Lietzmann, op. cit., p. 142ff.

It is in the writings of Irenaeus that the interpretation of the Eucharist as a first-fruit offering is clearest, and its implications in terms of the offering of a gift-sacrifice most fully drawn out. He explicitly states that Christ told his disciples to offer first-fruits in the form of the Eucharist, not because God needed such material offerings, but so as to express their gratitude to God for all his created gifts.[51] A gift to a king is a token of respect and honour, and God accepts the gifts of Christians because in so doing he recognizes the expression of gratitude intended by them, so "glorifying" the givers.[52] The idea of offering first-fruits to God in gratitude thus led to the interpretation of the Eucharist as a gift-sacrifice of thanksgiving for Creation and the provision of food, ideas which are more prominent here than thanksgiving for the salvation wrought by Christ. The gift-sacrifice is not, however, isolated from the communion-sacrifice even though it now has independent sacrificial status; Irenaeus includes thanksgiving for the spiritual food imparted in the rite, and the importance of the combination of both aspects is seen in his following remarks. He insists that if this sacrifice is rightly understood, it cannot be offered by heretics, because they do not believe in Creation, a fact which makes their Eucharist a mockery, the whole point of the rite being to show the communion and unity of flesh and spirit. The bread is a created thing taken from the earth, but by receiving the invocation of God, it does not remain common bread, but becomes "eucharist," composed of earthly and heavenly elements. The bodies that receive the "eucharist" do not remain corruptible, but have the hope of resurrection, being nourished by the gift of Christ's body and blood.[53] The important point for Irenaeus is that the sanctification of the bread becomes a parable of the Redemption of Creation, and his position is at this point clearly influenced by the need to oppose the heretics of Docetic or

---

[51] Adv. Haer. IX.17.5.

[52] Ibid., IV.18.1.

[53] Ibid., IV.18.4-5; IV.17.5.

of Dualistic tendencies.[54] But the actual sacrificial ideas involved are not specifically anti-heretical. The gift-sacrifice offered as first-fruits is expounded more fully than it had been before because it served Irenaeus' purpose, but the presence of the two types of sacrifice in conjunction with each other is not an innovation. In Irenaeus' exposition, however, the offering of the elements and the thanksgiving prayers are more clearly shown than ever previously to have sacrificial status in their own right, alongside the communion-sacrifice.

In the Alexandrians, the first-fruit idea is again used to describe the Eucharist. So far from giving first-fruits and sacrifices of thanksgiving to the daemons, Christians eat with thanksgiving to the Creator the things he has created for them.[55] "We give thanks to the Creator of the Universe and eat the loaves that are presented, with thanksgiving and prayer over the gifts, so that by the prayer they become a certain holy body which sanctified those who partake of it with a pure intention"; this is the Christian first-fruit offering.[56] The communion-idea is still associated with the offering of first-fruits, since clearly the elements offered are afterwards consumed by the worshippers. The Eucharist is a feast at which Christians enjoy God's created gifts and rightly praise him in psalms.[57] But although the elements are still closely associated with the communion, they have become also a gift-sacrifice to God in their own right, as a first-fruit offering and a symbol of the thanksgiving of the Church. It is a holy duty to give thanks to God for his favours and love to men,[58] and "we have a symbol of our thanksgiving to God in the bread which is called 'eucharist.'"[59]

---

[54] Ibid., IV.18.6; V.2.3ff.

[55] Origen, C. Cels. VIII.33-4.

[56] Ibid.

[57] Clem. Alex., Paed. II.4.43-4.

[58] Ibid.

[59] Origen, C. Cels., loc. cit.

The gift-sacrifice of praise and thanksgiving is reflected in the liturgies as the offertory of the elements on the altar.[60] The earliest description of the offertory as such appears in Hippolytus' liturgy, and although it cannot be stated without qualification that the Eucharistic prayer found in the present text has remained uncontaminated by later and foreign amendments,[61] the offertory-element is evidenced for the Second Century by Justin's description of how the president takes the elements offered by the people and offers praise and glory to God,[62] and also by Irenaeus' first-fruits interpretation of the gift-sacrifice offered in gratitude to God.[63] As early as I Clement we find that the bishop's office was to offer gifts.[64] In Serapion's Eucharistic prayer, the officiant describes how the worshippers have offered "this living sacrifice, this unbloody oblation."

The Eucharist, then, expressed the thanksgiving of the Church within a communion-sacrifice, and came to be also a gift-sacrifice of praise and thanksgiving in its own right. But we may say even more; for it has been suggested that the offertory of the Eucharistic elements was a preliminary offering which enabled the Church to share in the worship of heaven itself.[65] In this sense, the offertory was not a full sacrifice of worship, but a kind of passport to worship at the heavenly altar. A possible reconstruction of the Eucharistic prayer in the liturgy of Hippolytus

---

[60]For discussion, see Dix, The Shape of the Liturgy (Westminster, 1944), p. 110ff.

[61]See E. C. Ratcliff, "The Sanctus and the Pattern of the Early Anaphora," JEH (1950). In their editions, both Dix and Botte accept the Eucharistic prayer as that of Hippolytus, but Ratcliff disputes this.

[62]1 Apol. 65.

[63]See supra, at n. 54.

[64]1 Clem. 44.

[65]See Ratcliff, op. cit.; A. H. Couratin, "The Sacrifice of Praise," Theology (1955); and G. A. Michell, Landmarks in Liturgy (London, 1961).

expresses the thanksgiving of the Church for the divine work of creation and salvation, and for the privilege of being the Holy and Priestly People of God with the right to stand before God and minister to him before his face in company with the attendant multitude of heavenly ministers, there to join with them in perpetual adoration and to hear "the Sanctus" which, according to *Isaiah*, was the hymn eternally sung by the Seraphim. This has been inferred from the phrase "quia nos dignos habuisti adstare coram te et tibi ministrare"; it is supported by references to the Church as the priesthood of God in Justin and Irenaeus, by Irenaeus' statement that the Christian altar and temple are in heaven,[66] and by the fact that the use of the favourite *Malachi* prophecy implies that the Eucharistic offering is a glorying of the name of God.

This evidence increases in interest when it is noticed that the *Apocalypse*[67] seems to be influenced by the form of Eucharistic celebration to which the author was accustomed. The bishop in the center becomes in his vision the ineffable majesty of God; on either side of him were four and twenty presbyters arranged in a semi-circle, as at the Eucharist; and in the center, instead of the altar, was the lamb slain but now alive for evermore. It is particularly interesting from this point of view, that Ignatius speaks of the Bishop as representing God, not Christ; Christ, in this picture, is on the altar in the Eucharistic bread and cup. The hymns in the *Apocalypse* now take on further significance, since they may represent liturgical expression of the date at which the book was written. The three Eucharistic thanksgivings which appear later in the liturgies are present: thanksgiving for creation,[68] for redemption,[69] and for the priesthood of God's people.[70] The Sanctus is also

---

[66]Justin, *Dial*. 116; Irenaeus, *Adv. Haer*. IV.8 and IV.19.

[67]Esp. Ch. 3-4.

[68]Ibid., 5.9.

[69]Ibid., 5.9.

[70]Ibid., 5.10.

mentioned.[71] The *Apocalypse* gives us a pattern of thanksgiving and worship along the same lines as that deduced above for the Eucharistic prayer of the Second Century. Besides this, further evidence is provided in the New Testament by the *Epistle to the Hebrews*, which describes how the High-Priest entered heaven itself, so that Christians could with confidence draw near to the throne of grace[72] and enter the sanctuary,[73] which has already been identified with heaven;[74] then readers of the Epistle are exhorted to offer a sacrifice of praise to God through confession of God's name.[75] It has been suggested that the Church's participation in the worship of heaven and the glorying of God's name in the Eucharistic sacrifice lies behind this picture.[76]

If this reconstruction is right, Justin's subordination of the offering of the Eucharistic elements to the spiritual worship of prayer and praise is explicable.[77] It is the spiritual worship of heaven in which the Church shares at the Eucharist, and the material offerings of the elements merely "relieve the Church of that emptiness which would debar it from the presence of God."[78]

This does not mean that all we have said about the gift-sacrifice of the Eucharist is undercut. Rather it is confirmed. The Eucharistic elements are still offered as a gift-sacrifice of praise and in preparation for the communion-sacrifice. But the whole Eucharistic action and prayer becomes a complete sacrifice of perfect heavenly worship as well. The spiritualisation of sacrifice which was the basis of

---

[71]Ibid., 4.8. Couratin (op. cit.) draws attention to the fact that the form of the Sanctus in the LXX of *Isaiah* is "Holy, Holy, Holy is the Lord of Hosts," whereas later liturgies follow the *Apocalypse* version: "Holy, Holy, Holy is the Lord, the God of Hosts."

[72]*Heb.* 4.16.

[73]Ibid., 10.19.

[74]*Ibid.*, 8.2.

[75]Ibid., 13.15.

[76]See Couratin, op. cit.

[77]See *supra*, Ch. 11 at n. 46.

[78]Ratcliff, op. cit., p. 132-3.

the Christian position has affected even her central cult-act, and the material offering is subordinate to the Church's role in the spiritual worship of heaven itself. The Eucharist as a whole is a sacrifice of communion, a gift-sacrifice of praise and thanksgiving, and a sharing in the supreme worship of heaven. It is the highest conceivable sacrifice.

So far then, we have found the Eucharist summing up and fulfilling a number of the different types of sacrifice that we have analysed in this study. It remains to enquire whether it was in any sense a sin-offering, and if so of what type.

(c) The Eucharist as a Sin-offering

It is proposed to consider this kind of sacrifice by asking if the various types of sin-offering distinguished earlier were ever used to describe the Eucharist.

(i) The Eucharist as an Expiatory Sacrifice

We have already found earlier that positive use of the simple expiatory explanation of sacrifice is largely confined in Christian literature to the New Testament.[79] We must look here, then, for any suggestion that the Eucharist had expiatory significance.

The major passages in the New Testament concerned with the Eucharist have already been discussed. As we have seen, Paul interpreted it as a communion-sacrifice of the zebach/θυσία type, so that naturally praise and thanksgiving were associated with it. We should also expect that for such a sacrifice purity would be required, and as we have seen, this was so.[80] Paul warned of the dangers of partaking in the communion-sacrifice of the Eucharist in an unworthy manner, of not first examining oneself, of the possibility of eating and drinking judgment upon oneself.[81]

This is the only passage in the New Testament where the sacrificial aspect of the Eucharist is specifically discussed, and since purity from sin is clearly required, there can be no sense in which the Eucharistic

---

[79]See *supra*, Ch. 8.A.

[80]See *supra*, Ch. 11 at n.6.

[81]1 *Cor*. 11.27-9.

sacrifice was offered to expiate the sins of the worshippers. On the other hand, in the Institution accounts, the blood of Christ is treated as being the blood of the New Covenant sacrifice; in *Mark*, its atoning significance is made explicit by the phrase "poured out for many,"[82] and *Matthew* clarifies it further by adding "for the forgiveness of sins."[83] Any expiatory significance implied by this as far as the Eucharist is concerned is clearly only by association with the sacrificial death of Christ; the relationship between the Eucharist and Christ's sacrifice will be discussed in the next part of this chapter.

There is no evidence that the Eucharist ever acquired expiatory significance independently of its association with the death of Christ. It remained a rule that only those who were pure could partake of the sacrifice; a pure heart, a pure conscience and an irreproachable life were prerequisites. The Eucharist, according to Chrysostom, could only be received by those already baptised and purified by repentance;[84] Origen did not include the Eucharist among his list of sacrifices for sin.[85] We can therefore take it that the Eucharist was never regarded as an expiatory sacrifice in its own right.

(ii) *The Eucharist as an Aversion Sacrifice*

Our argument against the interpretation of the Eucharist as expiatory, should also tell against any other suggestion that it was a sin-offering. Even less likely than other types of sin-offering is the view that it was a sacrifice of aversion, since this would imply an offering made to the devil, and from what we have already seen, the Eucharist was quite clearly a gift-sacrifice to God.

Yet there is some indication that it had power to keep away the Evil One. Ignatius suggests that the mere act of coming together in unity and fellowship for the praise and glory of God (εἰς εὐχαριστίαν Θεοῦ καὶ εἰς δόξαν) destroys the power of Satan.[86] In the

---

[82] *Mk*. 14.24 [83] *Matt*. 26.28.
[84] Chrysostom, *Hom. Heb*. XVII, etc.
[85] Origen, *Hom. Lev*., II.4.
[86] Ignatius, *Eph*. 13.

Eucharistic Prayer of Hippolytus, we find that the rite was instituted by Christ "in order that He might abolish death and rend the bonds of the devil and tread down hell and enlighten the righteous and establish an ordinance and demonstrate the resurrection."[87]

Besides this, the treatment of the Eucharist as the Christian Passover could lead to the idea that the blood of Christ protects from the Destroyer, so implying that the Eucharist was in a sense an aversion sacrifice. It will be recalled that the Christian typological use of the Paschal lamb for Christ was based on a return to the original apotropaeic significance of the blood of the Sacrifice.[88]

None of these considerations, however, shows that the Eucharist was itself an aversion sacrifice, at any rate, in the sense of a sacrifice offered to the devil. Not even the analogy with the Passover necessarily implies averting significance. The celebration of the Jewish Passover feast had long since ceased to involve the application of blood to the doorposts to keep away evil. It had become simply a commemorative meal, linked to a past not a present act of salvation, though also anticipating the future goodness of God towards Israel.[89] Similarly, the Christian Passover commemorated the victory of Christ over the devil, and anticipated his final triumph at the Second Coming. In the present, like the Jewish Passover, it was a sacrifice of thanksgiving for an act of salvation that had occurred, not another saving act through sacrifice. It is true that Christians were exhorted to leave their personal Egypts of sin and subservience to the devil under the protection of the blood of Christ.[90] It is also true that communion in his body and blood strengthened the tempted Christian in his warfare against evil. But the Eucharist was not in any sense an offering to the devil to avert his powers. The

---

[87]Dix's translation; Dix ed. iv, Botte ed. 4.

[88]See supra, Ch. 7.C.

[89]See supra, Ch. 2.B.a.

[90]E.g., Greg. Naz., *Or*. I.3. Incidentally, this Paschal Homily makes no reference to the Eucharist.

elements were offered to God, and even though the wine represented Christ's blood, the ransom-price, there is never the slightest suggestion that is was offered to anyone but God. The Eucharist was an act of commemorative thanksgiving offered to the Saviour God; it was a meal of communion with him. It was not an aversion-sacrifice, though the presence of God and the holiness and purity of those gathered in communion with him inevitably kept the devil away. Even as a re-enactment of Christ's death (for discussion of which see the next section of this chapter), the Eucharist was not an aversion-sacrifice offered to the devil; it was always a sacrifice offered to God.

(iii) The Eucharist as a Propitiatory Sacrifice

A propitiatory sacrifice was one offered to God specifically to gain his favour after an offence. Since, as we have already seen, the offering-idea came to be of importance in the Eucharist, and the elements were offered to God as a gift-sacrifice, this is the type of sin-offering most likely to have been used of the Eucharist if it was ever understood as a sacrifice for sin.

In the later part of our period, there is plenty of evidence that the Eucharistic offering was understood in a propitiatory sense, as well as in the sense of a gift-sacrifice of praise and thanksgiving. This is clearly seen in the Eucharistic Prayer of Serapion which asks God to be merciful and to be propitiated (ἱλάσθητι). It is even more evident in Cyril of Jerusalem's Catechetical Lectures on the Eucharist:[91] he states that this memorial sacrifice is offered on behalf of the world, emperors, soldiers, those in sickness and trouble, and all who are in need, even on behalf of the departed, and it is a sacrifice of propitiation. "We offer Christ crucified for our sins, propitiating God, lover of men, for them and for ourselves." Even though God is called φιλάνθρωπος in the same sentence, the Eucharistic sacrifice is conceived in propitiatory terms. Admittedly the emphasis is on intercession for others, but "ourselves" are included, in spite of the fact that purity from sin was required of those joining in the sacrifice.

[91] Cyr. Jer., Cat. Or. V.8-10.

It is clear from what we have quoted from Cyril that the propitiatory aspect of the Eucharistic offering came about because it was thought to be a re-enactment of Christ's sacrifice. We shall turn to this aspect of the Eucharist in the next part of this chapter, but we should draw attention here to the fact that, because of this, the actual use of propitiatory language in connection with the Eucharist is found in the writings of those who accepted the propitiatory interpretation of Christ's death, namely those in closer contact with popular theology like Eusebius and Chrysostom, and those theologians, like the Cappadocians, by whom Athanasius' exposition of the Atonement was assumed. Propitiation was an idea foreign to the Alexandrians, and so it does not appear in their accounts of the Eucharist at all. This whole subject can only be discussed fully in relation to the idea of the Eucharist as a re-enactment of Christ's death, so to this we now turn.

B. The Relationship between the Eucharistic Sacrifice and the Sacrifice of Christ

The Eucharist, as communion-sacrifice and gift-sacrifice of praise and thanksgiving, was a sacrifice in its own right, offered by the Church to God. It was a pure sacrifice in which the Church confessed the name of God and entered into the very worship of heaven.

At the same time, it has an intimate relationship with the sacrifice of Christ. At the simplest level, the relationship consisted merely in the fact that the thanksgiving prayers concentrated particularly on the salvation brought about by Christ. It was a simple memorial of thanksgiving. But the ἀνάμνησιϛ certainly came to have much more significance as the idea spread that, in the Eucharist, the Church re-enacted the sacrifice of Christ. With this belief came assurance that the Eucharist had propitiatory power, though not as a sacrifice for sin in its own right, only as the re-enactment of Christ's perfect sacrifice for sin.

That the Eucharist and Christ's death were closely associated, is assumed by the use of two of the same typological analogies of both. Christ's death fulfilled the Passover, and the Eucharist was the Christian Paschal feast; Christ's death instituted the New Covenant, and the Eucharist was the sacrifice of the New Covenant. Since these ideas appear in the New Testament, they were clearly very early, and were likely to be influential because of their place in scripture.

We have already seen that Christ's death was believed to have been a sacrifice whereby the New Covenant was established, though only in the Epistle to the Hebrews was the typology with the sacrifice on Mt. Sinai explicitly worked out.[92] It is most frequently in relation to the Eucharist that we find references to the establishment of the New Covenant in the blood of Christ; this was what the wine of the cult-act represented according to the accounts of the Institution. It seems most likely that the idea that the Eucharist was a commemoration of the establishment of the New Covenant was early, most probably pre-Pauline.[93]

---

[92]See supra, Ch. 7.B. The idea of the New Covenant appears in Paul, but he does not speak of Christ establishing the New Covenant by his sacrifice. He uses the contrast between the covenants given to the Jews and the New Covenant of the spirit, confirmed in Christ (see 2 Cor. 3.6., 14; Gal. 4.24). In Eph. 2.22ff is found the expression "covenant of promise . . . brought new in the blood of Christ," and this probably represents Paul's thought, even if the Epistle was not written by him. This reference, and the implications of the "blood of the Covenant" in the Institution narrative are the only passages concerned with the New Covenant which are sacrificial, apart from the elaborate typology of Hebrews.

[93]On the grounds that the words "of the Covenant" in the Institution sayings cannot be translated into Aramaic, it has been strongly contended that Paul introduced this idea into his interpretation of the

In our earlier discussion of the Covenant-sacrifice it was pointed out that the Covenant-sacrifice was first and foremost a sacrifice of communion, whereby a "blood-relation" was established between Israel and God, but that simply because of the problem of failure to abide by the Old Covenant, the prophecy of the New Covenant was concerned with the final solution of the problem of sin. So the sacrifice which established the

---

Eucharist (e.g., by Jeremias,op. cit., p. 133; followed by Higgins, The Lord's Supper in the NT, pp. 33-4), and this contention is supported by the fact that the idea of the New Covenant figured centrally in the Pauline concept of the relation between Judaism and Christianity. Since, however, Paul makes no use of the idea in his exposition of the Eucharistic doctrine, and since it appears only in the traditional pericope of Institution which he quotes, it seems unlikely that he introduced the idea. He may well have influenced the form of the tradition so that the Covenant-idea was made more prominent, but one would expect him to have used the idea more positively if it was characteristically Pauline. It is not even absolutely clear that the words "of the Covenant" cannot be translated back into Aramaic: apparently it is not possible for both genitives, μοῦ and τῆς διαθήκης, to be contained in Aramaic construction, but M. Hokker (op. cit., p. 80ff) has enquired, why not regard the μοῦ as additional? There seems little ground for regarding the idea of the Covenant as appearing late in the tradition. It was an idea more intelligible to the Jew than to the Christian (see n. 102, infra). The most recent discussion of the origins of the Eucharist (Betz, Die Eucharistie in der Zeit der Griechischen Väter) regards the Covenant-idea as basic to the common tradition behind the Marcan version and the Antiochene version, which the author has already isolated from the Pauline and Lucan forms. (See Vol. II.1 pp. 16-8 for the Antiochene tradition and comparison with the Marcan; the Covenant-idea is contained in both, and is expounded as the kernel of the rite within the context of the primitive kerygma; pp. 34ff and 71ff.)

New Covenant was also atoning; it dealt with sin in order to make the establishment of a new covenant possible.[94] We have already noted that this aspect of the "blood of the New Covenant" was made explicit in the accounts of the Institution in Mark and Matthew, where the blood is said by the former to have been "poured out for many,"[95] and in the latter is added, "for the forgiveness of sins."[96] In Paul's account, there is no mention of this aspect of the Covenant-sacrifice, but in the light of his total theology, it is impossible to think that Paul did not believe that the establishment of the New Covenant in the spirit involved the removal of former sin.

The atonement idea is, however, only linked with Christ's sacrifice. The Eucharist itself is not an atoning sacrifice, either in the New Testament or in any of the writings which use the Covenant-idea. It is a proclaiming of the Lord's death; it is a memorial of an atoning sacrifice; it is the memorial of the establishment of the New Covenant. This is why it came to be linked with the Passover, and was regarded as the Christian fulfillment of the Jewish Paschal feast.

Paul himself concentrates on the communion-aspect of the Covenant-sacrifice, as far as the Eucharist is concerned. He does not connect the Eucharist with the sacrificial death of Christ outside the Institution accounts, and there its only connection is as a thankful memorial of that death. It is by Baptism that the Christian shares in Christ's death and is purified by his blood; in the Eucharist, he has communion in the Risen Life of the Lord, and engages in a joyful participation in the benefits of the New Covenant.

Thus, there is no clear indication in the New Testament that the Eucharist in any sense re-enacted the sacrifice of Christ. As a covenant-sacrifice, it was the actualising of the Covenant established by Christ. The Church, in the Eucharist, accepted the benefits of Christ's death, and joined in the very

---

[94]See supra, Ch. 7.B.

[95]Mk. 14.24.

[96]Matt. 26.28.

worship of heaven. The worshippers were sprinkled with the blood of the victim, Christ, and came up unto the Lord; they saw God, and ate and drank, as the people had on Sinai.[97] They were privileged to do this because in Baptism they had been purified by dying with Christ and rising again to a new life. Purity was required of all those who partook, and the action of the Eucharistic sacrifice was not in itself atoning; it recalled Christ's atoning death with thanksgiving.

The treatment of the Eucharist as a Passover celebration makes clear the intimate relationship of memorial between the cult-act and Christ's sacrifice.[98] Christ, the Passover lamb was sacrificed, and his blood protected the faithful from the Destroyer. Such was the typological relation between the death of Christ and the Passover; it depended on a return to the original Passover story in which God redeemed Israel from Egypt.[99] The typological relation between the Eucharist and the Passover, on the other hand, was based on the similarities between the Jewish annual Passover feast which recalled God's saving act of the past, and the memorial of Christ's death implied in the Eucharist. The blood of the Passover lamb was offered in Egypt to avert the Destroyer, but came to be offered to God at the altar in thanksgiving for the deliverance he had thus accomplished.[100] Likewise, the blood of the Eucharist was offered to God in thanksgiving, and as a memorial of the blood of Christ offered as a ransom-price to avert the devil. The Eucharist had the same function in Christianity as the Passover in Judaism, since both looked back with rejoicing and thanksgiving

---

[97]See Couratin, op. cit. He argues that the association of the Sanctus with the Eucharist, and the idea that the Church came into the presence of God in the Eucharist, depended on the typology of the Covenant-sacrifice on Sinai (*Ex*. 19 and 24). See esp. *Ex*. 24.1, 9-11, which are paraphrased in this sentence.

[98]See Additional Note III *infra*.

[99]See *supra*, Ch. 7.C.

[100]See *supra*, Ch. 2.B(a).

to the deliverance already brought about by God; they both also anticipated his future eschatological salvation. Certain similar characteristics in the celebrations drew attention to the parallel between them; both were meals of special thanksgiving and each was called a sacrifice.

The Passover and Covenant ideas originated in the New Testament and in a context of Jewish Christianity. They both expressed the relationship between the Eucharist and the sacrifice of Christ in terms of memorial of his saving death or actualising of the benefits of it. They did not explicitly imply a re-enactment of it. Neither of these two "types" seems to have dominated Eucharistic thought at any stage. They appear in the New Testament and then are of little importance until a much later stage when exposition of the canonised text became important. The Passover idea developed particularly when allegorical interpretation found intimate correspondences between the Jewish type and the annual Easter communion; the way in which the Passover was to be eaten was interpreted as the spiritual frame of mind required for receiving the Eucharist.[101] The Covenant idea is clearly Jewish, and would have most appeal to Jewish Converts.[102] In the context of a predominantly Gentile Church, the idea seems to have been allowed to lie dormant until Irenaeus made the specific claim that the Eucharist was the sacrifice of the New Covenant and contrasted it with the Old Dispensation when the Jewish Law had been in force.[103] The Eucharist thus became the

---

[101]See Additional Note III.

[102]Dix, Jew and Greek, p. 108. Nock, Early Gentile Christianity, p. 69ff describes the hellenising of the Covenant-idea which was essentially Jewish.

[103]Adv. Haer. IV.17.5. About this time, with the establishment of the Canon, the NT became known as the "New Covenant;" so, probably in opposition to Marcion's high-handed rejection of the OT the consciousness of being the people of the New Covenant became important in an entirely Gentile Church. The New Covenant idea was used mostly in the Pauline way to contrast the

characteristic cult-act of the New Israel's worship, and the theologians of the Eastern Church, conscious of the fact that they were heirs to the promises of the Old Israel, saw it as the example "par excellence" of the spiritual sacrifices which had replaced the old Law. The later liturgies contain the idea, at least partly no doubt by assimilation to the canonised Institution accounts in the New Testament.[104] The significance of the Covenant-sacrifice was now enshrined in the communion-idea, and in the continued belief that the Eucharist was a memorial of Christ's atoning death of which the blood was a symbol.[105]

For the earlier part of our period, the New Covenant and Passover typologies are confined to certain parts of the New Testament; the first appearance elsewhere of the New Covenant idea is in Irenaeus,[106] and of the Passover in Origen.[107] Apart from the occurrence of these typologies and the Institution accounts in the New Testament, there is little in the early part of our period to connect the Eucharist specifically with the <u>death</u> of Christ.[108] What

---

Jewish and Christian Dispensations, and the idea of the Eucharist being the Covenant-sacrifice implied that it was the characteristic sacrifice of the New Israel.

[104]Dix, loc. cit.

[105]Dix (op. cit., p. 109) remarks that the New Covenant became the Atonement.

[106]<u>Adv. Haer</u>., IV.17.5.

[107]<u>Comm. Jn</u>., 10.13; he allegorises the eating of the Passover Lamb with bitter herbs and unleavened bread as eating the flesh and blood of the Incarnate Word with repentance and sorrow.

[108]Even the use of an Institution account in the liturgy may have been a later development. This possibility seems to be generally admitted by those concerned with comparative liturgy. See Lietzmann (op. cit.) and Richardson's Supplementary Essay to the English translation of Lietzmann; also Dix. op. cit., pp. 226-7, 232-3. If this is so, I do not see how the Institution accounts could have been moulded by litur-

evidence there is concerning the nature of the Eucharist suggests a cult-meal centered on the ideas already discussed, namely communion, thanksgiving and the offering of first-fruits. The communion-elements impart Christ's Risen Life to the worshippers, and it is in Baptism not the Eucharist that the Christian enters into his death. This is true of the New Testament, the Apostolic Fathers, the Apologists, Irenaeus and the Alexandrians, whose discussions of the Eucharist have already been examined in earlier sections devoted to its character as a communion-sacrifice and thank-offering. There are a few exceptions in which communion in or memorial of the sacrificial death of Christ are emphasized: firstly, Ignatius' imagery for his martyr's death includes the suggestion that he is to drink the cup of the Lord, and to become the pure bread of Christ, and this implies that the Eucharist as well as Baptism could be a communion in the death of Christ;[109] secondly, Justin speaks on one occasion of the Eucharist as a memorial of his passion;[110] thirdly, the liturgy of Hippolytus

---

gical use before the writing of the NT. NT scholars assume that this accounts best for the form of the pericope but if the story had ever been recited in the liturgy, it is difficult to see why the practice should have dropped out.

[109]See Rom. VII.3; this should probably be interpreted as a reference to Ignatius' martyrdom, in the light of IV.1, where Ignatius says "I am God's wheat and I am ground by the teeth of wild beasts that I may be found a pure bread of Christ." Ignatius' language is often allusive and difficult to interpret. His combination of ideas is frequently due to his originality rather than to Church tradition.

[110]Justin's references to the Eucharist as a memorial are as follows: 1 Apol. 66; Dial. 41, 70, 117. Taken together, these passages support the view argued by Richardson in his Supplementary Essay (op. cit.), that Justin thought of the memorial as a memorial of the Incarnation, the whole redemptive act in Christ, and not a re-enacting of his passion or a participation in his sacrificial death.

uses the Institution account, speaks of the bread as his body "broken for you" and the wine as his blood "poured out for you," and associates the memorial specifically with Christ's death which freed the worshippers from death, sin and the devil.[111] But none of these exceptions necessarily implies a re-enactment of Christ's death, even though they associate his death more closely with the Eucharist than many other sources. According to our argument, even the Passover and New Covenant associations do not imply this, but like the phrases under consideration, simply draw attention to the nature of the Eucharist as a thankful memorial of Christ's sacrificial death, and as the means of receiving the benefits of his Covenant-sacrifice. The sacrifice of the Eucharist consists in its nature as a sacrifice offered by Christians in worship and thanksgiving, and shared in communion and by spiritual feeding. Any notion of re-enactment is implicit rather than explicit.

Yet, as we have seen, the eucharistic sacrifice was long regarded as a "memorial" of Christ's death, and while this does not necessarily imply a "representation" of that death,[112] it could easily develop into an

---

[111]Lietzmann (op. cit., p. 144) indicates that the concept of sacrifice in the liturgy of Hippolytus was similar to that involved in the offering of first-fruits and Christian fellowship-meals. There is no logical connection between the Institution account and the sacrifice, and nowhere is it claimed that Christ offered a sacrifice at his passion and that the Church offers a sacrifice analogous to it. If this is right, the presence of the Institution narrative in the liturgy does not signify anything more than a memorial of thanksgiving, such as we have found elsewhere.

[112]This is in contrast to Dix who assumes that for the whole of the pre-Nicene Church, the anamnesis was a "re-calling" or "re-presenting" of the thing in such a way that it is not so much "absent" as itself _presently operative_ by its effects (op. cit., p. 245). Others have this same view on the "azkarah" or memorial element in the Israelite cult, claiming that it implies a

explicit acceptance of this idea, particularly under the influence of the mystery-religions. The mystery-rites involved a secret, sacred drama, a presentation of the saving myth of the dying and rising god. As we have seen, the eucharist was regarded as analogous to a mystery-rite from very early on,[113] and this was increasingly the case as the Church became the "official religion" of the Empire, and sought to reserve its central mysteries for the truly initiated, that is, the baptised. It was a short step from drama to re-enactment, especially in the case of a cult-act which was already regarded as efficacious for the partakers in actualising the benefits of the saving event recalled. Cyprian was the first to state explicitly that "the Lord's passion is the sacrifice which we offer," and the way in which it is assumed by a writer who was no innovator suggests that it was a generally current assumption in the West in his time.[114]

Open acknowledgement that the Eucharist re-enacted the sacrifice of Christ had two consequences. Firstly, the sacrifice of the Eucharist became a sacrifice for sin, in spite of the requirement of purity for participation. The elements were offered to God as a re-enactment of Christ's saving action on the cross, and once his death was regarded as propitiatory in the same way. So, as we have already seen, Cyril of Jerusalem states that this memorial sacrifice is offered on behalf of the whole world and of the participants to propitiate God. Secondly, the sacrifice of the Eucharist ceased to have an independent significance of its

---

"re-actualisation." See J. de Watteville, _Le sacrifice dans les textes eucharistiques des premiers siècles_, p. 17ff. But I fail to see explicit evidence for this in the texts until a later date. I admit that the rite makes real the benefits of the saving act recalled, but does this really mean that the act itself is re-enacted? Adequate grounds for this common assertion have yet to be produced.

[113]See _supra_.

[114]Cyprian, _Ep_. lxiii.9.17. See M. F. Wiles, "The Theological Legacy of St. Cyprian," _JEH_ (1963).

own and became part of the one, perfect sacrifice of Christ. "We offer Christ crucified for our sins, propitiating God, lover of men, for them and for ourselves," says Cyril.[115] Gregory of Nazianzus later went so far as to speak of the time "when you sacrifice the Master's body and blood with bloodless knife."[116] So Chrysostom finds himself obliged to explain the relationship between the sacrifice of the Eucharist and Christ's sacrifice. Eusebius had reduced the Eucharist to a "memorial" to be offered continuously to God in place of a sacrifice;[117] but Chrysostom admits that the Eucharist was a sacrifice, so following long-standing tradition, and then claims that the sacrifice of the Eucharist is identical with the sacrifice of Christ.[118] His discussion occurs in a passage in his *Homilies on Hebrews* where he is commenting on the contrast which the Epistle makes between the repeated sacrifices of the Jews which merely kept sin in remembrance and had no power to cleanse, and the one, unique and all-powerful sacrifice of Christ; he raises the objection, "Do we not sacrifice every day?" He admits that we do in the Eucharist, but explains that it is "making a memorial of his death, and this sacrifice is one and not many;" and "that sacrifice was offered once for all and carried into the Holy of Holies . . . We offer always the same person, not one sheep now and tomorrow another, but always the same; so that the sacrifice is one . . . . Just as, while offered in many places, he is one body and not many bodies, so also there is one sacrifice. He is our High-Priest who offered the sacrifice which cleansed us.

---

[115]Cyril Jer., *Cat. Or.* V.8-10.

[116]Greg. Naz., *Ep.* 171. The word used is τεμνῇς which could mean simply "cut," but the context shows that he is using sacrificial imagery.

[117]Eusebius, *Dem. Evan.* I.10.25: Christ offered to the Father, for the salvation of all, a wonderful sacrifice and unique victim, and delivered to us a memorial to offer continually to God in place of a sacrifice.

[118]*Hom. Heb.* XXVII.

The sacrifice we offer now is the sacrifice which was then offered, which cannot be exhausted. This is done in memorial of what was then done . . . . It is not another sacrifice we offer, but always the same, or rather we perform the memorial of a sacrifice." Chrysostom is clearly trying to express a rather complicated relation which finally leads him to reduce the Eucharist to a memorial in the way that Eusebius had done. But on the way to this conclusion, he has identified the sacrifice of the Eucharist with the one, perfect sacrifice of Christ. His analogy with the unity of the body offered in many different places is an interesting one, since it recalls the emphasis of St. Paul on the unity of the loaf, and the prayer found in the Didache and the liturgy of Serapion that the Church may be united as the loaf is composed of the fruit of grains once scattered over the mountains. The mystic unity of the Church as the Body of Christ is represented in the loaf, and the unity of Christ's sacrifice is evident in the bread in spite of the fact that it is broken in many different places and at many different times. The Eucharistic sacrifice is not independent of the sacrifice of Christ, nor is it a repetition of it, but it has a mystic unity with it. The same interpretation is presupposed in the question raised by Gregory of Nyssa:[119] How could Christ give the disciples his flesh and blood to eat at the Last Supper while he was alive? His answer was that in some unspeakable and unseen way, by the power of him who arranged the mystery (τοῦ τὸ μυστήριον οἰκονομοῦντος), his body had already been sacrificed. The lamb sacrificed on the Cross for the sins of the world is identical with the body and blood sacrificed in the Eucharist.

At this stage then, the Eucharist not only acquired propitiatory significance and added to its character that of a sacrifice for sin, but it also tended to be subordinated to the sacrifice of Christ, becoming actually part of it. With this emphasis predominant, it ceased to be a sacrifice in its own right, though no doubt it may be felt that its significance was enhanced by this development. The

---

[119] Greg. Nys., In Christi Res., MPG 46/612 C-D.

mystical unity of the Church and Christ, and of the sacrificial action of Christ and his Body on earth, came to be represented in the mystical unity of his sacrifice on the Cross with the offering of the Eucharistic elements, presented on the altar as re-enactment of his propitiatory sacrifice.

C. Conclusion

The nature of the Eucharist is particularly complex because of the ambiguity of its relation with the death of Christ. It was and was not a sacrifice in its own right.

The meaning of the Eucharistic sacrifice throughout most of our period in the Eastern Church depended on its interpretation in terms of a communion-sacrifice and thank-offering of worship. Only those who were pure could partake of it, so it was not a sacrifice of purification; it was a partaking in the benefits of the New Covenant established through Christ's death by those already baptised and purified by repentance. Origen represents the predominant tradition when he fails to include the Eucharist among sacrifices for sin.[120] It was a sacrifice offered in memory of God's saving act in Christ and in anticipation of his future blessings; this Christian Passover was open only to those who had been saved by entering into the death of Christ in Baptism. In the Eucharist, the Christian bloodless and spiritual cult was consummated, as with humility the Church offered to God the supreme sacrifice of praise and thanksgiving, celebrating the memory of the great sacrifice whereby salvation was accomplished,[121] and entering into the worship of heaven itself. It was a sacrifice offered by the Church to God.

---

[120]See Hom. Lev. II.4.

[121]See Eusebius, Dem. Evan. I.10.28-38.

This tradition remained most important, even when explicit acceptance of the eucharistic sacrifice being a re-enactment of the sacrifice of Christ made it therefore dependent on Christ's sacrifice for its sacrificial character. Even as a propitiatory sacrifice, the eucharist itself did not deal with sin, for those who partook had already to be "pure," and God was "propitiated" by the presence of the purified and holy Christians rejoicing in the communion of the body and blood of his Son with thanksgiving, performing the memorial of his precious atoning death whereby man and God were reconciled. God was brought to men in the spiritual food offered for communion, and man was brought to God by the offering of the memorial of the sacrifice whereby God was reconciled to himself.[122] The Eucharist was intimately related to the death of Christ because it was the actualising of atonement in the Church and in the individual believer. Therefore there was a sense in which the Eucharist could acquire the overtones of _all_ types of sin-offering, depending which type was used to interpret Christ's death. Yet, it was only in the light of an atonement theory involving a sacrifice offered to God in propitiation that the eucharistic sacrifice could come to be identified with the sacrifice of Christ; and, in spite of this identification, the tradition remained predominant in the East that the Eucharist was a communion-sacrifice, in contrast to the predominance in the West of its interpretation as a "gift-sacrifice" offered to God to propitiate him for sins.[123] It was a communion-sacrifice which effected "new creation," actualised the New Covenant already established in Christ, and made atonement present in the life of the Church.

---

[122]Greg. Naz., _Poem. Mor_. XXXIV, 1, 228.

[123]This distinction is made by R. D. Richardson, "Eastern and Western Liturgies: the primitive basis for their later divergences," _HTR_ (1949).

Thus the eucharistic sacrifice was understood in terms of the three basic types of sacrifice analysed in this study, retaining its character as a sacrifice offered and shared in by Christian worshippers, as well as becoming an intimate part of Christ's sacrifice for sin. In this way it expressed the whole sacrificial thought and action of the Church.[124]

---

[124]Since this chapter was originally written, the comprehensive survey of texts by Jean de Watteville (op. cit.) has come to my notice. It is a useful work, but like other studies, makes no use of the distinction between different types of sacrifice employed here, and reads into the texts a greater element of "reactualising" Christ's sacrifice than I have tended to admit in the above discussion (cf. n. 112).

CHAPTER TWELVE

THE ROLE OF CHRIST AS HIGH-PRIEST AND SACRIFICE IN THE CHRISTIAN SPIRITUAL CULT

The aim of this chapter is to summarise briefly the conclusions so far reached concerning the relationship between the spiritual sacrifices offered by Christians and the sacrificial action of Christ; and to amplify the account we have already given by drawing attention to the role that Christ played in the Christian spiritual cult as High-Priest at the heavenly altar. We shall find that the sacrificial activity of Christ and the Church are intimately bound together, at least partly because the Church was incorporated into Christ himself, but also because the Church could offer no sacrifice independent of Christ's High-Priestly work.

In an earlier chapter on the types of sacrifice offered by Christians, it was argued that a general distinction could be made between the sacrifice of Christ and those of Christians, and that this distinction is found in a number of the relevant texts: namely, that the sacrifice of Christ was the final, supreme and perfect sin-offering, and the spiritual sacrifices of Christians were a response of praise and thanksgiving for the benefits of the sacrifice he had offered to save them from sin. Even at that stage, however, it was recognised that this distinction did not fully account for all aspects of the Christian spiritual cult and evidence was found for Christian offerings for sin, as well as sacrifices of praise and thanksgiving. In a later chapter, we had to take account of the fact that Christians were called upon to imitate the sacrifice of Christ in their own spiritual self-offering to God, and we found some grounds for regarding Christ's sacrifice not only as a sacrifice for sin, but also as a sacrifice of praise to God expressed in his offering of Man's perfect obedience, an offering Christians were naturally exhorted to imitate. The relationship was therefore more complex than the simple distinction made earlier.

In this section, we have devoted two chapters to tackling some of the most acute cases in which the relationship of the sacrifice of Christ and those of Christians needs elucidation: the problem of how Christians could offer any sacrifices for sin when Christ had offered the one perfect and complete sacrifice for the sins of the whole world; and the question of the nature of the Eucharistic sacrifice and its special association with the sacrificial death of Christ. In the case of the Eucharist, our original distinction seems, in general, to apply, the Eucharist being, in the early and Eastern tradition, predominantly a sacrifice of communion and thanksgiving offered by Christians in thankful remembrance of the great act of salvation which God had performed in Christ's sacrifice. Christ's sacrifice was the sacrifice for sin which was commemorated in the Christian sacrifice of thanksgiving and communion. This distinction was never explicit, however, and certainly broke down when the Eucharist began to acquire propitiatory power, but this depended entirely on its being a symbolic re-enactment of the one and only atoning sacrifice, that of Christ on the Cross. It was not a new and different sin-offering, but had a mystic unity with the one sacrifice for sin offered by Christ. Insofar as it was a sin-offering, it was not a sacrifice in its own right, but only in relation to the sacrifice of Christ. As a response of praise and thanksgiving, however, and as a communion in the spiritual food given by God, it was offered by Christians as a sacrifice with its own identity.

In the case of the other sin-offerings, Christians did offer them as sacrifices independent of Christ's sacrifice, for one very practical reason: it was found by experience to be too idealistic to expect men not to sin after Baptism, a requirement which had originally been binding because in Baptism the benefits of Christ's death were once for all received. But, again, there was a theologically more significant factor involved, the Christian consciousness of participating in Christ's sacrifice for the removal of evil from the creation. It was this participation in the sufferings of Christ that inspired, in particular, the courage of the Christian martyr in the face of cruel death.

The unity of Christ and the Church, of Christ and the Christian and of Christ and mankind as a whole accounts for the close relation between the spiritual sacrifices offered by Christians and his self-oblation. This unity was conceived in various different ways. To Paul, the Church was the Body of Christ and the Christian people were in Christ. In Baptism they died his death to sin; in martyrdom they shared in his sufferings. His resurrection was the first-fruits of the resurrection of those who believed in him. To Athanasius, humanity was summed up in Christ.[1] In his death, all men had died and so the debt to death was paid. In his ascension, mankind ascended, purified and perfected, fit to be presented to God. As we have already noted in Chapter Ten, this participation in Christ accounts for the belief that the martyr's sacrifice was efficacious for dealing with sin and was part of Christ's own conquest of the devil. So even when they were shy of speaking of Christ's sacrifice as being in itself one of praise to God, Christians still saw the perfect, willing self-sacrifice of Christ, accepted in obedience to the will of the Father, as the example and archetype of their own self-offering, whether in a life dedicated to God and lived "in Christ," displaying his humility, chastity and love, or supremely in a martyr's death died in imitation of him on the Cross.

The Christian was thus involved in Christ's sacrifice, and his own sacrifices were but a pale imitation of his perfect self-oblation. But it was also true that Christ was involved in the sacrifices of his followers. Christ's role in the Christian cult, especially as High-Priest, was to offer to God the sacrifices of the Church. Christ's priesthood applied not only to his own sacrifice in which he offered up his sinless self as victim; he was also the High-Priest of Christian spiritual offerings. "We praise God

---

[1]See Additional Note II.

through Jesus Christ, the High-Priest and Defender of our souls," says Clement of Rome, "Jesus Christ, the High-Priest of our offerings, the Defender and Protector of our weakness."[2] Origen stresses this particularly: "He who wishes to offer a sacrifice to God, ought to offer it through the hands of the High-Priest."[3] He even goes so far as to say that the priestly work of Christ is dependent on the spiritual offerings of Christians; we have to provide the offerings of pity, justice, piety, and peace which Christ, as High-Priest, needs to offer to God.[4] It is out of the "living stones" who are prepared to make time for prayers, to sacrifice victims of supplication, that Jesus (Joshua) builds his altar so as to offer up holocausts and a sacrifice for salvation: so Origen allegorises Joshua's building of an altar to celebrate a sacrifice of thanksgiving for victory.[5] The Church must be prepared to be built up as an altar of "living stones," to be the Temple of God and the Body of Christ, so that the saving work of Christ can take place. Christ and his followers were mutually involved, they in his sacrifice and he in their offerings. Christian prayers were offered through him as High-Priest:[6] he was never absent from anyone's prayers, and the Christian who prayed in fact shared in the prayer of the Word of God.[7]

Christ's role as High-Priest was very important throughout the tradition of the East concerning the Christian spiritual cult. Although, according to the standards of contemporary religions, the paraphernalia

---

[2]1 *Clem.* LXI.3 and XXXVI.1. Cf. Origen, *On Prayer*, X.2: "For the Son of God is the High-Priest of our offerings and our advocate with the Father."

[3]Origen, *Comm. Rom.* I.9; see also his use of the idea in *C. Cels.*: Christ our High-Priest taught us the pure way to worship God and offers our prayers to the Father (III.34; V.4; VI.20; VII.46; VIII.13, 26, 34-6).

[4]*Hom. Lev.* IX.6, 8. [5]*Hom. Jos.* IX.1.

[6]See 1 *Clem.* LXI,3 and *Mart. Pol.* XIV.3.

[7]Origen, *On Prayer* X.2, XV.2: "One must not make a prayer to the Father apart from him."

of a proper religious cult were absent, they had been entirely replaced for Christians by spiritual things. There was no visible temple, for the Temple of God was the Church, or the body of the faithful Christian.[8] There was no High-Priest because Christ was the priest of their offerings. There were no sacrificial victims, because Christians had in themselves the virtues and prayers to offer as worthy sacrifices to God.[9] Christ's function as the heavenly High-Priest who presented the offerings made by Christians to the Father was central to the whole scheme. The Christian altar was in heaven and the Christian High-Priest fulfilled his office there.

In the hands of the Antiochenes, Christ's High-Priesthood became linked with his continuing Manhood; as a priest involved in human suffering and temptation, he is able to have sympathy with men, even now that he is ascended to heaven, for there he not only sits on the throne as God, but he also remains the High-Priestly representative of mankind.[10] But this aspect of Christ's priesthood is not developed elsewhere in the Fathers, and is not directly relevant to our subject. Nor need we digress onto the subject of how Christ's priesthood was justified by more and more detailed exegesis of the Melchisedek allegory found first in _Hebrews_, and then throughout the literature from Justin to Chrysostom. It is the part that Christ played as High-Priest within the offering of the Christian spiritual cult that is of interest here, because it is another example of how closely Christ and his Church were associated in their sacrificial activity. This is the aspect of Christ's High-Priesthood that predominates in the Eastern tradition. For Origen, it is through him that spiritual sacrifices can reach the throne of a God who transcends all that man could offer.

---

[8]Temple of God = Church, e.g., Origen, _Comm. Jn._ X.20; = body of Christian, e.g., Origen, _C. Cels._ VIII.19.

[9]See _Hom. Lev._ V.2.

[10]This played considerable part in their exegesis of _Hebrews_; e.g., Chrysostom, _Hom. Heb._ XIV.1.

For later authors, he was the one who could so offer Christian sacrifices as to propitiate the Father: "The great High-Priest of the universe, Jesus himself, the only begotten of God receives, with shining eyes and upturned hands, the sweet-smelling incense of all the worshippers, and the bloodless and immaterial prayer-sacrifices, and transmits them to the Father in heaven, the God of the universe. He himself first adores the Father, and alone renders him the honour due; then he beseeches him to continue favourable and propitious towards us for ever."[11]

As High-Priest of the offerings of Christians, Christ was the priest who offered the Eucharistic elements on the heavenly altar to God, the Father;[12] this was how Christians entered into the very worship of heaven through this sacrifice. The Eucharist was the Christian sacrifice "par excellence," because it was a spiritual sacrifice of praise and thanksgiving offered through Christ, the High-Priest at the heavenly altar in response to God's act of redeeming grace in his Son; but also because it came to have an intimate unity with the sacrifice which Christ himself had offered to God on the Cross, acting as both High-Priest and victim. So Chrysostom could sum it all up in the words, "We have our victim in heaven, our priest in heaven, our sacrifice in heaven;" for, when the Lord Jesus lies as a slain victim, spiritual things are sacrificed which are worthy of heaven though celebrated on earth.[13]

The relationship of the sacrifice of Christ and the spiritual cult of the Christians is complex, because Christ and his Church are intimately bound together both in the fight against sin and evil, and in the offering of proper worship to God. In the work of Atonement, Christ offered a sacrifice to save

---

[11]Eusebius, Hist. Eccl. X.4.68. These words appear in a sermon reported in full by Eusebius as delivered at the dedication of the new Cathedral by "one of the moderately capable," presumably himself.

[12]See Dix, The Shape of the Liturgy, p. 252.

[13]Hom. Heb. XIV.1,2.

mankind, and insofar as the Christian joined in the expiatory work of Christ, he was given the power of God to enable him to conquer in the battle against evil. In his work as High-Priest, Christ was intimately involved in the sacrifices of the Church, providing the example of the perfect self-offering for Christians to follow and presenting to the Father their offerings of spiritual worship. This intimate relation is the reason why our simple distinction between Christ's sacrifice for sin and the Christians' response of sacrificial worship cannot entirely account for the evidence to be found in the writings studied.

CONCLUSION

The aim of this study was to examine the nature of the sacrifice of Christ in a broader context than that within which it is usually treated. With this purpose in mind, considerable space had been devoted to background studies, and to tracing contemporary Jewish and Greek influences on the formation, justification and interpretation of the Christian spiritual cult. Discussion of Christ's sacrifice has been placed alongside consideration of the sacrifices offered by his followers, and both have been examined in the light of relevant contemporary ideas.

In evaluating the results of this study, it must be admitted that the analysis of sacrifice according to types has been too neat. The scheme has to some extent been artificially imposed on a vast range of homiletic and other material, where consistency and logic are probably not to be expected; devotional language may use images of powerful emotional appeal without necessarily implying that a rational conception or theory lies behind their use. However, unexpressed assumptions about sacrifice must have been present, otherwise there would have been nothing to which sacrificial language could appeal, and it is these underlying possibly unconscious, interpretations that we have tried to uncover by analysis of sacrificial ideas into types based on consideration of the cults that formed the natural background to Christian usage. The weakness of this method consists in the fact that, though based on contemporary ideas, the writers with whom we have been concerned were not necessarily aware of the distinctions that we have drawn in our analysis. This generalisation is not entirely true: our analysis of Jewish sacrifices follows the same pattern as Philo's; distinctions in the purpose of Greek sacrifices were recognised at least by the Neoplatonists; and Origen differentiated between sacrifice "pro munere" and "pro peccato." But the mere fact that language implying different types was frequently applied to the same sacrificial action, for example, martyrdom or the

Eucharist, is enough to warn against too rigid an application of our analysis. In general, sacrifice language was used without too much discrimination, and with little concern over the resulting confusion. This is true even of Origen, whose predilection for conflicting allegorisations should warn us against claiming that all his statements are consistent.

In spite of these dangers in the basic approach adopted in this study, there have been some interesting results. The method of classification has served its purpose in highlighting aspects of sacrifice other than the commonly understood propitiatory interpretation. It has emphasised the importance and diversity of sacrificial ideas in Eastern worship, theology and ethics. It has shown that in the Greek Church, the Eucharistic sacrifice was far richer in meaning than is implied by the transactional character of the Western Mass; indeed, in our period, so far from being primarily propitiatory, the sacrifice involved in the Eucharistic rite was chiefly one of communion, thanksgiving and worship. Besides this, it has thrown considerable light on the very questions of Atonement theory, a narrow study of which was to be avoided.

It is some time since a full-scale History of Atonement Theory has been written, and the results of this study should modify earlier evaluations. As indicated in the Introduction, consideration of the treatment of Christ's sacrificial death in the writings of the Greek Fathers has been inadequate. While J. Rivière[1] seized on every sacrificial reference and read into it the complete expression of a theory of penal substitution, H. Rashdall[2] dismissed all such language as merely the use of traditional imagery. As a result, in Rivière's history, Eusebius' theory is regarded as the most important statement in the Greek Fathers and provides the basis for interpreting Athanasius, while in Rashdall's work, Athanasius is relegated to an Appendix, and Origen's views, expounded

---

[1]J. Rivière, The Doctrine of the Atonement.

[2]H. Rashdall, The Idea of Atonement in Christian Theology.

solely in terms of moral and intellectual response to the influence of the Logos, are represented as the culmination of Eastern thought. R. S. Franks[3] alone recognised that Athanasius produced the first complete and systematic treatment of the subject. Besides this, neither Rashdall nor Rivière recognised the importance of the "Christus Victor" theory. Since it is so prominent in the Fathers, they had to mention it, but Rashdall calls it "hideous," and Rivière regards it as "rank weeds;" both are thankful that the Church did not follow what they regard as such an unattractive side-track. Since then, G. Aulén[4] has redeemed the theory, and shown that it was the basic understanding of the Atonement found in the Fathers; but H. E. W. Turner,[5] while recognising the importance of this work, still regards it as only one of the ways in which the Fathers understood the work of Christ.[6]

It will be apparent from the present study that none of these earlier histories correctly emphasised either the Classic theory or the place of Christ's sacrifice within it. The consistency of Origen's rationale of Atonement and sacrifice within terms of the Classic theory has been overlooked,[7] and the

---

[3]R. S. Franks, History of the Doctrine of the Work of Christ.

[4]G. Aulén, Christus Victor.

[5]H. E. W. Turner, The Patristic Doctrine of Redemption.

[6]Since this was written, the situation has been somewhat improved by the publication of F. W. Dillistone's imaginative exploration of the variety of ways of expressing atonement; The Christian Understanding of Atonement (Philadelphia, 1968). See also F. R. Barry, The Atonement (Philadelphia, 1968).

7. Franks (op. cit.) recognises three features in Origen's ideas about the cross: (1) Christ overcomes the daemons by his death, (2) his death was a ransom paid by God to the devil, and (3) his death was a sacrifice to God. On the last, Franks says that Origen was the first to use this idea since Paul, and that it was an epoch-making move; he recognised that sin needs

achievement of Athanasius in reconciling conflicting elements of tradition has never been fully recognised.

It is impossible here to embark on re-writing the history of the doctrine of Atonement in the Greek Fathers, but a summary sketch of the lines along which it should go, may be attempted. The basic dualism of Christian thought must first be accepted, and this must be recognised in all the Fathers, including Origen, Athanasius and the Cappadocians. The pattern of soteriological thought apparent throughout our period must be seen as twofold: first, God's conquest of the devil and removal of evil and sin from his creation; secondly, his acceptance of recreated humanity in Christ. Sacrifice-language was used of both these aspects, but particularly of the first. It had a powerful appeal in the context of a society where sacrifice was a normal activity. No definition of sacrifice ever appears because there was no necessity for it; inevitably it was understood according to largely unconscious assumptions about how it worked, especially in popular theology. In the context of the Jewish Christian Church, it was understood as expiatory; in the context of the Greek-speaking Church, it was often assumed to imply propitiation, even though this was inconsistent with the usual interpretation of Christ's death as the action of God overcoming the devil. Origen reconciled the use of sacrificial imagery with the predominant theory of Christ's atoning work by understanding the sacrifice as analogous to aversion-sacrifices found in the Greek tradition, and there is some reason for thinking that this interpretation was common elsewhere also. The culmination of Eastern thought about Atonement is found in Athanasius, who reconciled the idea of a propitiatory sacrifice with insistence on the saving action of God in dealing with sin, death and the devil; and linked the tradition that Christ became human in order to make us divine, with his sacrificial offering of perfected humanity to the Father.

"propitiation." The important point for our argument is that Franks fails to see that, when pressed to rationalise, Origen in fact found a way of reconciling these three aspects in his thought. See <u>supra</u>, Ch. VIII.B.

But this study has not simply resulted in a re-evaluation of the history of Atonement. It aimed to broaden the whole context in which Atonement ideas were to be discussed. So we have found that the work of Christ cannot be treated in isolation from the sacrificial activity of the Church. Sacrifice-language is not only used to describe his atoning work, but is the expression of the faith and worship which must be the response to that work if it is to have any effect. Furthermore, it represents not merely response, but actual participation in the work of Christ. Worship and Atonement are shown to be commingled and ultimately inseparable. Sacrifice is properly treated as cult-language, not the language of juridical theory, and in such a context, it is clear that Christ's sacrifice was not substitutionary, but representative, a sacrifice in which Christians have to partake in order to receive its benefits.

It is clear that historical studies of the kind produced by Rashdall and Rivière were largely motivated by contemporary theological concerns. The present work has, as far as possible, been conducted solely with the purpose of uncovering the way in which the theologians of our period tackled explanation of the devotional language naturally employed by the Church. But it is inevitable that the results of the study should be considered from the present theological standpoint, and the value of the conclusions reached be assessed. This is not the place for an elaborate consideration of this question, but it is worth mentioning that a recent penetrating examination of the Atonement by H. A. Hodges,[8] not only offers a brilliant critique of the traditional Western theory of satisfaction and substitution, but restates in counterbalance to it, the very theory that is found in the Eastern Fathers. This is not to say that the concept of warfare with a personal devil is advocated. Clearly some "de-

---

[8]H. A. Hodges, The Pattern of Atonement. Barth's threatment of God's opposition to "das Nichtigs" is also a modern restatement of the Classic Theory. See also Dillistone (op. cit.) and Barry (op. cit.).

mythologising" is necessary. However, Atonement is treated in terms of the conflict between good and evil in the creation, with an insistence on the fact that Atonement comes <u>from</u> God rather than on the idea of offering satisfaction <u>to</u> God. The intention and result of Atonement is described as the ending of Man's enslavement to false ideologies and uncontrollable psychological forces. One real advantage of approaching the problem of Atonement along the lines of the Classic theory, is that instead of being limited to the riddance of one type of guilt-feeling, the salvation brought by Christ is shown to be relevant to all forms of alienation and all problems of human weakness, as well as to tremendous social evils. Another advantage is that emphasis is reserved for the saving action of God, and a division between the persons of the Godhead, Father and Son, is avoided. The sovereignty of God is preserved by the idea of self-reconciliation, the view that God himself found a method of reconciling with his goodness the fact that evil had been allowed to appear in his creation.

But, how did the Incarnation and death of Christ accomplish the victory over evil which is claimed for it? The mythological picture of God giving up his own Son to redeem mankind from the devil has the positive value of emphasising the cost to God of forgiveness, and the depths of the love that would bear such a cost for the sake of mankind; but it does not solve for us the problem of how evil was dealt with. The suggestion that the devil had rights over men out of which he was bought, or that he received Christ as a ransom for men, is not merely mythological, but morally indefensible. This aspect of the Classic theory can only be regarded as an unfortunate distortion of it - though in criticising it, it is as well to remember that the cruder statements of the penal substitution theory must likewise be regarded as morally repugnant distortions. The idea of God's self-reconciliation or self-propitiation eases the moral problems of both the Classic and the Western theories of Atonement, while retaining the essential emphases of both; but it only serves to explain how God solved his own "dilemma," otherwise expressed as the conflict between his justice and his mercy. It does not explain how the evil in the creation was in principle overcome by the life and death of Christ.

A satisfactory answer to this problem is impossible in this brief discussion, but it receives at least a partial answer in the other aspect of Christ's work emphasised in this study. Evil is dealt with by the restoration of perfection to corrupt human nature, and God, by becoming Man, and being involved in all that was wrong with Man, recreated human nature. Christ's death was not a straight substitute for the death of sinful men; rather in his death, all men may die and rise again. By identification with Christ through faith, mankind is restored to perfect worship of God and complete self-offering to God in a life of proper obedience. This is why there is such a close relation between the atoning death of Christ and the imitation of him which Christians called their sacrifice; this is why he is involved as priest in the offering of the spiritual sacrifices of perfected humanity. They in Christ, and Christ in them, offer the sacrifice. The healing of mankind's sin and weakness was not artificial or external, but was done in and through Man in Christ.

How the unity between men and Christ is to be conceived in modern terms is still a problem. Platonic concepts, like those of Athanasius, will not be acceptable; Christ is not the "Idea" of Man in which we all participate, nor is he collective humanity. The interpretation most easily visualised is an identification with Christ undertaken by the believing Christian as an act of will and with repentance - a moral and emotional identification by which the influence of the perfect, sinless life of one who reveals the full depths of God's love and forgiveness, is allowed full impact on the mind and will of the individual. This seems close to subjective views of the Atonement and may appear to undermine the objective emphasis of the Classic theory which is being defended. But only God has the power to remould the warped conscience and free the mind from slavery to favourite psychological sicknesses and pet sins. Man cannot free himself from his follies and idols simply by wanting to or trying hard. The perfectly objective influence of the creative love of God does the work of conversion. Our adoption as sons of God depends on the Spirit of God witnessing with our spirit that we are one with Christ through faith. The slogan "salvation by faith" is far more consistent with this interpretation than with the artificial substitution theory of Atonement with which it is usually associated. If Christ simply died in place of all sinners whether they recognise it or not, the Atonement is in danger of being so objective that faith is not required. Our identification with Christ is necessary, and only faith can make this identification.

One reason why this interpretation of Christ's unity with mankind seems subjective is because it is highly individualistic. But, in fact, it is through the Church that God's power to recreate human wills and consciences is mediated, however indirectly. It is the Church which preaches Christ who perfectly revealed the full depths of God's love and forgiveness. So when the Church is properly itself, it enters into Christ's work as a community, and is the means whereby God's saving influence is objectively expressed in the world. The believing Christian does not simply enter as an individual into a moral and emotional identification with Christ at a purely subjective level, but he takes his place in a community which attempts to be the Body of Christ on earth. This community not only continues the saving activity of Christ, but responds to it by offering spiritual sacrifices of worship through him; in this way, mankind within the Body of Christ is restored to perfect worship of God and complete self-offering to God in a life of proper obedience. The fellowship and unity of Christ and the Church is expressed supremely in the Eucharistic sacrifice which is a sacrifice of communion not only in the sense that the individual receives spiritual nourishment from it, but also as a fellowship-meal uniting the partakers in worship, faith and service. The unity of Christ and the Christian is objectively expressed in the communal life of the Church. Christ's work of Atonement can only be accomplished fully in the Church, and a proper understanding of it cannot be reached in isolation from consideration of the Church's life, service and worship.

These theological considerations need not be pursued further here. In summary of the results of this study, we may say that its main value has been in highlighting the importance and diversity of sacrificial concepts in the theological thought and spiritual life of the Greek Fathers, by drawing attention to meanings of sacrifice other than the propitiation idea, by re-appraising the significance of sacrificial ideas for their understanding of Atonement, and by emphasising the Church's spiritual cult, the sacrificial activity in which Christ and his Church were mutually involved. Our study of how extensive and varied was the use of sacrificial ideas in Greek Christian writers from the New Testament to John Chrysostom, has indicated that Atonement ideas should be considered in a much richer and broader context than is usual, and has provided lines of approach which should prove fruitful and suggestive in modern theological discussions.

ADDITIONAL NOTE I

The remarks on p. 81ff are based on the results of the study made by Marcel Simon in his _St. Stephen and the Hellenists of the Primitive Church_ (London, 1958). On the disputed question of who the Hellenists were, he argues that they were Hellenizers who, under the influence of Hellenistic philosophy and Jewish polemic against heathen idolatry, applied the same arguments to the Jewish sanctuary as to pagan temples: the Most High does not dwell in houses made with hands (_Acts_ 7.48). They called for a complete spiritualisation of worship and regarded sacrifice as always having been a form of idolatry, not God's will but a distortion of God's Law. Hence, Stephen's speech makes use of the prophetic anticultic passages and only depicts Aaron, from whom the priests proudly claimed descent, as opposed to Moses the true prophet, making use, too, of the Golden Calf, a blatant case of idolatry (_Acts_ 7.40ff). The entire speech of Stephen is negative and anti-Jewish whereas Peter, although he accuses the Jews of having killed the Prince of Life, excuses them and appeals for repentance (_Acts_ 3.17).

As against the positive attitude toward the Law adopted by Peter, Paul and the general Christian tradition (i.e., that the Law was given by God for the good of his people), Stephen regards the Jews as having always observed an idolatrous distortion of the Law, of which the very building of the Temple was an example. God never ordained sacrificial worship. "It seems obvious that Stephen stands, so to say, at the confluence of the two traditions: the prophetic tradition of the Bible and the philosophic tradition of the Gentiles" (Simon, op. cit., p. 88). Stephen's rejection would be blasphemous in the eyes of an orthodox Jew, and the false witnesses charge him with speaking against this Holy Place and the Law, saying that Jesus will destroy it and change the customs delivered to the Jews by Moses (_Acts_ 6.13-14). If this was the position of the Hellenists, then the fact that the subsequent persecution only affected them and not the more orthodox apostles is more understandable. If Stephen's speech does imply an anti-cultic, anti-Torah party in Jerusalem which has been concealed by the orthodox writing up of the incident by Luke (who makes Stephen a prototypical martyr) then Stephen stands virtually alone in the Christian tradition which, although later rejecting the cult for christological reasons, never rejected the idea that the Law was given to the Jews for their benefit by God. Stephen's rejection was fundamental: all sacrificial worship was idolatrous. The complete lack of any positive christological reason for the rejection of the Temple and sacrificial worship strongly argues against the idea of a connection between Stephen and *Hebrews*, an idea supported by C. F. D. Moule in his "Sanctuary and Sacrifice in the Church of the New Testament" (*JTS*, 1950), and argued in detail by W. Manson in his *Epistle to the Hebrews*. If this connection is rejected and the purely negative character of Stephen's opposition to the cult accepted, then it must be admitted that Stephen did not affect the mainstream of Christian thinking.

Similar views are found elsewhere in early Christian literature, apart from the exceptional case of the *Epistle to Diognetus* which likewise accuses the Jews of idolatry and takes a negative attitude to the Law. It is possible also that the Gnostics were in the same tradition, though evidence is very slim. In the *Epistle to Flora* (ed. Quispel) of Ptolemaeus, it is claimed that the Saviour commanded us to offer spiritual sacrifices, not irrational animals but spiritual praises and thanksgiving and charity and good deeds to our neighbour (5.10). The statement seems no different from many a Christian exposition of spiritual sacrifices, except for the claim that Jesus commanded it (which is not found in the canonical Gospels and may come from the *Logia Jesu* (ed. White, p. 26). On the other hand, there is no christological interpretation of sacrifice, and no evidence of a positive attitude to the Jewish Law. All that is involved is a spiritualisation like that found in the *Corpus Hermeticum*, although expressed in the characteristically Christian terms of charity, avoidance of evil works, etc. The evidence is too slim to claim dogmatically that the Gnostics stood for a radical spiritualisation as did Stephen, and nothing else; it does however seem to be a reasonable suggestion.

ADDITIONAL NOTE II

I have not felt it necessary to discuss Athanasius' view of the nature of substitution since I have been chiefly concerned to indicate the type of sacrifice involved in his theory. Eusebius' rationale (discussed _supra_, Ch. VIII.C) clearly means that the ransom or substitute is offered in place of the life of men. But various factors in Athanasius' treatment of the whole question of soteriology indicate that he did not regard this substitution as a crude quasi-legal device, but rather thought that in the death of Christ all humanity died. It was not a quirk of justice whereby God accepted the death of the body in which the Logos dwelt, in place of the death of other men, and regarded that as fulfilling the law of death. Rather, the death of all mankind was consummated in the Lord's body (_De inc_. XX.2). He did not come to die τὸν ἑαυτοῦ θάνατον, ἀλλὰ τὸν τῶν ἀνθρώπων ἦλθε τελειῶσαι (_De inc_. XXII.3).

In Athanasius' thought, the manhood of Christ and the death he died are expressed rather peculiarly and this has given rise to frequent discussion as to whether he meant the Logos dwelt in an individual man or in collective humanity--a sort of Platonic "idea" of man. (See Van Haarlem, _Incarnatie en verlossing bij Athanasius_; L. Bouyer, _L'incarnation et l'église corps du Christ dans le théologie de S. Athanase_, Ch. 3; J. N. D. Kelly, _Early Christian Doctrines_, p. 378.) Athanasius' only interest in details of the life of the individual man, Jesus, is soteriological: he wept at Lazarus' tomb to prove that he really had taken a human body and really bore our weaknesses. The significance lies, not in the individual man weeping, but in his solidarity with humanity. This could be explained in terms of the Pauline idea of being "in Christ," and his view that, in baptism, men die and rise again with Christ, crucifying the old life and accepting a new.

But Athanasius certainly seems to go further than this, since there are many passages which suggest that the incarnation automatically sanctified human nature: the very presence of the Logos in human flesh destroyed its passions, its weaknesses, its imperfection, and its subjection to death, and raised it to heaven (e.g., C. Arianos II.57, 53, 61, 65, 70, 75, etc.). On the other hand, sometimes in the C. Arianos, and especially in the Letters to Serapion, the transformation is not automatic, for he indicates that, for the work of the Logos to have effect, the individual must be in relation to the Logos through the Spirit. It is by participation in the Son that we become sons (see, e.g., C. Arianos I.39; II.56, 59, etc.). This is, however, very close to the Platonic idea that a thing has a certain nature by participation in the form of that nature. Man is purified by participation in the form of perfected mankind, the body of Christ. So in Athanasius' thought, Christ is identified with us in death, and we are identified with him in his death: "as by death we all die in Christ, so in Christ we shall all be exalted, rising from the dead and coming up to heaven" (C. Arianos I.41). His death was not an exchange for us, but gave us the opportunity to die with him and be re-created in him. Unless we are re-created in him, sin still has dominion over us (C. Arianos II.56). "He offered his body to death on behalf of all . . . and all now become free from sin and the curse of it and, raised from the dead, will remain forever clothed in immortality and incorruptibility" (II.69).

ADDITIONAL NOTE III

In actual fact, the evidence for the Eucharist being considered the Christian Passover is not as great as is often assumed. The Synoptic Institution narratives imply this, and some scholars argue that the Last Supper was historically a Passover celebration in spite of the conflicting evidence of John. (See Jeremias, The Eucharistic Words of Jesus. He is followed closely by A. J. B. Higgins, The Lord's Supper in the New Testament.) The character of the Last Supper is a controversial question and not immediately relevant to our purposes, but one argument against the theory that it was a Passover meal has not received a satisfactory answer: if the Last Supper was a Passover celebration and a Christian Passover was instituted on that occasion, why did not the Church adopt an annual celebration of the Eucharist? Acts gives the impression that it was daily, and later it certainly became a weekly service on the Lord's Day. (This argument is put by Dix in Jew and Greek, p. 101 against Jeremias and also by D. E. Nineham, Commentary on St. Mark, in the Appendix.) At a later period, when the Eucharist was interpreted as the Christian Passover, some people seem to have taken the logical step of only attending the Eucharist on Easter Sunday, and Chrysostom found it necessary to settle a controversy on the issue; see his Hom. Heb. XVII.

There is some indication that the Eucharist was not for some time generally accepted as the Christian Passover. Paul does not make the association. In his treatment of the Eucharist, he makes no mention of Paschal parallels at all and, in his account of the Institution, he does not say "on the night of the Passover," but "on the night in which he was betrayed" (1 Cor. 11.23). Paul's spiritualisation of the Passover is in no way concerned with the Eucharist: Christians celebrate the festival with unleavened bread of sincerity and truth, for Christ, their Paschal Lamb is sacrificed (1 Cor. 5.7-8). Since Paul reports the tradition that in the Eucharist Christians proclaim the Lord's death (1 Cor. 11.26), the connection could be made, indirectly, by associating these two passages, but clearly the association of the Last Supper or Eucharist with the Passover is not directly maintained or argued in the Pauline writings.

Similarly, John maintains that Jesus was crucified at the time when the Passover lambs were slain in the

Temple; Christ is the Passover lamb, as in Paul, and the possibility that the Last Supper was a Passover meal is excluded. (A hint of the tradition associating the Passover with the Eucharist may, however, be present in *Jn.* 6 where the Feeding story that gives rise to the discussion of the Eucharist is introduced by the statement that the Passover was at hand (*Jn.* 6.4).

As we have already seen, the Pauline tradition which associated the sacrifice of Christ with the Paschal victim developed into an elaborate typology whereby the blood on the doorpost in Egypt was seen as a type of the blood of Christ; the former was to redeem the children of Israel, the latter to redeem all mankind. But explicit association of these ideas with the Eucharist is rarely found in early literature, even though the Eucharist was a memorial of Christ's death. It is particularly significant that Justin never uses the Passover type at all in his discussion of the Eucharist, even in the context of a list of types where he explicitly associates the Passover with the sacrifice of Christ. The type of the Eucharist which he mentions is not the Passover but the meal-offering offered by cured lepers. In such a context, the association of the Eucharist with the Passover would seem to have been obvious, but Justin does not make the link (*Dial.* 40-1). The association does not seem to have been made explicitly until Origen; yet his use of it may not be very significant since it need not give evidence for the general belief of the Church. Origen makes every possible typological and allegorical association, whether traditional or not. Even Melito, in his *Paschal Homily* where the Passover-type was used so elaborately of Christ's death,never mentions the Eucharist.

The Synoptic Gospels are the only writings which connect the Eucharist with the Passover prior to the time of Origen. The liturgical nature of the texts shows that they definitely intended a reference to the origin of the Christian Eucharist and they state that the Last Supper was a Passover meal. It is probable however, that the reference to the Passover in the Marcan text belongs not to the original but to later expansions. (*Mk.* 14.12-16 is regarded as an expansion of the original Passion narrative, even by Jeremias. This applies equally to *Mt.* since his narrative is clearly dependent upon *Mk.*). This suggests that the Passover association may have developed late in the oral period and, since it appears nowhere else before Origen, that it may have originated in one area only and spread to the Church at a much later date. (The one difficulty with this theory is that *Lk.* 22.15-16 appears to be a genuine piece of independent tradition; but it has been suggested that this saying should be connected, not with the Institution of the Eucharist, but with the practice of some Christians of fasting on the Passover. See Kuhn, *The Lord's Supper and the Communal Meal at Qumran*, p. 90ff.)

Since the association with the Passover is clear in the Synoptic Gospels, it is surprising that an idea capable of such rich theological development was not used by any Christian writer before Origen who, in his *Comm. Jn.* 10.13, makes a clear Eucharistic reference in his discussion of Christ as our Passover. As the Jews ate the Passover lamb, so we eat the flesh and blood of the Incarnate Word. The lamb, he suggests, is to be eaten with bitter herbs and unleavened bread, that is, with repentance and sorrow. Following Origen, the idea becomes common, especially in the Paschal Homilies which were preached on the occasion of the celebration of the Easter Communion. Allegorisations of how the Passover should be eaten depict the spiritual frame of mind demanded for eating the Eucharist. The annual Easter Communion was the real equivalent of the Jewish Passover and, at least in this context, was recognised as the Christian Passover. It was the memorial of the saving act which founded the New Israel, and that saving act was the sacrifice of the Lamb of God to redeem mankind from the devil. (See Hippolytus, *On the Passion*, 4, 25-6, 41, 49; the Origenist Homilies, II.17 and III *passim*; Greg. Naz. *Or.* XLV.15-6.)

SELECT BIBLIOGRAPHY OF SECONDARY SOURCES

Armstrong, A. H. Plotinus. London, 1953.

Aulén, G. Christus Victor. London, 1931.

Baron, S. W. & Blau, J. L. Judaism, Postbiblical and Talmudic Period. New York, 1954.

Baumgarten, J. H. "Sacrifice and Worship among the Jewish Sectarians of the Dead Sea Scrolls." Harvard Theological Review, 46 (1953).

Bernays, J. Theophrastus' Schrift über Frommigkeit. Berlin, 1866.

Betz, J. Die Eucharistie in der Zeit der Griechischen Väter. Frieburg, 1961.

Bevan, E. Stoic and Sceptic. Oxford, 1913.

Bigg, C. The Christian Platonists of Alexandria. Oxford, 1866.

Black, M. The Scrolls and Christian Origins. London, 1961.

Bouyer, L. L'Incarnation et l''Eglise-corps du Christ dans le théologie de Saint Athanase. Paris, 1943.

Bultmann, R. Theology of the New Testament. London, 1955.

Capelle, D. "L'Anaphore de Sérapion." Muséon, 59 (1946).

Chadwick, H. (ed. & trans.). Origen: Contra Celsum. Cambridge, 1953.

Couratin, A. H. "The Sacrifice of Praise." Theology, 58 (1955).

Cross, F. L. The Study of St. Athanasius. Oxford, 1945.

Daniélou, J. The Development of Christian Doctrine before the Council of Nicaea, Vol. 1: The Theology of Jewish Christianity. London, 1964.

______. Origen. New York, 1955.

Dewar, L. "The Biblical Use of the Term 'Blood.'" Journal of Theological Studies (n.s.), 4 (1953).

Dix, G. The Egyptian Church Order: The Apostolic Tradition of Hippolytus. London, 1937.

______. Jew and Greek. Westminster, 1953.

______. The Shape of the Liturgy. Westminster, 1944.

Dodd, C. H. Commentary on Romans. London, 1932.

______. The Apostolic Preaching and its Development. London, 1936.

______. The Bible and the Greeks. London, 1935.

______. The Interpretation of the Fourth Gospel. Cambridge, 1953.

Dodds, E. R. The Greeks and the Irrational. Berkeley (Calif.), 1951.

______. Euripides: The Bacchae. Oxford, 1944.

Downing, J. "Jesus and Martyrdom." Journal of Theological Studies (n.s.), 14 (1963).

Festugière, A. J. Personal Religion among the Greeks. Berkeley (Calif.), 1954.

______. Epicurus and His Gods. Oxford, 1955.

Franks, R. S. History of the Doctrine of the Work of Christ. London, 1918.

Frazer, J. G. The Golden Bough. London, 1913.

Frend, W. H. C. The Donatist Church. Oxford, 1952.

______. Martyrdom and Persecution in the Early Church. Oxford, 1965.

Gray, G. B. Sacrifice in the Old Testament. Oxford, 1925.

Haarlem, A. van. Incarnatie en verlossing bij Athanasius. Wageningen, 1961.

Hallie, P. Scepticism, Man and God: Selections from the Major Writings of Sextus Empiricus. Middletown, Conn., 1964.

Hanson, A. T. The Wrath of the Lamb. London, 1957.

Hanson, R. P. C. Allegory and Event. London, 1959.

Harl, M. Origène et la fonction révélatrice du verbe incarné. Paris, 1958.

Harrison, J. E. Prolegomena to the Study of Greek Religion (3rd ed.). Cambridge, 1922.

Hick, J. Evil and the God of Love. London, 1966.

Hicks, R. D. Stoic and Epicurean. London, 1910.

Higgins, A. J. B. The Lord's Supper in the New Testament. London, 1952.

Hodges, H. A. The Pattern of Atonement. London, 1963.

Hooker, M. Jesus and the Servant. London, 1959.

James, E. O. Sacrifice and Sacrament. London, 1962.

Jeremias, J. The Eucharistic Words of Jesus. Oxford, 1955.

Johnson, A. R. The Cultic Prophet in Ancient Israel. Cardiff, 1944.

Kelly, J. N. D. Early Christian Doctrines, London, 1960.

Koch, H. Pronoia und Paideusis. Berlin, 1932.

Kuhn, K. G. "The Lord's Supper and the Communal Meal," in K. Stendahl (ed.), The Scrolls and the New Testament. London, 1958.

Lampe, G. W. H. A Patristic Lexicon. Oxford, 1961.

Lietzmann, H. Mass and Lord's Supper. Leiden, 1953.

Lindblom, C. J: Prophecy in Ancient Israel. Oxford, 1962.

Manson, W. The Epistle to the Hebrews. London, 1951.

McKeating, H. "Divine Forgiveness in the Psalms." Scottish Journal of Theology, 18 (1965).

Merlan, P. From Platonism to Neoplatonism. The Hague, 1953.

Michell, G. A. Landmarks in Liturgy. London, 1961.

Molland, E. The Concept of the Gospel in Alexandrian Theology. Oslo, 1938.

Montefiore, H. W. The Epistle to the Hebrews. London, 1964.

Morris, L. L. The Apostolic Preaching of the Cross. London, 1955.

______. "The Biblical Use of the Term 'Blood.'" Jour- of Theological Studies (n.s.), 3 (1952), 6 (1955).

Moule, C. F. D. The Birth of the New Testament. London, 1962.

______. "Sanctuary and Sacrifice in the Church of the New Testament." Journal of Theological Studies (n.s.), 1 (1950).

Mowinckel, S. O. P. The Psalms in Israel's Worship. Oxford, 1962.

Murray, G. Five Stages of Greek Religion. Oxford, 1925.

Nairne, A. The Epistle of Priesthood. Edinburgh, 1913.

______. The Epistle to the Hebrews. Cambridge, 1917.

Nineham, D. E. Saint Mark. London, 1963.

Nock, A. D. Conversion. Oxford, 1933.

______. Early Gentile Christianity and its Hellenistic Background. New York, 1964.

North, C. R. The Suffering-Servant in Deutero-Isaiah. London, 1948.

Osborn, E. F. The Philosophy of Clement of Alexandria. Cambridge, 1957.

Perler, O. "Das vierte Makkabäerbuch, Ignatius von Antiochen und die ältesten Martyrerberichte." Rivista di archeologia cristiana, 15 (1949).

Pelikan, J. The Light of the World. New York, 1962.

Pohlenz, M. Vom Zorne Gottes. Göttingen, 1909.

Porteous, N. W. "Prophecy," in H. W. Robinson (ed.), Record and Revelation. Oxford, 1938.

Rad, G. von. Old Testament Theology, 1. Edinburgh,

______. Studies in Deuteronomy. London, 1953.

Rashdall, H. The Idea of Atonement in Christian Theology. London, 1919.

Ratcliff, E. C. "The Sanctus and the Pattern of the Early Anaphora." Journal of Ecclesiastical History, 1 (1950).

Rawlinson, A. E. J. "Corpus Christi," in G. K. A. Bell & A. Diessmann (ed.), Mysterium Christi. London, 1930.

Richardson, R. D. "Eastern and Western Liturgies: The Primitive Basis for their Later Divergences." Harvard Theological Review, 42 (1949).

______. "Supplementary Essay" to E.T. of H. Lietzmann, Messe und Herrenmahl. Leiden, 1953.

Rivière, J. The Doctrine of the Atonement. London, 1909.

Robinson, H. W. Redemption and Revelation. London, 1952.

______. Inspiration and Revelation in the Old Testament. Oxford, 1946.

______. The Cross in the Old Testament. London, 1955.

Rose, H. J. Religion in Greece and Rome. New York, 1959.

Rouse, W. H. D. Greek Votive Offerings. Cambridge, 1902.

Rowley, H. H. The Meaning of Sacrifice in the Old Testament; republished in From Moses to Qumran, London, 1964.

Schmidt, H. R. Veteres philosophi quamodo iudicaverint de precibus. Giessen, 1908.

Simon, M. St. Stephen and the Hellenists in the Primitive Church. London, 1958.

Soury, G. Aperçus de philosophe religieuse chez Maxime de Tyre. Paris, 1942.

Sowers, S. G. The Hermeneutics of Philo and Hebrews. Zürich, 1965.

Spicq, C. L'Epitre aux Hébreux. Paris, 1952.

Taylor, V. Jesus and his Sacrifice. London, 1959.

Turner, H. E. W. The Patristic Doctrine of Redemption. London, 1952.

de Vaux, R. Ancient Israel. London, 1961.

______. Les sacrifices de l'Ancien Testament. Paris, 1964.

Wiles, M. F. "The Theological Legacy of St. Cyprian." Journal of Ecclesiastical History, 14 (1963).

______. "One Baptism for the Remission of Sins." Church Quarterly Review. 165 (1964).

Wolfson, H. A. Philo. Cambridge, Mass., 1947.

Yadin, Y. The Scroll of the Wars of the Sons of Light against the Sons of Darkness. Oxford, 1962.

Yerkes, R. K. Sacrifice in Greek and Roman Religion and in Early Judaism. London, 1953.

Zimmerli, W. & Jeremias, J. The Servant of God. London, 1957.

A Committee of the Oxford Society of Historical Theology. The New Testament in the Apostolic Fathers. Oxford, 1905.